EVERY FARMER SHOULD HAVE ONE!

AWTHORP'S HYDRAULIC RAM

he Most Approved and Cheapest Plan of Supplying Dwellings and Barns with Water.

A number of them are already in use in Baltimore ounty and they are giving the utmost satisfaction, as e number of testimonials from well-known citizens, now my possession, will show. They are simple and will st a lifetime, one farmer having had one in use for wenty years and in all that time it did not cost $10 for pairs.

Fitzhugh Horse Hay Fork!

o be rigged in Barns and Barracks for the rapid unload- g and storing of hay. The best thing of the kind in the market. Safe and easily operated.– any already in use. Get one for the coming harvest.

THE SUCCESS FORCE PUMP!

With a few feet of hose attached to one of these, Pumps you can force water over your house, ater your lawn or garden and sprinkle the streets. The best Pump made, and it never fails o give satisfaction.

I am the Authorized Agent for the above mentioned articles, and will take pleasure in iving all necessary information in regard to them. Call on or address,

J. WESLEY LEE,
Towson P. O., Baltimore County, Md.

ay 25 1y.

JAS. L. RIDGELY, JR.,
—DEALER IN—
HARD LUMBER,
And WAGON MAKER'S MATERIALS,

Felloes, Spokes, Shafts, Axles, Tongues, Dray Tails, Single and Double Trees, &c., &c. All kinds Bill Stuff for Framing, Bridging, Etc., Cut to Order on Short Notice.

HARRISONVILLE.

CHAS. C. WITTIG, SR.,
MERCHANT TAILOR.

A full assortment of Gentlemen's Furnishing Goods, such as Cloths, Cassimers, Vestings, &c., constantly on hand, which he is prepared to make up at Lowest Prices.

FITS GUARANTEED;

Also READY-MADE CLOTHING.

HEREFORD.

DEAD ANIMALS

DEAD HORSES, MULES and COWS promptly removed. JOHN G. MILLER, 2695 Wilkens Ave., Baltimore, Md.
Phones Gilmor 1149; Fork 51. tf

DR. A. C. McCURDY,
SURGEON DENTIST,

(Graduate of Baltimore College Dental Surgery, Class of 1878,)

TOWSONTOWN, MD.,

Office and Residence--York Road, near the M. E. Church.

Having a newly fitted office, with all modern appliances, I am now prepared to skillfully perform all branches of operating, &c.

Irregularity in Children's Teeth successfully treated. Artificial Teeth inserted from one tooth to an entire set.

Having had an extended and varied practice I feel no hesitancy in saying that I can guarantee satisfaction in all cases.

Charges moderate. A call respectfully solicited.

REFERENCES:—Judge Yellott, Judge Grason, J. C. Carpenter, John E. Owens, Caleb S. Taylor, Washington Stevenson, Dr. J. H. Jarrett, G. Frank Morgan, J. E. Standiford, John I. Yellott, Chas. E. Fendall, C. Bohn Slingluff, Longnecker Bros., Capt. E. Herman and many others.

Oct. 13.—tf.

SOLDIERS' BOUNTY!!
ENSIONS! PRIZE MONEY!!
BACK PAY, &c.
Government Claim Office,
70 W. Fayette strett, near St. Paul street,
BALTIMORE, MD.

IDOWS of Soldiers who have died in the service of the United States, are entitled pension for life, in addition to the Bounty 100, and all arrearages of pay, &c.

hildren and Heirs of deceased soldiers, ere there is no widow living,) are entitled ounty, &c. &c.

oldiers who have been wounded and disa- are entitled to Pension.

oldiers who have been Prisoners of War are tled to Commutation of Rations.

eamen in U. S. Service are entitled to Prize ney, Naval Bounties, &c.

rompt attention given to all claims against United States.

WM. B. HILL,
Government Claim Office,
No. 70 W. Fayette street, Baltimore.

. B.—*No letters answered unless a postage np is enclosed.*

arch 7.—tf

August Loose,
MERCHANT TAILOR,
AND
READY-MADE CLOTHIER,
Towsontown, Baltimore county, Md.,

RESPECTFULLY informs his friends and the public in general, that he has removed to his new house, on Main street, opposite Ady's Hotel, where he has always on hand a full assortment, of CLOTHS AND CASSIMERES, which he is prepared to make up in the latest styles, and on reasonable terms, *cheap for cash.* He requests his old friends and the public to give him a call.

A large variety of FALL AND WINTER GOODS on hand, which I invite the public to examine.

The best of LINEN BOSOM SHIRTS always on hand. Clothing made to order at short notice. Nov. 3, 1860.—tf

The Celebrated Spanish Jack Corporal.

THIS fine young Jack will stand the present season, commencing 14th April and end July 14th, as follows: On Tuesday, Wednesday, Thursday and Friday of every other week at Chew's woods, Towsontown; the balance of the time at my stable, except Saturday, when he will be at Kemp's Hotel, near Black Rock.

Terms:—$15 to insure. Any person parting with an insured mare before she is known to be in foal, will be held for the insurance. Two mares belonging to one person insured for $25.

May 2.–3t* SAM'L H. COLE.

OTICE IS HEREBY GIVEN,

HAT an election for DIRECTORS OF THE ASHLAND IRON COMPANY OF BALTI- RE COUNTY, for the ensuing year, will be at ASHLAND, on

Thursday, March 26th, 1863,

een the hours of eleven and one o'clock.

BARTOW LATIMER, Secretary.

shland, March 7.—3t

SPRING AND SUMMER GOODS.

I AM receiving weekly fresh additions to my stock of DRY GOODS, GROCERIES, QUEENSWARE, &c., which consists in part of—

Persian Cloth; Ladies' Black Dress Silks; Valencias and De Baize; assortment of Purples and Mournings (English Prints); Manchester and Domestic Ginghams; Ladies' Shawls in great varieties, and Mantillas; Nubias; French Worked Collars; Undersleeves; Insertions and Edgings; Furniture Calico; Ladies', Gentlemen and Childrens' Hosiery in great variety; Black Alpacas from 18¾ to 75 cts; Bleached and Unbleached Muslins; Shirting Linens from 25 to 87½ cts.; Table Diapers from 25 cts. to $1, and Cloths from 25 cts. to $2 50; Sheetings, bleached and unbleached; Napkins from 75 cts. to $3 per doz.; Linen, Habakuk, Diaper, and Linen Crash, bleached and unbleached.

Gentlemens' Black Doeskins, Cassimeres, and a beautiful quality of French Cloths, Cassinetts, Tweeds, Kentucky Jeans, with every variety of gentlemens' wear.

Sugar from 9 to 12½ cts. per lb.; Molasses at 37½, 50 and 62½ cts. per gal.; Green and Browned Coffees of the best quality always on hand; Green and Black Teas; Best Sugar-Cured Hams, Middling and Shoulder Bacon, Baltimore cured —with a general assortment of Groceries, Provisions, Hardware, Medicines, Boots, Shoes, Hats and Caps, &c., &c., in great variety.

MRS. M. A. SHEALEY,
Towsontown, Md.

March 1.—tf

SPECIAL
SUNDAY DINNER
$1.00

MENU
Fresh Shrimp Cocktail
Choice of Soup
Choice of—
Broiled Shad Roe and Bacon
Roast Half Spring Chicken
Broiled Beef Tenderloin
(Mushroom Sauce)
Chicken A-La-King

Potatoes Green Peas
Lettuce and Tomato Salad
Thousand Island Dressing
Choice of Desserts—Pie, Ice Cream
Tea Coffee

Special Week-day Dinners
50c, 75c, $1.00

Maryland Restaurant
York Road and Penna. Ave.
TOWSON, MD.

Cockeysville Hotel.

HIS CELEBRATED HOTEL, for the last year in the occupancy of Hugh Horner, is in operation under his management, to which notice he in- s the attention of the trav- g public, soldiers, and citi- s of Baltimore County.

is table will at all times be supplied with very best that the market affords. His ors and segars he guarantees equal to any t in the county. A careful and obliging ler always in attendance.

y strict attention to business he flatters self that he will merit the continuance of patronage heretofore so liberally bestowed n him. HUGH HORNER.

eb. 8, 1862.—1y*

BALTIMORE COUNTY PANORAMA

BALTIMORE COUNTY PANORAMA

NEAL A. BROOKS
RICHARD PARSONS

Published by
Baltimore County Public Library
Towson, Maryland

Produced by

Editors for The Donning Company:
Nancy O. Phillips
Richard A. Horwege, Senior Editor
Design by Sharon Varner Moyer

A Baltimore County Heritage Publication

Baltimore County Public Library
320 York Road
Towson, Maryland 21204

Library of Congress Cataloging-in-Publication Data:

Brooks, Neal A., 1944-
Baltimore County panorama/by Neal A. Brooks. Richard Parsons.
p. cm.—(A Baltimore County Heritage Publication,
ISSN 0270-0344)
Bibliography: p.
Includes index.
ISBN 0-937076-03-1
1. Baltimore County (Md.)—History—Pictorial works. 2. Baltimore County (Md.)—Description and travel—Views. I. Parsons, Richard. II. Title. III. Series.
F187.B2B328 1988 88-22953
975.2'71—dc 19 CIP

Printed in the United States of America

For

Nancy, Jeffrey and Gregory Brooks

who patiently understood the passion history engenders

and

Jane A. and John B. Parsons

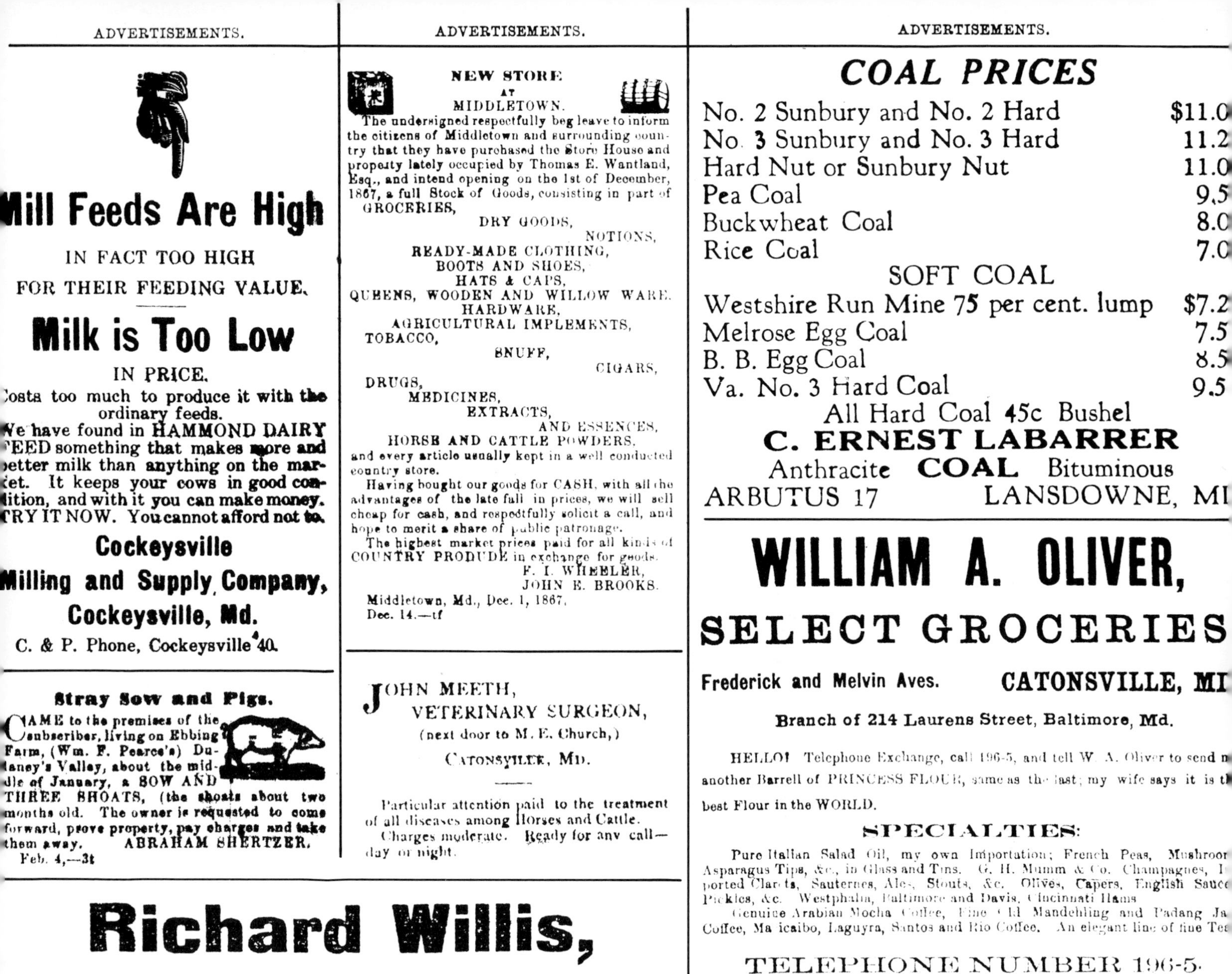

Mill Feeds Are High

IN FACT TOO HIGH

FOR THEIR FEEDING VALUE.

Milk is Too Low

IN PRICE.

Costs too much to produce it with the ordinary feeds. We have found in HAMMOND DAIRY FEED something that makes more and better milk than anything on the market. It keeps your cows in good condition, and with it you can make money. TRY IT NOW. You cannot afford not to.

Cockeysville

Milling and Supply Company,

Cockeysville, Md.

C. & P. Phone, Cockeysville 40.

Stray Sow and Pigs.

CAME to the premises of the subscriber, living on Ebbing Farm, (Wm. F. Pearce's) Dulaney's Valley, about the middle of January, a SOW AND THREE SHOATS, (the shoats about two months old. The owner is requested to come forward, prove property, pay charges and take them away. ABRAHAM SHERTZER.

Feb. 4,—3t

NEW STORE

AT

MIDDLETOWN.

The undersigned respectfully beg leave to inform the citizens of Middletown and surrounding country that they have purchased the Store House and property lately occupied by Thomas E. Wantland, Esq., and intend opening on the 1st of December, 1867, a full Stock of Goods, consisting in part of

GROCERIES,
DRY GOODS,
NOTIONS,
READY-MADE CLOTHING,
BOOTS AND SHOES,
HATS & CAPS,
QUEENS, WOODEN AND WILLOW WARE.
HARDWARE,
AGRICULTURAL IMPLEMENTS,
TOBACCO,
SNUFF,
CIGARS,
DRUGS,
MEDICINES,
EXTRACTS,
AND ESSENCES,
HORSE AND CATTLE POWDERS.

and every article usually kept in a well conducted country store.

Having bought our goods for CASH, with all the advantages of the late fall in prices, we will sell cheap for cash, and respectfully solicit a call, and hope to merit a share of public patronage.

The highest market prices paid for all kinds of COUNTRY PRODUDE in exchange for goods.

F. I. WHEELER,
JOHN E. BROOKS.

Middletown, Md., Dec. 1, 1867.
Dec. 14.—tf

JOHN MEETH,
VETERINARY SURGEON,
(next door to M. E. Church,)
CATONSVILLE, MD.

Particular attention paid to the treatment of all diseases among Horses and Cattle.

Charges moderate. Ready for any call—day or night.

COAL PRICES

No. 2 Sunbury and No. 2 Hard	$11.0
No. 3 Sunbury and No. 3 Hard	11.2
Hard Nut or Sunbury Nut	11.0
Pea Coal	9.5
Buckwheat Coal	8.0
Rice Coal	7.0
SOFT COAL	
Westshire Run Mine 75 per cent. lump	$7.2
Melrose Egg Coal	7.5
B. B. Egg Coal	8.5
Va. No. 3 Hard Coal	9.5

All Hard Coal 45c Bushel

C. ERNEST LABARRER

Anthracite **COAL** Bituminous

ARBUTUS 17 LANSDOWNE, MI

WILLIAM A. OLIVER,

SELECT GROCERIES

Frederick and Melvin Aves. CATONSVILLE, MI

Branch of 214 Laurens Street, Baltimore, Md.

HELLO! Telephone Exchange, call 196-5, and tell W. A. Oliver to send m another Barrell of PRINCESS FLOUR, same as the last; my wife says it is th best Flour in the WORLD.

SPECIALTIES:

Pure Italian Salad Oil, my own Importation; French Peas, Mushroor Asparagus Tips, &c., in Glass and Tins. G. H. Mumm & Co. Champagnes, I ported Clarets, Sauternes, Ales, Stouts, &c. Olives, Capers, English Sauce Pickles, &c. Westphalia, Baltimore and Davis, Cincinnati Hams

Genuine Arabian Mocha Coffee, Fine Old Mandehling and Padang Ja Coffee, Maracaibo, Laguyra, Santos and Rio Coffee. An elegant line of fine Tea

TELEPHONE NUMBER 196-5.

REMEMBER: All these Coods at City Price

Richard Willis,

DRUGGIST & PHARMACIST,

TOWSONTOWN, Md.,

Near the Postoffice,

Keeps constantly on hand a supply of FRESH DRUGS & MEDICINE, PERFUMERY & TOILET ARTICLES and all goods usually kept in a first-class Drug Store.

☞ Physicians' Prescriptions carefully and accurately compounded at all hours, day and night.

SODA, VICHY, DEEP ROCK AND CHLORINE STRONTIA WATER always on draught.

☞ ALSO, CHOICE CIGARS AND TOBACCO.

May 26.—tf.

JOSEPH A. NEUMAYER,

Justice of the Peace.

All business promptly attended to.

CLAIMS OF ALL KINDS COLLECTED. &

—OFFICE—

Gardenville, Baltimore County, Mc

C. P. & Telephone, Hamilton 4 K.

NESTER N. EDWARDS,

LOCKSMITH,

Rear of Elks' Hall,

1-12-3m TOWSON, MD.

CONTENTS

LETTERS OF APPRECIATION 8
PREFACE 10
ACKNOWLEDGMENTS 12
INTRODUCTION 14
COLOR PHOTOGRAPHS 19
LIFE & LEISURE 40
TRANSPORTATION 102
PUBLIC SERVICE 124
SCHOOLS 152
EVENTS 172
CHURCHES 194
AGRICULTURE, BUSINESS, AND INDUSTRY 212
HOUSES 272
HOSPITALS AND INSTITUTIONS 290
POSTSCRIPT 296
BIBLIOGRAPHY 300
PICTURE CREDITS 303
INDEX 305
ABOUT THE AUTHOR 319

Letters Of Appreciation

I enthusiastically invite my fellow citizens to read and enjoy *Baltimore County Panorama*, this beautiful pictorial history of our county. While Baltimore County is a jurisdiction on the move, getting better each day, we must never lose sight of our heritage of rolling hills, of small rural villages, and of caring for each other. Whatever direction we take in the future, the best of the past must and will be protected.

Dennis F. Rasmussen
County Executive

Baltimore County
a Great County!

The County Council notes with pleasure the care with which the authors have searched for and found history in every community of the county. Few stones seem to have been unturned; the authors found events, people, and buildings in every corner of our great county. Surely this is a book which all of us can read and enjoy over and over for years to come.

Dale Volz, Chairman
County Council

The Board of Library Trustees of Baltimore County has a serious commitment to the preservation of local history. In 1980 the Board of Trustees authorized the library to begin a Heritage Publications series. The books in this series have been very well received and critically acclaimed. The present handsome book is a credit to the library and its staff, and one which the Board of Trustees is proud to offer to the citizens of the county.

Dorothy Beaman, President
Board of Library Trustees
for Baltimore County

Preface

Baltimore County Panorama does not pretend to be *the* pictorial history of Baltimore County or even *a* picture history of Baltimore County. What we hope is that this review is a celebration of two hundred years of life in this interesting county of 610 square miles. Each photo may be viewed (in part) as being representative of its type: a hotel, a Victorian house, a parade, a school group, or whatever is similar to all old hotels, or all Victorian houses; parades do not change much from decade to decade; school groups still look very much as they did a century ago—grimly stolid! We were favored with such a flood of interesting pictures that, like the sorcerer's apprentice, we had to struggle to keep from going under. We were limited by the printer to a certain number of black and white pictures and pages in color. The choices were difficult to make. Many important pictures from every section of the county had to be put aside, to be used another time.

A dearth of early pictorial material has given the present collection a strong tilt towards the late nineteenth and early twentieth centuries. Our intention has been not only to record some of what has changed or vanished but also to try to find the thread of continuity with the past. Although some pictures may be identified with specific people in a specific place and at a specific time, there are qualities about many of them which make them timeless. The children playing in the pictures of the 1980s might readily see themselves reflected in the happy faces of children playing in the early 1900s. Only the peculiarities of costume or the structural changes in equipment separate the tennis and ball players of today from those at the turn of the century.

The gaps are large, and, inevitably, every community in every part of the county will regret the absence of some favorite building or place: the bridge one used to fish from; the demolished school one went to; the church one was married in; the old barber shop or salon where one got the first haircut; the woods in which the family picnicked, now occupied by a development; and an endless list of vanished businesses and companies that paid the wages which supported generations of countians. Because of the quantity restrictions imposed on us, and because of the volume of excellent photos, arbitrary decisions had to be made about what would *not* be considered for inclusion.

The first decision was the acceptance of the present boundaries of Baltimore County as the area we would portray. We excluded, except for two pictures, those parts of what is now Baltimore City but which were part of Baltimore County before the 1888 and 1918 boundary expansions by the city. Thus eliminated from consideration were Govans, Highlandtown, Canton, Dickeyville, Calverton, Roland Park, Guilford, Mt. Washington, Woodberry, and Hampden, all regions that gave Baltimore County a rich diversity.

Also excluded were charming pictures of animals which could have been taken anywhere but added nothing to the reader's knowledge of old Baltimore County other than a reinforcement of the sense of ruralness. Withdrawn from consideration were escaped horses on the Beltway, cattle fording streams, sheep grazing in meadows, swans at the Woodlawn Cemetery and geese at Druid Ridge, the K-9 dogs of the Baltimore County Police Department, and an assortment of citizens with their pets. Pictures of repetitive events—fires, floods, parades—have been used selectively, and those included were picked because they represented significant events, or because the photos had other elements worth noting. The photos of many interesting people had to be passed up. Pictures of some well-known buildings have not been repeated here. We regret not having had the space to cover the housing developments of the last forty years.

Sincere attempts were made to balance activities, people, structures, and events so that each of the regions in Baltimore County was represented. What was left may not have achieved the complete fairness we sought, as the quality of a picture of a structure or an event may have been so superior to similar pictures from other jurisdictions that its selection was inevitable, even though this created an imbalance in the number of pictures selected from any region. We endeavored to find pictures that were unique, of good quality, and not available in other still in-print collections of local area photographs, and that also reflected interestingly on life in Baltimore County. We excluded fascinating material dealing with the nineteenth-century textile industry which will be used in Volume II of John McGrain's *From Pig Iron to Cotton Duck*, a future library publication. This does not mean that we intentionally shunned difficult material. We wished to present slavery, segregation, social and political conflict, the Depression, natural disasters, and life in all its many forms, for we approached the subject in the belief that a pictorial panorama dictates that the present must confront the past in all its variety.

Instead of adopting a conventional segmented time-frame approach (eighteenth century, nineteenth century, twentieth century), or a town-by-town review as has been done by some local historians elsewhere, we preferred to use a general essay to tell the story of Baltimore County's development. We then adopted nine categories into which we grouped all of our pictures, enabling us to show comparative pictures on like subjects from different areas of the county at different times. We cross time and geographic locations back and forth regularly within each category. We have tried to identify those experiences that residents of Baltimore County hold in common, rather than perpetuate the long-cherished insularity of our communities.

We tried to eliminate evidence of our personal preferences except in one area, where we failed miserably! Like little boys in a candy store, we became transfixed by the photos of trains, trolleys, biplanes, and classic automobiles, and by turbines, generators, laundry machinery, commercial bakeries, vinyard equipment, dam construction, quarry work, road repair, and the computerized heavy industrial presses, drills, and cutters at major Defense Department contractors. We hope our readers will appreciate what our editorial committee suggested that we cut.

We have made a sincere effort to identify people in the photographs, believing this to be both a useful service to genealogists and of interest to descendants of the people shown. We realize that there are gaps and probably inaccuracies, as we had to rely on easily misinterpreted and often sketchy material. Where possible we have tried to list women by their own names. In some cases it was not possible to uncover that information, and in a few instances, first names of both men and women were not found. We hope interested readers will fill in the gaps for us and correct our errors so we can furnish better information should the book be reprinted.

The Baltimore County Public Library hopes that interested readers may be willing to share their old picture collections with the library so that copies may be made for use in future publications. Readers whose favorite places and cherished events were not included should contact the library and share their pictures or those of friends and neighbors. Those interested in lending the library family or company photographs are invited to contact Richard Parsons at the Towson Administrative offices of the library. The library encourages the use of its photo archives by the public.

Neal A. Brooks
Richard Parsons

Towson, Maryland
June 1988

ACKNOWLEDGMENTS

The following institutions, organizations, corporations, and individuals contributed significantly to this book. Without their help there would be no book.

AAI Corp., Walter A. Friend; American Bank Stationery Co., Douglas J. Saunders; Baltimore Bicycling Club, Robert B. Bennett; Baltimore County Chamber of Commerce, Hank Johnson and Nancy Lax; Baltimore County Historical Society, Amelia and Elmer R. Haile; Baltimore Museum of Industry, Dennis Zembala and Peter Liebhold; Baltimore Museum of Art, Victor Carlson; Baltimore *Sun*, Clem Vitek; Boordy Vineyard, Inc., Robert B. Deford; *Catonsville Times,* Paul Milton; Enoch Pratt Free Library, Maryland Department; Essex Community College, Richard Trent; Franklin Square Hospital, Debbie Rosen McKerrow; Friends of the Catonsville Library, Lisa Vicari; General Instrument Corporation, Worldwide Wagering Systems Division, Thomas K. Robbins; Georgetown University, Department of Special Collections, Jon Reynolds; Grumman Aerospace Corporation, Paul F. Causey and Vic Martorana; Historical Association of Dundalk and Patapsco Neck, Hulett C. Baird; Historical Society of Essex and Middle River, Paul M. Blitz, Jr.; Lansdowne Historical Society, Inc., Howard H. Olver; League of Women Voters of Baltimore County, Kitty Stierhoff; Legum Chevrolet, Jeffrey A. Legum; Lovely Lane Museum-Library, Baltimore Conference United Methodist Historical Society, Rev. Edwin Schell; Marriott's Hunt Valley Inn, Norma S. Tomkinson; Maryland Marathon, Inc., Les Kinion; Maryland Public Television, Carol Wonsavage; Maryland Racing Commission, William Linton; Maryland State Archives, Christopher Allan and Mame Warren; Maryland State Law Library, Michael S. Miller; Maryland State Police, Col. Elmer H. Tippett; Mass Transit Administration, Maryland State Department of Transportation, Anita Presses, Kathleen Kohls; State Department of Transportation, Anita Presses; McCormick and Co., Allen McBarrett; McDonogh School, Anne Body; Nottingham Properties, Inc., Bruce Campbell, P. Douglas Dollenberg, Richard Jones; Patapsco Valley State Park, Maryland Department of Natural Resources, Walter F. Brown; Patuxent Publishing Co., Tenney Mason; Peale Museum, Richard Hall, Dean Krimmel; Provincial Curia of the Maryland Province of the Society of Jesus, the Very Reverend James A. Devereux, S. J.; Social Security Administration, Michael Brennan; St. Joseph Hospital, Jane L. Jubb; State's Attorney of Baltimore County, Judith A. Almon; Towson Senior High School, Dr. Andrew H. Dotterweich; *Towson Times*, Jonathan Witty; Trustees of the *Bunker Hill* Foundation, Mrs. Charles H. Taylor and Mary Baldwin Baer; University of Maryland, College Park, Department of Social Collections, Lauren Brown and Anne S. K. Turkos; the following departments of the Baltimore County government: Administrative Offices, the late B. Melvin Cole; Commission on the Arts and Sciences, Lois K. Baldwin; County Council, Thomas Toporovich; Recreation and Parks, Robert Staab and Francis Dearman; Fire Department, Ted Tochterman; Police Department, Lt. Malcolm Niefeld, Cpl. Janet Stabile, Officer Robert Deale, E. Jay Miller; Public Library, Pat Erdman, Angela McArthur, Marilyn Murray, Cathy Saulsbury, Ruth Schaefer, Cindy Schweinfest, Tom Sollers, David E. Turner, Angela Vogel; Public Schools, Elaine B. Isennock, Dr. Anthony G. Marchione.

Unique material was given or lent to us by all of the following people: Judge William S. Baldwin; Rich Burton; Lida May Berry; Lydia A. Berry; Hon. Helen Delich Bentley; George Blakeslee; Gerry L. Brewster; former Senator Daniel B. Brewster; Carsten S. Brinkmann; Vernon Bush; Mrs. Benjamin H. Bussey; Katherine H. Buxton; Roberta Carter; Mildred S. Cassen; Andrew C. Clemens; Mr. and Mrs. Shearman Dance; Walter M. DeVilbiss, Sr.; Marie Duncan; Margaret East; Regina E. Fox; Beryl Frank; Edna Gorfine; Mrs. L. W. Gorfine; Robert Bruce Hamilton, Jr.; Louis Hergenrather; Mrs. C. S. Hewitt; William Hollifield; Mrs. Douglas Horstman; A. Michael Isekoff; Mrs. Robert W. Johnson; Mrs. John Kade; Gary Kadolph; Jacques Kelly; Edmund T. Kenney; Thomasine F. Kibbe; Dale Kief;

Christyne Lategano; Ethel and Helen Lins; Rev. Joseph Lucca; Robert Lyon; Jay Lyston; Reverend Heyward H. MacDonald; Norton C. McDonough; John W. McGrain; Rieman McIntosh; Marjorie E. Miller; Jeff Morgenstern; Rev. Frederick O. Murphy; James D. Officer; B. E. Von Paris, Sr.; Henry B. Peck, Jr.; Carroll Radebaugh; Judge John E. Raine, Jr. (ret); Julia Randall; Dorothy Maisel Reis; Rev. David Remington; Canon Sally Robinson; Rev. Phillip B. Roulette; Walter Rubeling; Douglas J. Saunders; Raymond Carlton Seitz; Regina B. Shepperd; Mrs. Samuel M. Shoemaker III; George L. Small; Crompton Smith, Jr.; Angie Spicer; Wilmina Sydnor; B. Marvin Thomas, Jr.; Charles L. Wagandt II; M. Cooper Walker; Jean S. Walsh; Helen Hale Weed; the late Madeline G. Weis; Rev. Edward Whetstone; Ben Womer; Hilda N. Wilson; and the late A. Leister Zink.

Jacques Kelly, John McGrain and Jean Walsh read the manuscript, lent us pictures, and answered many research questions. We are very grateful.

Next, a word about our photographers. James K. Lightner and his daughter Theresa worked as a team with us on the copy work. Jim Lightner copied four of the large collections on site, to comply with organizational concerns and restrictions. Theresa Lightner worked extraordinary hours in the darkroom to have the prints ready in time to meet the printer's schedule. Their work speaks for itself; Jim Lightner took the stunning picture of the *Queen Elizabeth II* included in the book.

We wish to express our thanks to people who are, unfortunately, no longer able to receive them. The contributions they made to the preservation of local history in their respective areas has placed them in the lasting debt of the citizens of Baltimore County: Pikesville, Mrs. T. Newell Cox, Sr.; Reisterstown, Louise Bland Goodwin; Essex, Helen and Alex Baumgartner; Lansdowne, Frances Bannon.

INTRODUCTION

The pageant of this community has played for more than three centuries, evolving from a simple wilderness to a complex society with a dense population. Founded in 1659, Baltimore County rested on the upper western shore of a province developed by the Calvert family. The Calverts initially directed the founding of their feudal grant in 1634 in St. Mary's, but the colonists quickly moved up the coastline in search of rich land situated on tidewater. The Chesapeake Bay and its tributaries served as the main route for travel in this wilderness; therefore the earliest settlers sought property adjacent to the colonial "highway." Only when the choice sites on the waterfront had been claimed in the proprietor's land office did the latecomers move inland.

Of course, these lands were already occupied. Indians resided in the region and others passed through the present-day confines of the county as they moved in search of game, cropland, or enemies. Although most of the Eastern Woodland tribes in Maryland lived in the lower portions of the Western and Eastern shores, there were confrontations between the early white settlers and the local tribes, as the early county court records indicate. On the other hand, part of the reason for early settlement in the upper bay apparently involved trade with the Indians. Even without warfare, the tribes were destined for near-elimination simply by contact, for the Europeans brought deadly diseases that destroyed the native population.

The white settlers spread along the coast and gradually moved inland. Their land grants were technically leaseholds; that is, they owed rent to the Lord Proprietor based on the amount of acreage. Although the landholdings of seventeenth- and eighteenth-century Baltimore County seem high to suburbanites today, the average size of 50 to 150 acres was in reality a hedge for an uncertain era. First, the amount of land that might be cultivated was quite small—perhaps only 5 to 10 percent of the total owned—because of the toil involved in preparing, hoeing, and planting. Second, the main cash crop (tobacco) rapidly depleted the soil and the planter needed larger areas for the future. Third, at least some of the land was in timber for lumber and firewood. That left a portion that might be slowly cleared for pasture. Therefore, the average planter was in reality a small landowner. Increasingly in the eighteenth century, the population consisted of indentured servants and slaves, neither of whom owned land.

How did these settlers live? The court records, inventories from their estates, and letters reveal quite a different image from the usual picture of big eighteenth-century homes and jolly, bewigged gentlemen with dazzling ladies at their sides. Most of the landholders in the eighteenth century had modest homes—two rooms and a loft were common. Fireplaces provided the heat, at least the pittance that did not escape through the chimney. These families owned little in the way of clothing or personal luxuries. Their tools, the items with which they made a living, are their most frequently listed possessions in the old records. Not that these settlers eschewed the good life, for those who could afford it purchased fine furnishings and cloth from England, but such affluence was the exception. Although the paintings we have (in effect, the graphics from the pre-1840 era) often depicted comfort, these portrayed only the upper class at that time, consisting of only a small percentage of the population. Most people lived a meaner existence. Their lifespans proved the hardship; the seventeenth-century Chesapeake area was noted for its high mortality rates. As the colonists became seasoned, the eighteenth century still had no cures for the dreaded smallpox, fevers, dysentery, or complications in childbirth that carried off many in the population. But the data show that the county (with considerably wider territory than now) grew consistently.

Baltimore County Population (Colonial Period Estimates)

1715	1756*	1771*
3,000	18,000	28,000

* Includes Baltimore Town

What we have concluded is that life in the colonial period was not easy. Although most colonists lived in humble circumstances, they were able to improve their lives by supplementing farming returns through crafts or merchandising enterprises. The population grew and by comparison to early settlers, became wealthier, but a rural population with little economic diversity could not produce the riches that the later mercantile-industrial class of Baltimore created in the nineteenth century as the port city grew.

Nevertheless, institutions were developing in outline. There were also some fine residences, at least parts of which are original to the colonial period, such as *Perry Hall Mansion* or *Hampton Farmhouse*. The clergy began to have an impact on society, particularly so in the cases of men like Francis Asbury or Thomas Cradock. The political leadership came then from the higher rungs of the social order, and like their latter-day brethren, they connected the holding of office with special privileges for gaining more wealth.

The activities or recreation, however, were less organized, even primitive. Yet some of those, such as horse racing or tavern socializing were well established. But the kinds of organized recreation that came in the nineteenth century and that have carried over into the modern era waited for a more ordered society that had wealth and leisure.

In the era following the American Revolution, profound changes occurred in the region. One of the most significant involved the growth of Baltimore City, then part of Baltimore County. As a thriving port and the third largest city in the fledgling nation, Baltimore's urban energies allowed it to dominate the region. Because the port offered an outlet for the county's agricultural surplus, the city's domination was vital to the surrounding county's economic health. But the city also had an appetite for political power and developed a need for services that forced a divergence from the county by the mid-century. The city's extension of the boundaries in 1816 (the northern line became what is now North Avenue in Baltimore) served notice of the new political and demographic muscle. In 1854, what had been essentially a joint governing arrangement between Baltimore City and the county was broken when the county separated all of its functions and established a county seat in Towson.

Towson was then a crossroads location marked especially by its taverns; it absorbed the county court functions without disturbing its bucolic setting. There were other locations represented in our photo collection that mimicked Towson in all but political ways. Catonsville and Reisterstown, too, grew because of their turnpike connections.

Transportation improvements in the nineteenth century unified what was then a truly sprawling jurisdiction. The building of private turnpikes that replaced some trails and inadequate roads improved access to the port of Baltimore. But the speed and ease of transportation brought by the railroads were improvements on a scale only comparable in modern times to a transatlantic crossing via the Concorde instead of the *Queen Elizabeth II*. When the Baltimore & Ohio Railroad opened the iron way from Baltimore to Ellicotts Mills, it cut an entire day's journey to one hour. The breath-taking speed and the later improvements in comfort made the railroads a marvel for the people who used them—and made great fortunes for the entrepreneurs who owned them. Shortly after the mid-nineteenth century, the streetcars (first horse-powered, then electrified) improved the access to the city and allowed the suburbs to sprout in every direction along the city boundaries. Both of these transportation advances literally kept people out of the muddy ruts such as the ones on Sweet Air Road in front of Chestnut Grove Church, where unfortunately no one had a choice in the mode of travel.

For its citizens, Baltimore County provides a commendable level of services that grows with each decade. Its 1988-1989 fiscal year operating budget of $960.9 million is an almost unfathomable contrast to a nineteenth-century budget that paid merely for a few clerks, the part-time county commissioners, the judges, and a relatively small number of school personnel. No regular police or fire services even existed until the 1870s, when the suburban fringe around the Baltimore City boundaries required them. Even then there was considerable reluctance on the part of the citizenry or political leaders to expand these services unless they were pressured by reform movements or citizen uproar. Three such reform periods took place, with the Progressive era at the beginning of the twentieth century, the suburbanization movement in the 1940s and 1950s, and the political reform movement, with its new vision of public service, in the 1970s and 1980s.

Schools, too, have undergone significant change as a result of both professionalization and societal expectations. Even when inadequate, as they were in the nineteenth century, schools have always gobbled up tax dollars and resulted in the highest expenditures of any county service department. But their effect has been more a reflection of what the citizens wanted them to do, as we can see in the photos illustrating the efforts to provide both academic and vocational preparation. It is hard to imagine that we would now tolerate the employment of a fourteen-year-old substitute in an elementary classroom, as occurred once in 1916. In addition, an entire generation has passed since separate black schools, which were clearly unequal to white schools in equipment, curriculum, or physical plant, were outlawed. Before this crucial change, a black community on Schwartz Avenue (South Towson) literally raised the funds to rent school space. Furthermore, there were no black high schools in the county until the 1939 openings of Carver in Towson, Bragg in Sparrows Point, and Banneker in Catonsville. Obviously, these were impossible locations for many blacks; black students simply quit after seventh grade, if indeed they went that far.

It may be noted that even white students in remote locations had great difficulty attending high school, too, although they had many more choices (eleven sites). But what the high schools offered in curriculum had at least improved from an earlier period; between 1886 and 1903, Franklin High School in Reisterstown was the only state-accredited high school in the county.

Several other factors aid in understanding county politics and public service. The first of these is the overwhelming predominance of the Democratic party since the Civil War. With only a few brief years when they were tossed out by contrary voters, the county commissioners and their successors (the county executives and county councils) have been Democrats. Generally, true reforms have arisen within the Democratic party because the Republicans had little hope of winning and in numerous cases failed to contest offices. This imbalance has been adjusted to an extent by the increased Republican registration and election of Republicans to state office (the Maryland Senate and House of Delegates) in the 1980s.

The second factor in understanding county government is bossism. Since the Reconstruction era, the leaders of the Democratic party machinery until recently have controlled county patronage and privileges in a tightly knit arrangement. There have been intraparty squabbles, but until the advent of home rule in 1957, unchecked power was in the hands of the Democratic leadership. Democratic domination exists to some extent in the present decade, but the rearrangements of councilmanic elections and reapportionment of state legislative districts have dispersed the decision-making procedures.

A third factor in county political life is unquestionably the corruption in various bribery and kickback schemes which have been proven in court. These cases include the conviction of a county executive (Dale Anderson). Former county executive Spiro T. Agnew pleaded *nolo contendere* before his trial date. Several state officeholders from the county and other county officials also faced legal charges and were convicted. Much of the corruption relates broadly to the land-use decisions, integral to planning and zoning, that county leaders must arbitrate. Corruption is perhaps an unfortunate by-product of one-party control, citizen apathy, and rapid growth patterns; governmental policies, as well as personal failure, play a role in permitting it to occur.

Early religious history for the county, in several ways, has been overemphasized. While it is true that Lord Baltimore had a religious purpose as one reason for founding the colony, his other purpose was to make money by developing a feudal barony. That is, he expected to attract settlers who would become landholders and pay annual quitrents to the Lord Proprietor. Lord Baltimore was a Catholic, but at no time were Protestants discouraged from migrating to Maryland. In fact, the second Lord Baltimore attempted to soothe disputing religious factions among colonists with the Toleration Act of 1649. Later, when the Anglican Church became the established (meaning official) church of the province, other denominations openly worshipped, with the exception of Catholics. Yet in Baltimore County, the number of churches remained small and the area's sparse population did not attract clergymen.

In addition, few settlers participated in church affairs, partly because of the problem of distance, which was compounded by the miserable condition of roads. Second, most colonists came for economic opportunity and not for religious reasons, and their connections to organized religion were often tenuous or nonexistent. Also, the formality of the established (Anglican) church apparently generated little enthusiasm. It was not until the beginning of Methodism, shortly before the American Revolution, that any religious excitement occurred. The Methodist movement grew quickly, in part because of the dedicated clergy willing to ride the circuit, the receptiveness of the audience, and the informal worship arrangements (often meeting in homes).

In the nineteenth century, the ability of a more settled and larger population to travel resulted in great interest in organized churches. Other factors encouraging organized religion included the ending of legal restrictions on Catholics (at the time of the Revolution) and later for Jews. Large attendance at camp meetings in various locations also stirred religious development. The sites of such meetings, such as the Camp Chapel in Perry Hall or Emory Grove in Glyndon, attracted throngs of people, making them some of the most important gathering places anywhere in the nineteenth century.

Organized religious observances have remained significant for many present countians. Religious diversity continues, and new congregations are still forming. By a recent count, there were 464 places of worship in Baltimore County. Methodists were the leading denomination with nearly one-fourth of that total.

Until the twentieth century, the county remained essentially agrarian, with only an occasional cluster of stores and services for the farming community. The agricultural presence is now hard to recreate in a panorama that has changed so radically, but photos of the barns, hay wagons, dairies, livestock, and farm implements should remind us of the rural nature of nineteenth- and early twentieth-century Baltimore County. The rural legacy is now rapidly disappearing in the face of housing demands, coupled with the dramatic rise of land values that are incompatible with agricultural profitability.

Farming was the leading economic activity in Baltimore County until recently. The pace of life reflected this agrarian setting as life was dictated by the needs of crops and livestock. These needs are also reflected in the abundance of outbuildings appearing in the farm photos, as farmers used different structures for different purposes, and in nearly all instances that we found, constructed substantial barns—even larger than many homes. These barns and outbuildings have mostly departed; much of the hay and silage is stored under temporary covers, returning to earlier techniques. Large timbered barns cost a great deal to construct and to maintain compared to metal pole buildings, which are also more compatible with modern-day farm equipment and operations.

In the late twentieth century, one is also struck by the amount of home production that has now passed into the commercial sphere. Families had regular periods to butcher the hogs, preserve the produce from the gardens, and stockpile firewood for heat and cooking. But even for farmers, the power of technology affected their lives. The thresher and steam tractors significantly reduced the amount of labor needed and, with other advances, increased the amount of land one person could farm. The advent of electricity, improved transportation, and new equipment radically changed the dairy business. After the New Deal rearrangements, and subsequent revisions of rules in the agricultural markets, the once-vigorous dairy industry gradually dwindled to a mere handful (thirty-eight dairymen in 1988, according to the county extension agent.)

Another major economic entity in the county was the mill. The county's situation on the fall line, with its numerous streams, had very early provided locations for thriving mill complexes. When the money of the city sought investment opportunity, it went to the textile mills, such as Oella, Warren, or Phoenix, where hundreds of men, women, and children traded the drudgery of farm labor for the monotony of tending mill machinery, perhaps no less nor more exciting than the fields. These textile mills, the flour mills such as Gambrill's, and the smaller grist and sawmills that once dotted the landscapes symbolized economic diversity and vitality. Photographers have certainly found them interesting, judging by the numbers of surviving images, only a few of which have been reproduced here.

Of course, many of the region's mill sites passed into the confines of Baltimore City, especially after the 1888 annexation of county land which took in the Hampden-Woodberry complex. But the mills that remained, such as Oella, Warren, Alberton, and Phoenix, wove themselves into the twentieth century. Flour mills, too, continued to produce for a regional market. These large-scale capitalistic ventures visually broke the small town and pastoral landscape in a distinct manner that attracted photographers. Why was that? We suggest several theories. The mills were major employers, particularly when the economy boomed. The sheer size of the buildings and surrounding townscapes must have been attractive. They were clearly not the norm, and although we have several represented here, they were isolated geographically. Also, the mills represented economic concentration and wealth, at least for the owners. Lastly, they existed for long periods; even Warren might have produced for another decade or two had not the Loch Raven Reservoir project quieted its looms.

If the textile mills offered the photographer a massive subject, the country gristmills, which now seem quaint, offered a variation on the agrarian theme. They stood as symbols of an era when there was less centralization, where the small farmer might grind his grain without shipping it to an impersonal market. Economics and technology were unyielding forces that eventually led to the demise of country millers, but these mills represented both a vitality and commercial success through the nineteenth and for some, into the twentieth century. Although rapid technological change typifies the 1980s, both the textile and gristmills used essentially the same methods of production that with business acumen remained profitable from the early Industrial Revolution well into the twentieth century.

Judging the impact of these enterprises on the local economy is made more interesting by the social connotations. Historians and social analysts have long argued the merits of the mill town. On the one hand, there is the overwhelming evidence that mill jobs meant long hours, dangerous conditions, low pay, child labor, and patronizing mill owners. On the other hand, there was obvious affection (at least in oral recollections) of many workers toward their jobs and managers, the excitement provided in town activities, and the enjoyment of higher wages than they could earn from seasonal agricultural work. These ideas probably are all part of the mill town experience. The pictures give more of a sense of human contact in the milltowns than in the agricultural environs.

Small businesses such as country stores, artisans' work such as blacksmithing, and public accommodations such as taverns or hotels also contributed to the town landscapes of Baltimore County. In the nineteenth and even well into the twentieth century, these facilities tended to serve a local population that did not commute long distances. They also reflected a simpler method of marketing in communities where there was decidedly less money than current suburbanites enjoy. These businesses were far more personal affairs—the owners knew and trusted their customers to pay their bills, and the consumer expected to receive quality goods and services. One expectation apparently was that one stop generally would provide all items. The pictures of the Guttenberger, Weis, or Foley stores indicate a wide variety of products and as much inventory as space allowed. No next-day delivery or just-in-time inventory procedures were in effect for these retailers.

The inns and taverns also reflected a slower pace and less hurried travel than is the case in the late twentieth century. Until the roads improved to handle automobiles, a plethora of inns was required for frequent overnight stops. Even in the twentieth century, for example, those who had business in the Circuit Court in Towson might need a room if the proceedings dragged on for more than a day. From shopkeeper to smith, from tavernkeeper to cabinetmaker-funeral director, county towns provided all the necessary services.

In the post-World War II era, the individual community stores gave way to the regional shopping centers. Eastpoint (1956) and Westview (1958) opened the new direction and a continuous development of new strip centers and malls has devoured open fields and clogged the traffic arteries, but also provided a significant gain for the county tax coffers and the local job market. A problem has been that the outermost (or latest ring of malls) proved detrimental to the inner ones. Security Mall economically undermined Westview; Owings Mills Mall is not assisting Pikesville to retain a viable business district. One of the latest of these, Nottingham Properties' White Marsh Mall, contains 190 leased locations and five department stores covering 152 acres. As such shopping centers attempt to provide for every possible family need or desire, the modern mall with its emphasis on frequent visits may have indeed become a new cathedral to the suburban consumer.

Overall, Baltimore County's continued economic development has provided a base for citizen prosperity; Census Bureau data from 1985 indicates over sixteen thousand establishments providing employment for more than a quarter million people at a payroll exceeding $4.5 billion.

Baltimore County contains every type of house from the grandiose to the merely sufficient, with many in the middle. To select photographs reflecting all the myriad styles would be impossible. The examples chosen are here because we believe that the way we live is reflected in these houses. They are important in judging how a generation viewed itself; each era has distinct values that are reflected in the structures.

Even the oldest buildings extant, however, have endured countless alterations to bring them up to modern standards. Therefore, using *Clynmalira* as it now stands to represent eighteenth-century housing is simply ahistorical. The 1988 version barely resembles the beginnings. Much the same happens to even more ordinary houses as owners frequently update them to suit new styles and to meet the legal requirements of codes prior to sale. Housing tended to reflect current notions in popular magazines as much in the nineteenth century, when *Godey's Ladies Book* offered patterns, as it does in the twentieth century, when *House Beautiful* or *Better Homes & Gardens* offer the latest notion.

Of the county's 257,000 (1985 data) dwelling units, we have tried simply to offer an interesting choice by size, geographic location, and architectural style.

Baltimore County has always been an attractive place to live. Its rolling hills have provided appealing landscapes for communities to nestle in, as well as the water power that generated early industrial energy—and jobs. The county has also consistently offered property tax rates that were half those of Baltimore City, while its proximity to an urban area and its own active society offer access to many lively activities and events. Small wonder that the county historically has drawn in not only out-of-staters but also newcomers from all parts of Europe, from Asia, and from Latin America. Major groups coming into the county have included blacks, Hispanics, Asians, Irish, Germans, Eastern Europeans, and Southern Europeans. The table below illustrates the growth of population.

Baltimore County Population*

1800	1850+	1900+	1920+	1950	1985 (e
25,434	41,592	90,755	74,817	270,278	665,2

* All totals exclude Baltimore City
+ These are misleading numbers compared to earlier years because they reflect population lost in the 1816, 1888, and 1918 extensions of Baltimore City boundaries, and the 1837 creation of Carroll County.

The ways in which the populace of Baltimore County enjoyed themselves, also captured our attention. By the latter decades of the nineteenth century, there were numerous pastimes that apparently attracted both the rich and the poor. Sports tended to be carefully orchestrated, with teams in all locales for boys and girls in schools, and for men and women in search of leisure. Picnics and outings, church entertainments, organized forays of mill operatives, swimming in the bay and the tributaries, fishing trips to the shores of the eastern county, or visits to amusement parks all attest to the growing importance of leisure and the recording of it on film. These citizens seemed to enjoy themselves. There is a connection between the decline in farms and the increase in a suburban population that required more organized or planned sports rituals.

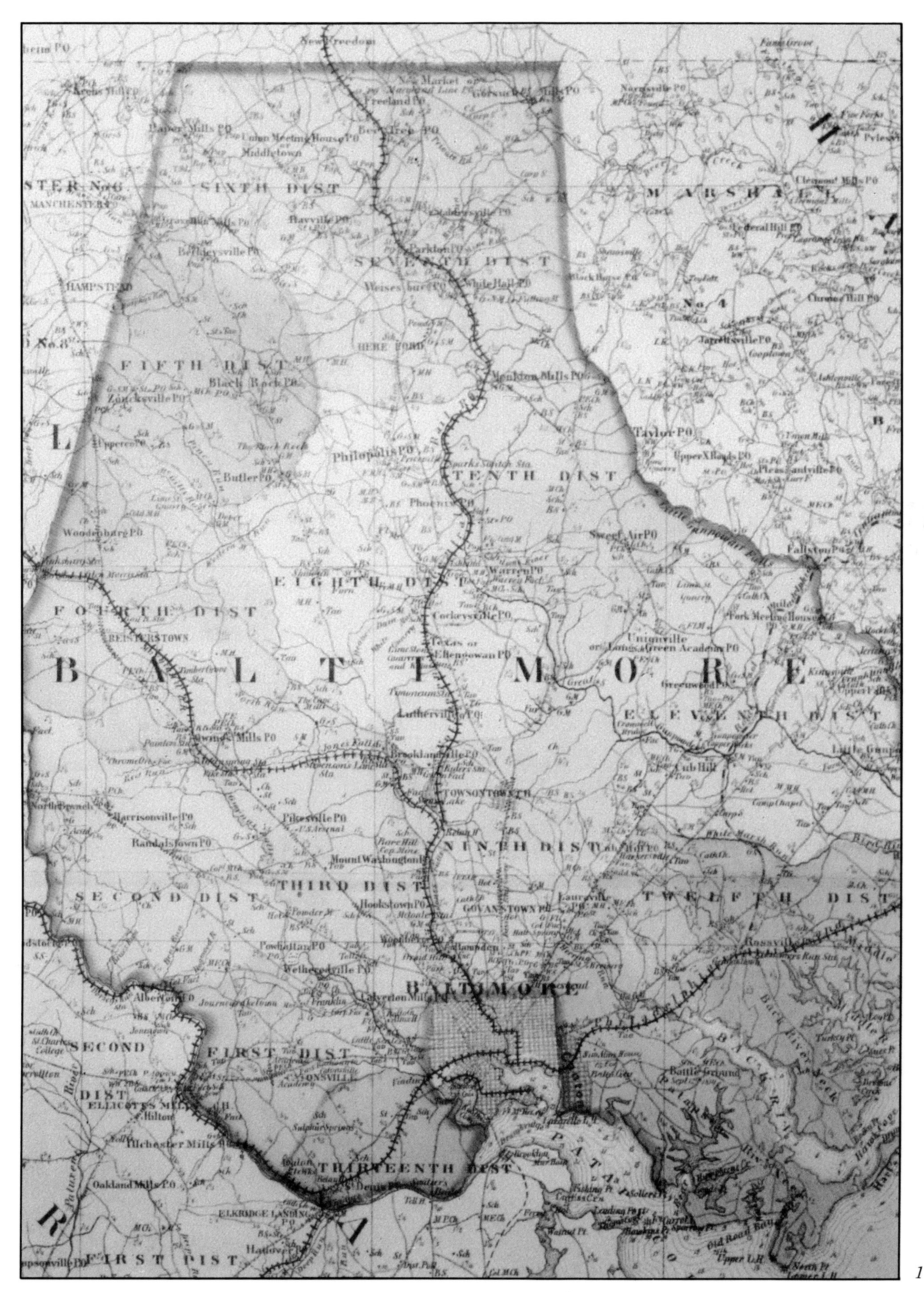

1

Baltimore County as it appeared in the 1866 Martenet map. See postscript, page 296 for modern-day analysis.

2

Hampton, *Hampton Lane, Towson, built by Capt. Charles Ridgely between 1783 and 1790. It was held by the Ridgelys until 1948, when it was purchased by the Avalon Foundation and presented to the United States. It is now a National Historic Site administered by the National Parks Service, Department of the Interior.*

Hampton, *like* Wye *on the Eastern Shore, is a five-part mansion, having a large central block surmounted by a unique cupola, balanced by two hyphens and two wings which were service areas. One side housed the kitchen and pantries, and the other the business offices of both the estate and the Northampton Iron Works, the source of the Ridgely fortune. The main block contains the essential rooms for entertaining—dining room, drawing room, music room, and parlor. In the terraced front lawn the estate has six formal parterres, which were landscaped over many years. There are magnificent stands of ancient trees, a tea room which utilizes the old estate offices, a gift shop in the former kitchen wing, a restored Orangery which can be rented for receptions, and the brick-walled Ridgely burial grounds. Preservation Maryland, a private organization, maintains the graveyard.*

Hampton *is made of stone covered with terracotta-tinted stucco. The coloring is caused by the iron-bearing sand used in making the stucco.*

3

Francis Asbury was the first general superintendent or bishop of American Methodism. He was born in 1745, in Handsworth near Birmingham, England. Apprenticed to a Methodist blacksmith who converted him, Asbury became a minister and answered John Wesley's 1771 call for volunteers to go to America.

The Revolution left the Methodists with a shortage of clergy. Wesley "laid hands" on Dr. Thomas Coke and sent him to do likewise with Asbury, which he did at the Christmas 1784 Conference, when the Methodist Episcopal Church in America was established as the world's first independent Methodist Church.

An important meeting place for Methodists, which also provided lodging for the bishop, was Perry Hall, *then owned by Harry Dorsey Gough. Weak and in declining health, Asbury died on circuit in 1816 in Spottsylvania, Virginia. His remains were interred in Mt. Olivet Cemetery, Baltimore.*

4

Ballestone, *Rocky Point Golf Course, poses problems for the title searcher as no substantial houses are reported on the site in the 1798 tax list index. By 1813, however, owner Isaac Stansbury did have two hundred dollars worth of improvements listed, which was probably a modest house. An 1836 advertisement is the first evidence of a brick house on the site. The Miller family owned the house from 1850 to 1969, when it was acquired by the county's Department of Recreation and Parks to celebrate the American Bicentennial. It has been sensitively restored and outfitted as a living museum. Its tours and programs are a source of great community pride.*

5

Panoramic View of the Scenery on the Patapsco River for 7 miles Above and Below Ellicott's Mills, Md. . . . . *A key to E. Sachse's lithograph circa 1855 shows Alberton at the top, followed by Oella, then the Granite factory (totally destroyed in 1868), the Patapsco Flour Mills on the Baltimore County side, opposite Ellicott City, Gray's Mill, and the Thistle Mill. By the 1920s Thistle was making automobile tire composition. The Dismal Mill, opposite Thistle, is on the Howard County side of the river.*

6

View of Ellicott's Mills, Md. . . . *This E. Sachse lithograph of 1854 is noteworthy for the border views of the old Patapsco River mills and Ellicott City buildings.*

7

8

Liverpool-born John E. Owens (1823-1886) was the most celebrated comedian in America when he purchased Edward Taylor's 197-acre farm near Towson in 1853. He built a mansard-roofed mansion which he called Aigburth Vale. *Owen's hospitality was legendary; his landscaped grounds were distinctive. After his death, Sheppard-Pratt Hospital, the holder of a mortgage on the estate, sold the main portion of the land at auction in 1889.*

John Hubner, a Catonsville developer, acquired the property. By 1919 he had sold the house and 4.9 acres to Dr. George F. Sargent for a mental hospital, which operated until 1950. Hubner sold the agricultural land to Towson Nurseries. The nurseries sold to the Board of Education in 1943 and 1946, and Towson High School was built on the site. The mansion, still used by the board, served as its headquarters for a time.

Owens is credited with giving the Confederacy its anthem. He had taken a four-year lease on a New Orleans theater at the beginning of the Civil War, and selected the minstrel walk-around tune "Dixie" for a military drill routine performed by forty girls in Zouave costumes. Soon everyone was whistling the catchy tune in march time.

Pimlico Race Track was still in Baltimore County until 1918. Racing began at the track on October 25, 1870. As the idea for a Maryland track had formed at a dinner at Saratoga, New York, attended by Governor Oden Bowie, the main race on opening day was called the Dinner Party Stakes. The winner was a horse named Preakness, which had been sired by Lexington, America's then-leading horse at stud. Governor Bowie requested that the race be renamed the Preakness, thus beginning the history of racing's Middle Jewel of the coveted Triple Crown.

The track is pictured here during a harness race in a Hoen lithograph from about 1895.

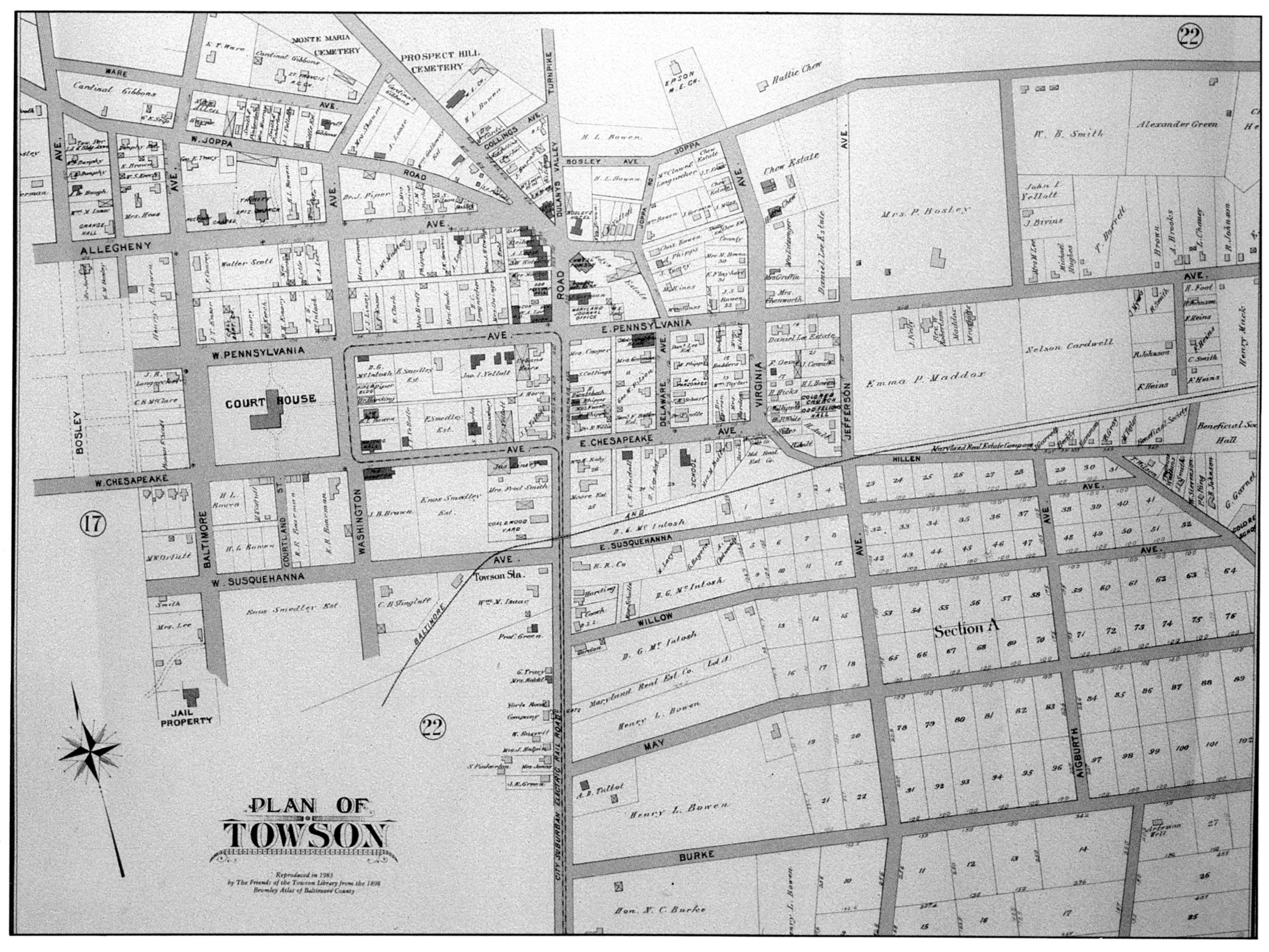

Towson as it appeared in 1898. See postscript, page 296 for modern-day analysis.

10

An electronics class at a Southeastern Vocational-Technical Center, at Sollers Point Road, Dundalk, is at work in 1974.

11

A teacher checks the work of her pupils at Pinewood Elementary School, Timonium, in 1978. Besides the well-financed, up-to-date public school system, Baltimore County has a large number of excellent parochial and private schools.

12

This 1976 aerial view of the 148-acre Essex Community College campus on Rossville Boulevard indicates how important community colleges had become. Essex and its sister campus in Catonsville had begun as part-time colleges in 1957, meeting in temporary facilities. By 1988 each served approximately ten thousand full and part-time students. A third campus opened in Dundalk in 1971.

Franklin Square Hospital and the Eastern Regional Health Center stand beyond the trees at the center rear of the photo.

This is the kindergarten class at Logan Elementary School in Dundalk, 1974.

13

14

A class in choral conducting is under way at the University of Maryland, Baltimore County, Catonsville, during the 1978 academic year.

15

A modern chemistry lab is shown at Goucher College, Towson, 1978.

A high altitude 1987-1988 photograph of the entire White Marsh area shows the mall in the center, with the ribbon of Interstate 95 to the right. The white area to the right of Interstate 95 is the old White Marsh quarry, expected to be worked out by 1991 and slated for future commercial development. North of the mall are three residential areas; from left to right: Ambermill, Woodfall, and Lawrence Hill. Immediately to the left of the top left corner of the mall is the police station. Southeast of that is White Marsh Plaza, a shopping area which includes a chain food store. South of that are (top) the health center, and, below, professional center buildings numbers one to three. To the right of the health center and professional buildings is the White Marsh Branch of the Baltimore County Public Library. East of the library, bordering Interstate 95, (bottom to top) are American Bank Stationery Company, Williams Mobile Office, the White Marsh Business Center and White Marsh High Tech (two equal-size buildings), Stump Electric Company, and the post office (one square building across the road from Lawrence Hill).

18

Taken from the top of one of the Washington Avenue bank buildings in Towson, this photo shows Dixon and Dixon's 1854 courthouse, the 1910 Baldwin and Pennington north and south wings added onto the original facade, and the 1926 and 1958 additions (making an H shape). Toward the top of the picture looms Gaudreau's massive County Courts Building of the 1970s.

17

The expanding business community at Hunt Valley was photographed on July 21, 1983. Near the top of the picture, to the right of Interstate 83 are the low buildings of Marriott's Hunt Valley Inn. To their right are the Executive Plaza office towers, and to their right, off by itself, is the world headquarters of the PHH Group. Across Shawan Road from PHH is the low-lying Hunt Valley Mall. On the hill above the mall, and to the left of it, is the Masonic Home of Maryland, originally known as Bonnie Blink, *once the Weiskittel estate. It is now a retirement home for Maryland's Freemasons and their families. Across Shawan Road from the mall and to the right of the picture is a C & P Telephone Company office building. The bridge crossing Interstate 83, mid-point in the photo, is Beaver Dam Road.*

Baltimore County provides a welcoming and cooperative environment for business and industry. An active and effective, forward-looking Baltimore County Chamber of Commerce supports and advises businesses and corporations of all sizes, from the internationally renowned to the fledgling one-or two-person enterprise.

19

The AAI Corporation had started in 1950 as Aircraft Armaments Industries on Reisterstown Road, Pikesville, and moved to Cockeysville in 1955. This major defense contractor has made a varied line of products over the years, including cartridge cases, riot control equipment, armored vehicle turrets, fuses, ammunition parts, and sophisticated computer-driven training and simulation devices. The view shows computer-controlled machining of ammunition parts in 1978.

20

A Grumman mechanic is refining the finishes left by machine cuts in the lower wing-pivot fitting for the F-14 Navy fighter plane. The F-14 ("Tomcat") was a featured part of the movie Top Gun.

The Grumman Corporation's Aircraft Systems Division in Glen Arm started out as General Engineering, Inc., at 2401 and 2527 Frederick Road in 1946. It had been started by Irvin C. Tillman as a subcontract machining shop. Purchased by Grumman and moved to Glen Arm, it garnered some notable contracts: parts for the PSM patrol aircraft for Martin; parts for the F86 fighter and F105 fighter, both for Republic; parts of the B70 bomber for North American; major wing tips for both the F106 fighter and B58 for General Dynamics; and parts for the F14, the A6, and the F111 for Grumman. The facility covers 380,000 square feet on both sides of Long Green Pike.

21

An engineer in 1978 tests personnel air samples submitted by coal miners, to assure safe working conditions. He is attached to the Bendix Corporation Environmental and Process Instruments Division on Taylor Avenue.

22

Making cardboard boxes in 1976 at the Ward Machinery Company, Cockeysville.

Carroll's store in Jacksonville, at the intersection of the Jarrettsville Pike and Paper Mill Road, served area residents from 1902 until 1987. Carroll family members who ran the store over the years were Perry; Miles, Sr.; Miles, Jr.; another Perry; and then Thomas (son of Miles, Jr.), who helped run the store with his uncle Perry. After the store closed, developer P. F. Obrecht and Company razed the structure and erected Paper Mill Village, which opened in the spring of 1988.

The scene here was a familiar one to country store users throughout the county. In this case, Perry Carroll is slicing fresh deli meats behind his refurbished counter.

23

The Hunt Valley Inn was started in 1971 on the site of Gerar, E. Gittings Merryman's horse and cattle farm. The Marriott Corporation began operating it on January 15, 1977. Shown here is the inn's restaurant, the Cinnamon Tree.

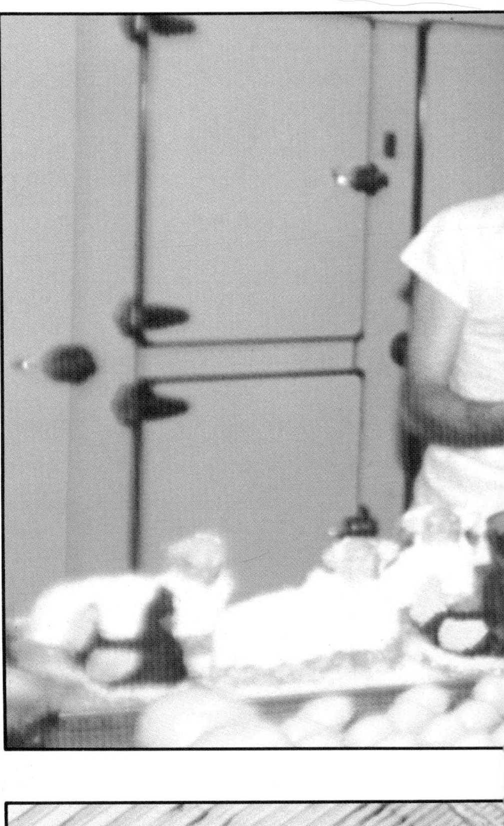

24

26 All of the county's malls are in a constant state of rejuvenation and modernization. This restful scene was in Security Mall in Woodlawn in 1976.

28

Gerhard Kadolph arrived from Germany in 1952. He began to work in the Strand Bakery, next to the Strand Theater, Shipping Place, Dundalk. The bakery, which had been in operation since the 1930s under a Mr. Schroeder, was sold to Kadolph and a co-worker, John Wafer, in 1955. Kadolph bought out his partner and continued in business until 1971. After he closed the bakery, Kadolph worked as a pastry specialist in a number of places, including Haussner's. He is shown decorating pastries.

25

Boordy Vineyards is a central Maryland winery which was started by Evening Sun *writer Philip Wagner in 1945 in Riderwood. In 1980, Robert Deford, whose family grew some of Wagner's grapes on their Long Green farm, bought the business and the name and moved the wine production to Long Green Pike. Boordy makes highly regarded Seyval Blancs, Chardonnays, and Cabernet Sauvignons. Rob Deford is surrounded here by casks in one of the cool aging rooms. The handsome stone winery building on the farm, originally a Gittings family holding, is very old.*

27

George W. Radebaugh, from Harford County, started the family florist business in Towson in 1921. An impressive show of poinsettias was displayed in 1966.

29

The Baltimore Bicycling Club lines up for the Towsontown Gran Prix on April 16, 1977. The old courthouse and the new County Courts Building are in the background.

30

In 1983 champion golfer Cathy Whitworth participated in this playing of the Lady Carling Open at Pine Ridge Golf Course in Timonium. Towson's Carol Mann was a frequent winner of this and other golfing events.

31

A skylarking boy shows off his skill on the swing above the Beaver Dam swimming quarry in Cockeysville in 1978. In some places the water in the flooded quarry is over two hundred feet deep.

Split-second action at a football game at Pot Spring Elementary School in Timonium in 1974.

32

33

The Baltimore County Department of Recreation and Parks maintains an outstanding countywide network of free public tennis and basketball courts, golf courses, public beaches, and ball fields. Here an agile senior citizen makes a sharp return at the net.

34

The Baltimore Symphony Orchestra left its summer home on the Goucher College campus in 1977. On July 31 that year it began an unbroken tradition of offering summer concerts under a striped pavilion on the slopes of Oregon Ridge Park, Hunt Valley. These events are much loved by county residents, especially the Fourth of July fireworks extravaganza and the gala that ends the season. The concerts provide opportunities for relaxed, informal family picnic outings.

Throughout the year Baltimore County agencies schedule a variety of interesting and mostly free events in this park: nature walks, festivals, balloon ascensions, and sledding, as well as outdoor concerts of blue grass, jazz, pop, rock, and classical music.

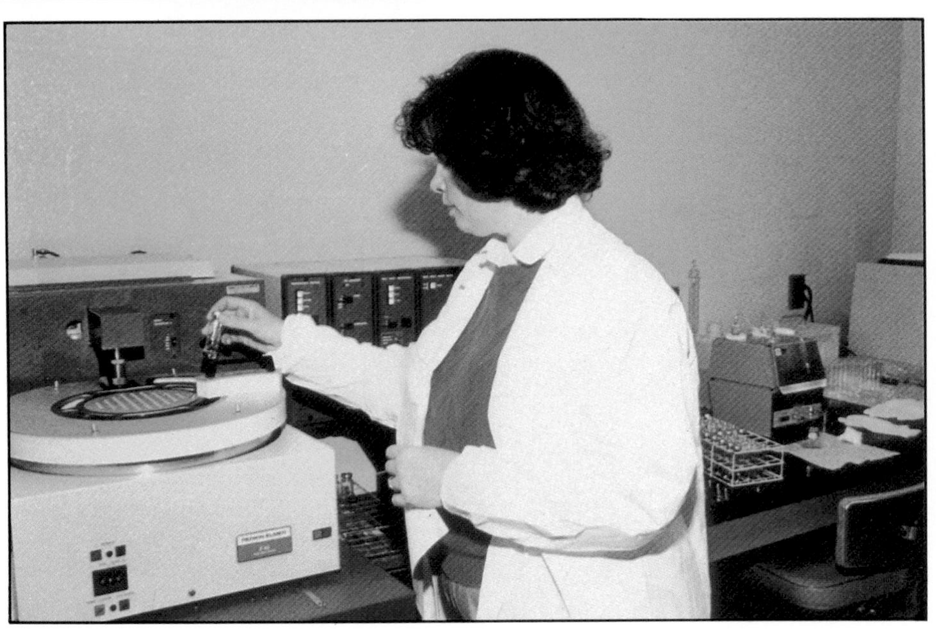

36

Katherine E. Sullivan, Forensic Chemist III, at Maryland State Police headquarters, Pikesville, is utilizing a gas chromograph machine to perform a blood alcohol analysis for a drunken driving case.

Tracing its origin to the mass-produced automobile, the state police grew from the establishment of the position of commissioner of motor vehicles in 1910. This one individual had to police Maryland motorists by himself. By 1914 he was assisted by a few motorcycle deputies. In 1920 the murder of a bystander during a holdup created the uproar needed to fund an appropriate police department. In 1921, thirty-five trained motorcycle deputies, called the State Police Force of the Commissioner of Motor Vehicles, were hired. By 1935 the force had become a separate state agency under a superintendent appointed by the governor. The Maryland State Police took over the renovated Federal Arsenal (and former Confederate Soldier's Home) on September 9, 1950.

35

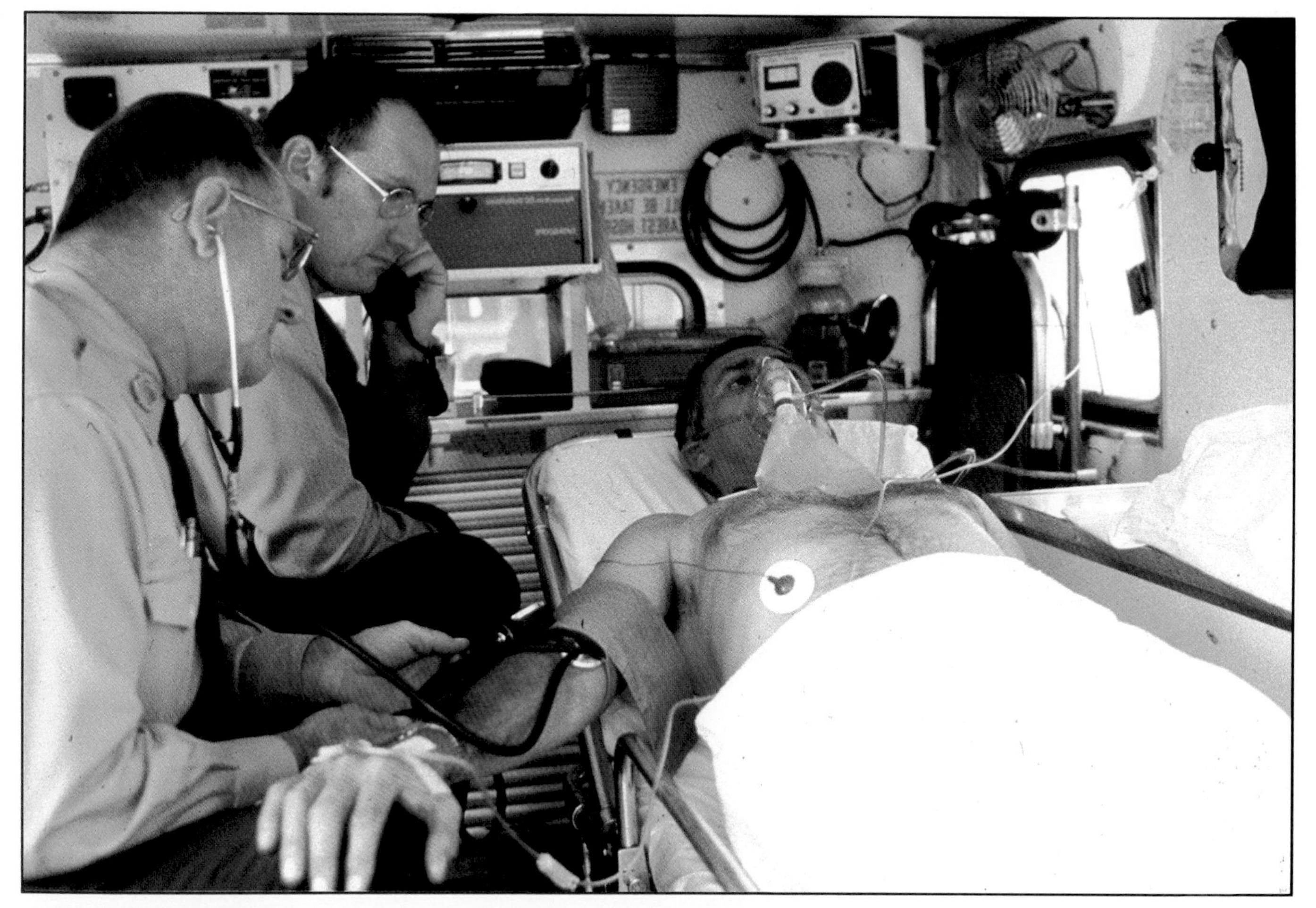

The Baltimore County Fire Department's mobile coronary care unit is in action in 1974. All areas in Baltimore County are now within reach of hospital or outreach clinic care. The Baltimore County Health Department has up-to-date clinics in all major areas. They provide a total range of services, including rabies shots for pets, dental services, mental health and substance abuse counseling, free flu shots, and testing for AIDS.

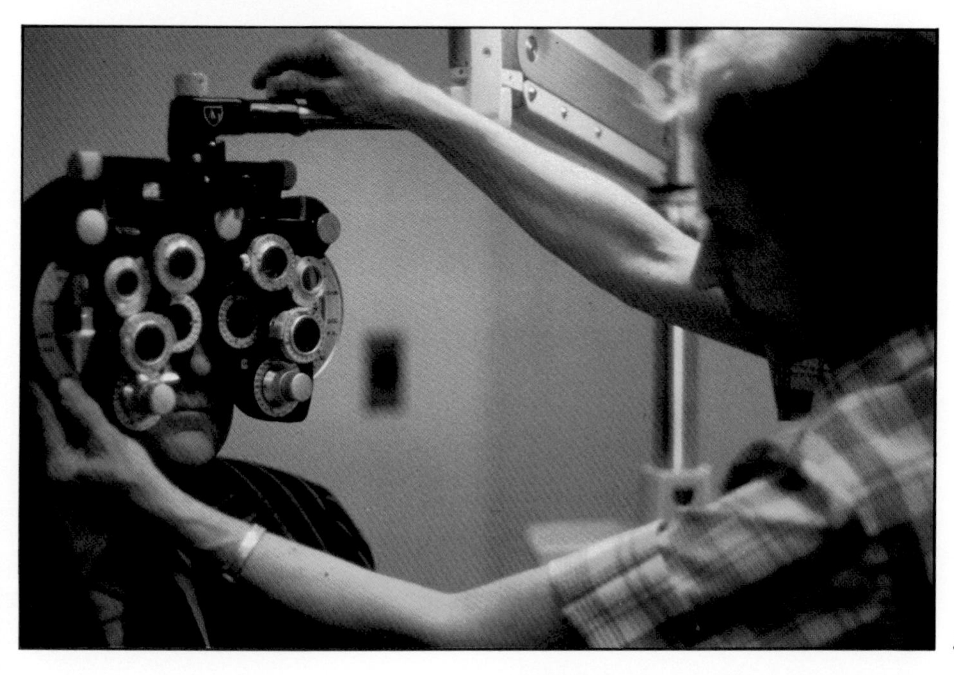

37

An ophthalmologist at the Greater Baltimore Medical Center at North Charles Street, Towson, prepares to give an eye test in 1978.

38

When an Amtrak passenger express slammed into a Conrail train with three locomotives on January 4, 1987, the community of Chase helped the rescue groups and succored the shocked and injured people so magnificently that it was commended by President Ronald Reagan.

The Conrail engineer and the brakeman, who had been smoking marijuana, had failed to replace a signal bulb in the cab, had not activated a taped warning whistle, and had deactivated the deadman's pedal, which would have stopped the train. The Conrail engineer's sense of timing was undermined by the narcotic; he overlooked warning lights and got onto the main line just ahead of the Amtrak engine, which hit the third Conrail locomotive and jackknifed. Many Amtrak cars were badly crumpled, and 16 people died, with 175 injured Conrail engineer Ricky Gates pleaded guilty to one count of manslaughter by locomotive and was sentenced to five years in prison. As a result of this accident, federal regulations covering substance abuse by transportation workers were adopted.

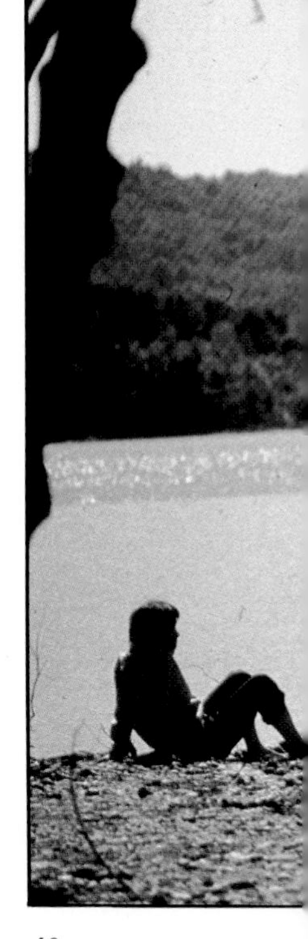

40

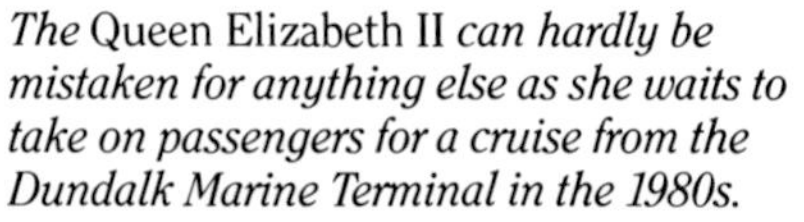

The Queen Elizabeth II *can hardly be mistaken for anything else as she waits to take on passengers for a cruise from the Dundalk Marine Terminal in the 1980s.*

39

41

The beauty of Loch Raven has made it a refuge for boaters and fishermen and nature lovers generally. On weekends much of the most scenic road around Loch Raven is reserved exclusively for bicyclists.

Dappled light reflects off the Chesapeake Bay as a lone boat with colorful sails glides off into a 1974 sunset.

42

Beer and crab feasts are common summer get-togethers in Baltimore County. These people are digging in during the summer of 1983.

LIFE & LEISURE

Many of the amusements of the late nineteenth and early twentieth centuries were quiet and unadventuresome by late twentieth-century standards. Common pastimes were quiet rowing on lakes; mannerly riding on extremely heavy, old-fashioned bikes; a hike; a Sunday ride with horse and carriage; a family picnic in a grove, or a family reunion; a slow-moving game of tennis or croquet; a trip in a friend's steam-powered launch or early gasoline chug-chugger; parlor games, charades, and costume parties. For the more vigorous there was hunting of one kind or another, and for the boys (big or little) football and baseball were the attractions.

Recreation taken for granted by most in 1988 would have been unacceptable for social or religious reasons even fifty years ago. Pool had stag connotations at best and a seedy reputation at worst; girls did not participate in baseball games or join marching bands. Fashions have changed, too, in just how much skin it is acceptable to show at a beach or pool. Indoor card games today are a little more exciting than whist or euchre. Sports are played on Sunday; indeed, even stores are now open Sundays. Twenty-five years ago it was difficult to find an open gas station on Sunday.

Some earlier popular amusements are now either genuine curiosities or are fading fast: examples are croquet, quoits, rolling hoops, hopscotch, and dancing around Maypoles. When was the last time anyone saw a group of boys shooting marbles?

Thornton Nimmo ran an organ manufactory and sales office in Baltimore. He lived in a very large house set on a hill above York Road in Towson, part of the present Towson Branch Library site at 320 York Road. After his death, and before the house was torn down in the 1950s, it served as county Democratic party headquarters and was known as "the castle on the hill." Here Nimmo, abut 1921 or 1922, is enjoying his power boat in Middle River with, front left to right, Mrs. Hess, Mrs. Elizabeth Kenney (wife of the Towson banker, William C. Kenney, who took the picture), Thelma Hess, Elizabeth Watson Gessford, Edmund Kenney, and Virginia Merryman Thomas (a real estate agent and sister of Elizabeth Kenney).

43

In the rowboat, on Lake Roland in 1886, two proper young men in hats, ties and waistcoats, rowing on alternate sides, take a break. (Photo by A. H. Brinkmann)

The Popke family relaxes on their classic wooden launch, the Alvida J. *(named for Alvida Jensen) at Turkey Point, Rockaway, in the early 1900s.*

44

45

The well-maintained power boats at Joe Blazek's Stansbury Yacht Basin in the 1950s epitomize the close relationship many county residents have to their watery playgrounds.

The Baltimore Yacht Club, in a Blakeslee-Lane Studio view of the 1950s, is located on Sue Island, Sue Creek.

46

48

Jerome Smith, the boy on the tricycle, is with his mother, Harriet Jones Smith, in Catonsville in the early 1900s.

Eating watermelon in the 1890s was just as messy then as it is now. Here, members of the Watkins and Bowen families struggle with their slices (to the detriment of their clothes, no doubt) on the grass outside the George Vinton Bowen farmhouse on what is now property of the Greater Baltimore Medical Center.

49

50

Being pulled in their donkey cart, about 1896, were Walter, Arnold and Helmuth Brinkmann of Catonsville.

President Benjamin Harrison visited Bowley's Quarters at least twice, as reported by the Baltimore County Democrat, *on November 16, 1889, and by* Frank Leslie's Illustrated Weekly, *on April 8, 1891, from which the illustration is taken.*

51

Two young women while away a summer afternoon about 1899 on a wide veranda cooled by breezes from the Gunpowder River. Clara Brown (later Mrs. Lee Marshall) and Dorothy Baldwin (later Mrs. James Garrettson) played crokinole, a now obscure board game, at Hillside Farm, *Warren.* Hillside *was the summer estate of Dorothy's father, Summerfield Baldwin, who owned the cotton manufacturing village.*

52

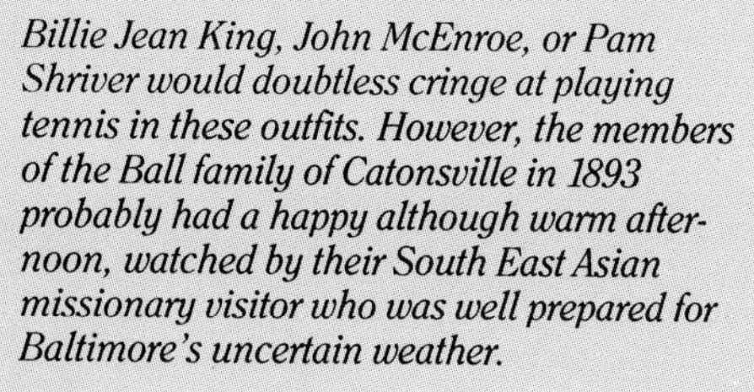

Billie Jean King, John McEnroe, or Pam Shriver would doubtless cringe at playing tennis in these outfits. However, the members of the Ball family of Catonsville in 1893 probably had a happy although warm afternoon, watched by their South East Asian missionary visitor who was well prepared for Baltimore's uncertain weather.

53

54

55

In the summer of 1892 Juliet Gambrill Sewell Baldwin, wife of Summerfield Baldwin, the owner of the Warren Cotton Mill and its village, enjoyed tea with her daughters and their friend on the wide, wraparound porch of Hillside Farm. *Although substantially dressed by today's standards, they could enjoy cooling breezes near the Gunpowder River, as they were on a high hill overlooking the mill and village. From left to right are Juliet Baldwin, Anne Louise Baldwin, Juliet Catherine Baldwin, and Alice Woodward Leakin. Mrs. Baldwin was a niece of Charles A. Gambrill, the flour milling king of Maryland, who had taken her into his family when she was orphaned. Interestingly, Charles Gambrill had actually been the manager of the Warren mill about 1832, at the beginning of his career and before he moved from cotton to flour milling. At Warren, the Baldwins lived in the same old stone house as had her uncle.*

Members of the Myer family of Rosland, *Roslyn, near Pikesville, and friends, with Phineas their oversized dog, in 1894. In the back row, from left to right, are Anna Myer and Michael Keyes; in the middle, Rosalie Shriver and Elizabeth Myer; and in the front James Whedbee and Robert J. Myer.*

We would like to know more about this dignified Catonsville couple, Mamie Williams and her husband Oden, a Union Army veteran.

1909

THE ELKRIDGE HOUNDS

WILL MEET

MARCH

WEDNESDAY 17TH, AT 2.00 P. M.	HUNT, EUDOWOOD SANTARIUM GATE
SATURDAY 20TH, AT 1.00 P. M.	HUNT, HAMPTON GATE
WEDNESDAY 24TH, AT 4.30 P.M.	DRAG, KENNELS
SATURDAY 27TH, AT 1.00 P. M.	HUNT, MEREDITH'S FORD BRIDGE
WEDNESDAY 31ST, AT 4.30 P. M.	DRAG, LOCH RAVEN

APRIL

SATURDAY 3RD, AT 1.00 P. M.	HUNT, TIMONIUM
WEDNESDAY 7TH, 4.30 P. M.	DRAG, SHERWOOD
SATURDAY 10TH, 1.00 P. M.	HUNT, HAMPTON GATE
WEDNESDAY 14TH, 4 30 P. M.	DRAG, TIMONIUM
SATURDAY 17TH, 1.00 P. M.	HUNT, HILLENDALE GATE HILLEN ROAD
WEDNESDAY, 21ST, 4.30 P. M.	DRAG, MEREDITH'S FORD BRIDGE

THE ELKRIDGE HOUNDS WILL LEAVE THE CLUB HOUSE 5 A. M. ON MONDAY MORNINGS DURING MARCH AND APRIL UP TO AND INCLUDING MONDAY, APRIL 19TH.

GRAEME TURNBULL
SECRETARY

THOS. DEFORD
M. F. H.

58

The annual "fixture card" for the Elkridge fox hunters listed the assigned meeting places for each meet of the season. The club was formed in 1878, moved its meets from Anne Arundel County to Baltimore in 1881 (near the Pimlico Race Track), and in 1883 to Slingluff's Road near Highland Park (adjacent to Mondawmin, *banker George S. Brown's estate). The club incorporated in 1888, purchased former governor Augustus Bradford's estate* Montevideo Park *on Charles Street, and built stables and kennels. They used what is now the present golf clubhouse, once a large tenant house on the estate, as the mansion itself had been burned by Gen. Bradley T. Johnson's Confederate raiders during the Civil War.*

In 1920 the club purchased the 307-acre property of Mrs. Howard Ridgely, called Long Quarter Farm, *at 1609 Pot Spring Road. Neighboring landowners augmented the acreage. In 1935 the club moved to its present site on Pocock Road in Harford County.*

In the early years it was not unusual for hunters, horses, and hounds to board a train to travel to some distant meeting sites, such as to Doughorhegan Manor *in Howard County, to the* Viaduct Hotel *in Relay, to Ellicott City, or* Brooklandville.

The Greenspring Valley Hunt Club, founded in the 1890s, kennels its hounds at Stamford, *a former Philpot estate on Mantua Mill Road, Glyndon. The annual "blessing of the hounds" at St. John's in the Valley Episcopal Church is a much-photographed event of this club.*

57

Since 1962 the St. John's Evangelical Lutheran Church, formerly on Dance Mill Road, has occupied this field at the corner of Dulaney Valley and Manor Roads. Called Knoebel's Corner in the old days, it is being crossed by the Elkridge Fox Hunting Club and Elkridge Hounds in 1930.

60

These two pictures of Boy Scouts need no comment. The older one shows a Lutherville troop on the banks of the Gunpowder River, near Paper Mill Road in 1916 under the direction of its scoutmaster, the Reverend Paul F. Bloomhardt of St. Paul's Lutheran Church, shown helping a pre-scout youngster hold up the flag. Troop 32A is at a 1945 jamboree in Dundalk and looks more relaxed, perhaps because the relatives were not around!

61

59

The St. Denis Glee Club, with mandolins, guitars, drums, and trumpet, was ready for action about 1904.

62

The county's bands and orchestras provided summer enjoyment for thousands of county residents over the years. Every mill town or large village at one time or another had one. The public schools had them, too, and in them this grand old American tradition lives on. The Lansdowne Volunteer Fire Department Band is shown, about 1920.

63

The Towson High Band, about 1917, is a study in instruments and expressions. Some of the Towson boys look about thirteen or fourteen, too young for high school today. At that time, however, state standards defined any school offering more than three grades beyond the sixth as a high school. Twelve full years of schooling were not offered in Baltimore County until after World War II.

64

The Army Band at Fort Howard, photographed about 1910, is typical of the period.

65

The boys in the Catonsville High School orchestra of 1918 were identified as, from left to right, E. Ogle, H. Rosenthal, B. Brinkman, E. Hupfield, and W. Topp.

The Alberton Cornet Band, founded in 1879, appears here in the early 1980s, when it was known as the Daniels Town Band, under the direction of William Webb. This is the last nineteenth-century town band left in the area that still performs, truly a remarkable tradition.

66

67

According to the information on the back of this photo, the women's choir of Dundalk in 1955 sang for special meetings, church meetings, veterans groups, hospitals, and USO's. In the first row, from left to right, are Isabelle Martin, Margaret Kent, Grace Deily, Ember Williams, Mary Simpson, Mim James, Merle Heilman, Ellen Thornton, Minetta Waters, and Roberta Lewis; second row, Ruth Armstrong, Elizabeth Fisher, an unknown woman, Dorothy Jones, Betty Wheeler, Ruth Menicon, Marion Kella, and Virginia Padgett.

68

In 1918 Rosa Ponselle, aged twenty-one, was the youngest dramatic soprano ever to debut at the Metropolitan Opera House. When she retired in 1938, after twenty glorious years, she married Carle A. Jackson and moved to Baltimore County. The Jacksons bought at auction 155 acres of the old Nacirema estate of Gen. Felix Agnus, the Baltimore American *publisher. The house they built for five hundred thousand dollars was appropriately named Villa Pace, after the famous operatic aria "Pace, pace, Mio Dio." Villa Pace was erected on the hilltop where Agnus's house had stood. Now in private ownership and restored following the diva's death in 1981, Villa Pace is visible from Greenspring Valley Drive and overlooks Villa Julie College.*

Rosa Ponselle gave generously of her time and talents to help young singers in their careers. James Morris of the Metropolitan Opera was a friend and protege. The great singer was also a guiding force in the development of the Baltimore Opera Company.

The Villa Pace dining room is seen at Christmas time in 1961, in a Jack Shipley photo. From left to right are Mrs. H. Guy Campbell; Mrs. J. Harold Grady, and Rosa Ponselle. Mrs. Campbell was the wife of a member of the Harry T. Campbell and Sons Stone Products Company. Mrs. Grady's husband was mayor of Baltimore at the time. Later he became a judge.

69

The old Catonsville County Club, or Catonsville Casino, stood on Bloomsbury Avenue, at a site later used by the Catonsville Middle School (formerly the high school). The club lasted from 1891 to November 11, 1906, when a 5:00 a.m. fire in the bowling alley caused it to burn. The building was a focal point for the community, and a wide variety of sports were played there. Famed John McGraw (of the Orioles and New York Giants) came to scout its baseball games; a challenge round for the Davis Cup was played on the grounds; and other events included bowling and cricket, Fourth of July activities, horse shows, and picnics.

Nostalgia buffs tried to resurrect the club; in 1908 a new clubhouse was built on the site. It was later used as the Catonsville High School cafeteria until it was razed in the 1950s. Finally, the clubless Catonsville residents acquired the old Lurman estate, Bloomsbury Farm, *and opened the Rolling Road Golf Club.*

70

The Surburban Club, at the corner of Park Heights and Slade avenues in Pikesville, was established by affluent German Jews in 1903 on land leased from Thomas Beale Cockey of neighboring Lyal Park. The picture dates from the 1930s. The old clubhouse was torn down and a modern one erected in 1960.

The Woodholme Country Club and golf course, Woodholme Avenue, Pikesville, was started in 1926 by the Amity Club of Baltimore for Jews of East European descent. There was a charter membership of a hundred. The picture shows the clubhouse in 1928. When it was rebuilt in 1937, a large swimming pool was added and the overall holdings were increased to 237 acres.

72

Don Swann, Jr., was associated with the Hilltop Theater from its 1938 inception in Ellicott City. In 1942-1943 the theater utilized the Vagabond Players Read Street (Baltimore) space; in 1944-1945 it was at the Mt. Washington Casino. In 1946-1947 it was housed at the Maryland College for Women in Lutherville. For ten years, until 1958, the theater was at Emerson Farms, Brooklandville. Before it closed permanently in 1960, Hilltop was at Therapia Farm, Reisterstown, now the site of Morningside Apartments. The Baltimore Sun photo dates from 1951, as the building program at Emerson Farms was being completed.

Capt. Isaac Emerson, a chemistry graduate of the University of North Carolina, acquired title to the Brooklandwood estate on Falls Road in 1916. The inventor of Bromo-Seltzer and owner of the Emerson Hotel, he ran a spring water bottling works from the large estate, as well as a hundred-cow dairy farm. Most of this milk was sold over the counter at the farm.

Sunday drivers in the Greenspring Valley paused at the farm for dishes of cooling ice cream or a glass of fresh milk, which cost ten to fifteen cents. In June 1976 the old dairy barn was remodeled for use by the Montessori School. The photo shows the entrance to the Brooklandwood Dairy, also known as Emerson Farms.

74

The 1908 Franklin High School, Reisterstown, baseball team was dressed to the nines (or almost!) for the annual portrait. Among the group are young men identified as Stocksdale, O'Meara, John Thomas, Donald Munroe, Mosner, Leslie Oursler, Charles Watters, Cameron, and Hoffman. Most of the first names, as well as which names belong to which players, are so far unknown.

75

The 1932 issue of Sidelights, *the Towson High School's annual, pictured the lacrosse team with its period equipment. Shown from left to right are, in front, W. Watson, G. Schaffer, L. Davis, G. Owens, R. Merrifield, J. Loizeaux, G. Watson, G. Klingelhofer, D. Buck, and T. Wilson; in the back row, Coach MaDan, R. Litsinger, J. Spindler, D. Tillman, R. Loizeaux, H. Webb, H. Reckord, T. Richardson, R. Burke, and J. Harris.*

76

John Ridgely, the fifth master of Hampton *received some friends on the lawn outside his front door, about World War I. From left to right are Otho Ridgely, Sr., John's brother, who lived at the* Furnace Farm*; Charles E. Treadwell; Mrs. Charles E. Treadwell, Grace McGowan, Mrs. William McGowan, Ethelwyn McGowan, William McGowan, and John Ridgely.*

77

These women in the early 1900s are shelling peas on the porch of the Bowen farmhouse, which still stands on Greater Baltimore Medical Center property. From left to right are Alice Gorsuch, Mrs. George Vinton Bowen (widow of the quarryman-farm owner), Rebecca Jemima Bowen, Mary G. Bowen (the wife of Charles Bowen), and Annetta Stitt Bowen Watkins (daughter-in-law of the Towson political figure, J. Maurice Watkins, and wife of the Circuit Court stenographer, J. Maurice Watkins, Jr.).

80

79

Joshua Fitze of Cockey's Mill Road, Reisterstown, took these three photos. A very elegant John Franklin on July 10, 1904, must have been headed for church or to pay a courting call. The Benson family of Cockey's Mill Road, Fitze's neighbors, had a reunion on October 26, 1907. Mrs. William Gore is a study in dignity, in August 1904.

Early in this century a group of Parkton friends posed on the rocks in a county stream. In the front row are R. Walton East, Jr., and Catherine Calloway; in the rear, Mr. and Mrs. Frank Cox, Henrietta East, and Walton East, Sr.

82

The Pearce family, from near Hartley's Mill, Long Green Branch, sat on the back porch sometime between 1906 and 1910 for this portrait. In the top row, from left to right, are Joe Pearce, who lived to be ninety-one; Bill Pearce, who was a machinist; Ellie Pearce, Stella Pearce; and Frank Pearce, who was a mail carrier. In the lower row, are John Pearce, a machinist and farmer; Martha Pearce; Greenberry Pearce, a mail carrier at Glen Arm and a Civil War veteran, Mary Jane Pearce; Arthur Peace, Greenberry's son, who died at the age of nineteen; and an unidentified person.

83

The Gray family of Reisterstown in the early twentieth century. In the top row, from left to right, are Blanche Shurlock Gray, Frances Noyes Gray, Pearce Choate, and Mary Rebecca Gray; in the lower row, David William Gray, Ellen Ely Gray, Ellen Hepburn Gray, and Joseph Percy Gray. The Grays lived in a fieldstone house called the Elms, *which was built around the 1760s. Francis Scott Key lived in that house from 1835 to 1850. The property was taken for the Liberty Dam reservoir project in the early 1950s.*

84

A group of unidentified guests at Brightside, *the Poseys' summer lodge for paying guests off Bellona Avenue, near Lake Roland. The date is 1886. Baltimoreans looked to summer retreats in Baltimore County such as Relay, Ruxton, Sherwood Station (Riderwood), and Towson as spas to escape the heat, insects, and cholera, among other illnesses. Working-class people also fled to quality summer cottage housing on the county's bays and inlets; some city parishes with a heavy church attendance suffered a 70 percent dropoff in the summer. The wealthy, many of whom owned summer estates, closed their town houses and moved linens, silver, children, and servants out to their country places in June and did not return until October.*

85

Nicholas Bosley Merryman, treasurer of Baltimore County in the early years of this century and master of Hayfields, *is with his family on the porch of the mansion. In the top row, from left to right, are Mrs. William S. Carroll (of* Duddington*) Sallie Love Merryman Dugan in the lap of her mother, Sally Love Merryman, Miss Howaton; Anna Merryman Carroll; and Mrs. Nicholas Bosley Merryman. Second row, Mrs. Norton Merryman Jessop; Norton Carroll McDonough (in lap); Henry Carroll, son of Mrs. W. S. Carroll; Betty Merryman Kemp; Nicholas Bosley Merryman; Mary Wright Merryman; and Nicholas Bosley Merryman III. Front row, Freddie Wright, brother of Mary Merryman; Anne Merryman Carroll; John Merryman in the lap of Nicholas Bosley Merryman II; and Eleanor Merryman Roszel. The girls' names include their future married names.*

86

87

Confederate veteran E. Scott Dance sat in the garden of the family property, on Dance Mill Road in the Blenheim area about 1900. Standing are, from left to right, Ernest, Lawrence, Beulah, and Willard Dance. Seated are Gilbert, Susan Jenkins Dance, E. Scott and Milton Dance. E. Scott Dance (1843-1945) was the bailiff of the Orphan's Court after the mid-1920s.

Although the area now known as Double Rock Park, east of Harford Road, Parkville, did not get county park status until 1952, it nevertheless had long had its fans, as shown by this photo from early in the century.

88

Nineteenth-century Towson haberdasher August Loose's stone house, which was probably built in the 1840s, stood on Joppa Road, on what is now the Roy Rogers Restaurant parking lot (619 York Road). In 1926 the house was occupied by house painter Aquilla C. T. Bosley and his family, shown here all decked out to march in the July 4 parade. Even the house is festooned! From left to right are Catherine Bosley, on the horse; John E. Hurst Bosley; William Henry Bosley; Margaret Bosley Zimmerman; Gertrude Bosley Strack; Eleanor Bosley; Clinton Bosley; Marie Bosley Kade; and behind the children, M. Eliza Hahn Bosley; and Aquilla C. T. Bosley. The girls' later married names have been included.

89

90

The Dunty family lived at Perry Hall *mansion from 1888 to 1915. They were photographed there about 1903. In the back row, from left to right, are Robert P., Florence M., Mary E., Susan Clayton (nursemaid to the younger children), William George Dunty, Jr., Edith R. and Bess V. In the front row are James H., Hazel W., Hannah Elizabeth Ransom Dunty, William Dunty III, Osborne Yellott (the baby, named for a prominent Towson lawyer). Dunty ran a sawmill and gristmill on the Gunpowder River and, according to old family members, managed the rock crushing operation at the old Ashland Iron Works for J. F. C. Talbott, Emmanuel Herman, and Joshua Horner. The stone was used on Baltimore County's roads.*

Edith Miller of Towson was extremely proud of her new coupe in 1932, as she sat beside her beaming father and his friends. From left to right are Katherine Miller, Mrs. W. C. Kenney, Frank Miller, and Edith Miller. Caught with a lot of real estate in the slow market of the Depression, Miller lost a lot of money, became depressed and killed himself. People remembered him as a very nice person.

91

The Sparrows Point High School Soccer Team won the Baltimore County championship in 1914. Long-time principal Joseph Blair is at the right in the back. The Towson High School team won the championship in 1929. In the front row, from left to right, are C. Hart. R. Codd, N. Hope, G. Magness, and W. Schiller. In the middle row are W. Gonce, C. Mace, W. Osenburg, A. Rubeling, and coach MaDan (hands behind back). The back row includes an unidentified person, J. West, C. Fowble, and R. Gagliano, who is standing between Osenburg and Rubeling. Albert Rubeling (1913-1988) had an active baseball career. Beginning in 1930 he played for local league teams; between 1935 and 1939 he moved up from class D to class A teams, when he joined the Phillies, then led by Connie Mack. He spent time with both Toronto (in the minors) and the Pittsburgh Pirates. Rubeling ended his career with Atlanta in the Southern League in 1952. He worked for Eastern Stainless Steel for the next twenty-three years.

92

93

The Lansdowne Football Team was the Monumental League champion in 1934. In the first row, from left to right, are L. Ziolkowski, R. T. Olver, W. C. Olver, and E. Knauf. In the second row are M. Bodner, J. Biggs, W. Riedel, E. Johnson, H. Stem, G. Bowser, W. Knoblock, T. Buckmaster, O. Simmons, E. Holler, and C. Loudenslager The top row includes Dr. L. S. Tawney, C. Heales, J. H. Reinhardt, S. Holler, J. Ziolkowski, W. Ebbert, J. Saxon, E. Singer, F. Ryan, E. Woods, B. Harris (coach), J. McCubbin, A. Haberkorn (manager), and H. Reinhardt.

94

History records many famous skinny-dippers, including Lord Byron the poet and Leander of Greek legend! These anonymous strippers are cooling off in an unidentified county stream in 1903.

While this boy is tubing on the Patapsco in the early 1980s,a he could just as well have been on the Gunpowder, an equally good float for tubers.

95

Blessed with bayside beaches, creeks, and rivers, Baltimore County also has many man-made pools and worked-out quarries turned into swimming holes, such as Milford Pool, shown here in the 1950s.

96

97

A sandy beach, North Point, in 1921. A later view shows beach lovers in 1947.

98

The entrance to Rocky Point Beach, Back River Neck, in 1946-1947, is blocked by two period cars. The ticket booth is at the right.

99

About 1912, Lutherville photographer Emma K. Woods found a member of the Leisenring family swinging in the back yard at Oak Grove, *at one time the home of Dr. John Morris, the Lutheran educator who had founded the village in 1854.*

100

101

Charles Edward Thomas, Jr., of Towson was fourteen when his uncle photographed him on his father's porch in the summer of 1910, reading the Sunday funny paper.

102

Edmund T. Kenney was eleven in 1922 when his father photographed him with the family dog Tutankhamen at One Terrace Dale, Towson.

103

This boy's pride in his pet sheep is clear as a judge squats to evaluate the animal more critically at the Timonium State Fair in September 1933. It should be noted that while the correct title of this fair is the Maryland State Fair, Timonium, we refer to it as the Timonium State Fair, which is what everyone calls it.

104

105

106

Bay Shore *was a favored spot for countians from August 11, 1906, until it was bought and later closed by Bethlehem Steel in 1947. The steel company had bought the tract to prevent rival U.S. Steel from acquiring water frontage. Company picnics, sponsored by such firms as Consolidated Gas, Alberton Cotton Mills, and W. J. Dickey Company, hired buses or arranged for streetcars to take the entire work force to the beach for a day's enjoyment paid for by the company. Typical of the huge crowds which came on any one day were the seven thousand Gas and Electric Company employees and their families who arrived September 12, 1924, on ninety-five streetcars and a whole acre of private cars. The sunbather is Emma Vogel at* Bay Shore *on July 16, 1922.*

107

While F. Scott Fitzgerald was writing his novel, Tender is the Night, *in 1934, he stayed at* La Paix, *the Towson home of noted Baltimore architect Bayard Turnbull, now the site of St. Joseph's Hospital's power plant. Here a tense Fitzgerald and his troubled wife Zelda (then receiving treatment at Sheppard-Pratt Hospital) are on the lawn after a fire which, it was thought, she might have started.*

The Sunday roast is waiting to be cut at 322 Hopkins Road, Rodgers Forge, about 1946. From left to right are Jane Feder, Anne Lyston, an unknown person, Josephine Feder, Fred Feder, Pauline Feder, and Jay Lyston. Fred Feder had a photography studio in Towson through approximately the 1920s to the 1950s.

108

109

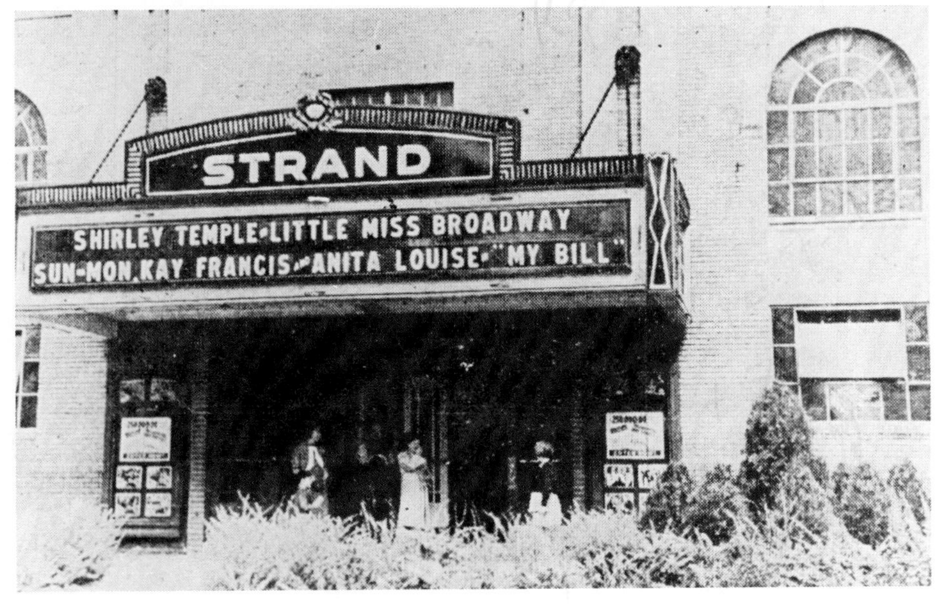

110

Cox's bowling alley at the corner of Reisterstown Road and Sudbrook Lane is shown here about 1910. Repeal of Prohibition in 1933 brought a new owner, Frank Spalding, a liquor license and a bar. Spalding's continued as a popular restaurant until 1977, when it was sold.

The Strand Theater, Shipping Place, Dundalk, opened in February 1927 and closed in 1985. Although not a gaudy Byzantine-revival masterpiece, it was a serviceable, pleasant neighborhood cinema, which gave countless hours of pleasure to its customers, as did the Alpha in Catonsville, and the Towson Theater, to mention only two others of the same era. The New in Reisterstown and the Pike in Pikesville, both now closed, opened in the 1930s.

Vernon Bush started his popular Vernon's Roller Rink on Oella Avenue in 1948 and kept it open for twenty-eight years. Both inability and reluctance on his part to meet the "hidden costs" of obtaining zoning which would have allowed him to expand, prevented him from getting the zoning, although he had wide community support. There is some feeling that letters of complaint filed against him were fraudulent, from nonexistent people at nonexistent addresses. As he would not play the game by the rules of the times, the bogus letters were accepted as evidence. Bush closed the business, leased the building, and retired to Anne Arundel County. Interestingly, others did get the zoning requested by Bush on the contested site. A couple at Vernon's in the 1960s, pose for their wedding-on-skates picture.

111

115

Mrs. Cull and her horse Punch at the Timonium State Fair in 1909. Mrs. Cull is presumed to be the wife of Baltimore attorney Roger W. Cull. They lived at 1415 Park Avenue, Baltimore.

Daisy Keidel and her horse stood by the porte cochere of Homewood, *on Edmondson Avenue, Catonsville, about 1900. The house, built by Joseph P. Fusting in 1830, was purchased by Dr. George Frederick W. Keidel in 1864. Although sold in 1924, plans to level the house for a new road in connection with the development of the estate were halted by the 1929 stock market crash. The Spittel family bought the house in 1935.*

116

114

Gwynn Oak Park opened in 1895. Shown are a hot air balloon in 1906 and the carousel about 1911. Two employees sit in the sun listening to a third play the banjo in 1905. The park became integrated after being targeted by frequent demonstrations in the middle 1960s. After seventy-nine years of operation, the facility finally closed in 1974.

117

Photographers have always had a good time at the state fair. One was intrigued by the exuberant girl on the swing, October 10, 1962; another was fascinated by the people spinning on the wheel in September 1966. (Swing photo by Charles Hart; wheel photo by Harold Spicer) Produce contests are always popular; this one caught the eye of Richard Childress on August 27, 1978. Gerry Brewster, an assistant state's attorney in

118

11

120

Baltimore County, is also a jockey licensed to compete in Maryland's great timber races. He took an elegant series of photos of a horse auction at Timonium in 1988. Big money changes hands at such sales. Appropriately, the handler wears a tuxedo even though the buyers are casually dressed. An earlier horse lover caught the action as trotters raced on the track on September 13, 1908. The Midway is shown as it looked about 1909.

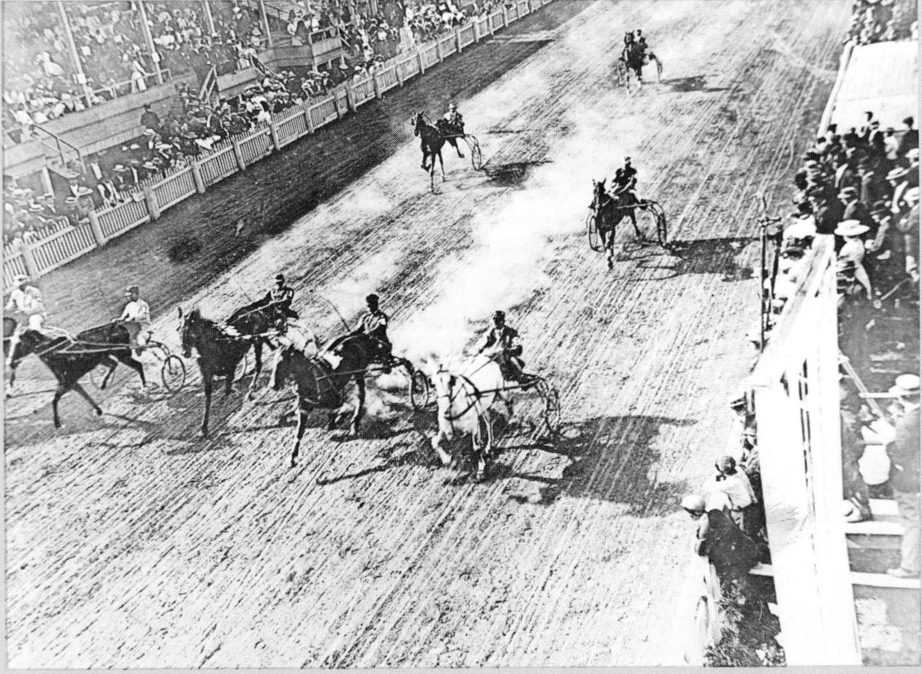

121

122

123

This September 24, 1950 aerial view of the Timonium State Fair and its half-mile race track show only dirt fields used for parking on the east side of York Road. Interstate 83 has not been built; Greenspring and Deereco roads and the heavy development along them did not exist. At the left of the picture, woods occupy the space where there is now a restaurant, a car dealership, and a gas station. (Photo by Richard Tomlinson)

124

Roaming the Timonium State Fair on September 11, 1936, Baltimore News-Post *photographer Pete Rowe caught a moment of indecision on the face of the boy in the dark suit. Does he have enough money in his pocket to buy what he is longing for at the Midway stand?*

125

Typical of the many county street fairs, ethnic celebrations, free public lawn concerts, and festivals is the annual Towsontown Spring Festival. This major Baltimore-area spring event, sponsored by the Towson Business Association, is shown here in a Richard Childress photo of April 1972. Started in 1968 as the inspiration of long-time community leader and civic activist Hilda Wilson, the food, flower, crafts and other booths, live music, and displays by the National Guard, police, fire, and other governmental services attract more than a hundred thousand people each year.

The opening race at the Baltimore Raceway at Martin Boulevard and Pulaski Highway may have been in 1947, or it may have been in 1949. No one is sure. People do agree that the last race was in 1962.

126

Brady Mann (at left), a friend, and their coon dogs were photographed by Joshua Fitze in the Reisterstown area on March 21, 1909. They obviously had a successful night.

127

128

Crompton (Tommy) Smith, Jr., left on Jay Trump clears a fence at England's 1965 Grand National, the first American horse and rider to win the event. The pair won the Maryland Hunt Cup so many times that they retired it. The other rider is Pat McCarron on Freddie, a Scottish horse; they finished second.

Even more important than the Maryland Hunt Cup, My Lady's Manor Steeplechase Race, and the Grand National—Baltimore County's spring timber races—are the tailgate parties which precede them. This restrained picnic was at the Point to Point Race on April 4, 1965. Some party lovers go all out with catered picnic hampers, good crystal and china, silver candlesticks, wine—the works!

129

The North Point-Edgemere School Mother's Club had an authentic white elephant sale on May 23, 1931. From left to right are Wayne Hisleir, Mary Cleveland, Ruth Silver Lee, Estell(e) Roberts Spencer, Helen Johnson, Theresa Peters, Mrs. Nells, Mrs. Welch, Mrs. May Thoebus (Phoebus?), and Mrs. Thomas.

The North Point-Edgemere School Mother's Club manned its battle stations for a May Day festival in the early 1930s. The giant pots of coffee indicate that the women were in charge of the food. From left to right are Estell(e) Roberts, Helen Johnson, Estelle(e) Spencer, Nellie Heeter, Mrs. Thomas, and Mrs. Benlion.

131

132

On September 3, 1938, young Joe Blazek perches on the spare of his 1932 Chevy Roadster, undoubtedly the envy of every young man in Middle River.

133

The Governor's Cup Regatta, at Cox's Point on Back River, Essex, is a Labor Day weekend event that began in 1966. Here a group of boats are gunning it in the late 1960s.

Although forty years separate the boy fishing at the Avalon dam on the Patapsco and the amateur fisherman at the Lake Roland dam in 1937, the peacefulness and beauty of both scenes are the same.

134

135

Robert Dieter baits his line at Diamond Ridge, Woodlawn, on September 4, 1982.

136

Pictures of happy children: carefree snowballers in Catonsville in the early 1980s; sledders on Pembroke Avenue near Flannery Lane, Woodlawn on March 4, 1960, photographed by Harold Spicer; Michael Crosby, Catonsville, in a fifth grade Jumpathon—the joy on his face says it all. Marcus Lynch, Jr., prepares to throw a mean dart at a 1980s Banneker Festival. J. Jefferson Miller, Sr., as a boy, lights a firecracker half as big as he is on his birthday, July 4, 1912. Son of a clothing manufacturer, Miller spent his childhood summers in Catonsville, often visiting the Charles Wackers in Eden Terrace, where this photo was taken. Miller grew up to head Baltimore's Charles Center. He died on April 4, 1972.

137

138

139

140

141

Photographer Keith Weller caught a tense moment at an Arbutus PAL center pool game on December 4, 1981.

143

Airborne Ric Wallen is a study in concentration as he flips his skateboard down two steps at the old courthouse in Towson in March 1988. The photographer was Gail Burton.

144

Fast film and high-resolution cameras froze the action of these competing athletes. Bob Dryden and Dan Barnes scramble for the puck on the frozen pond at Woodlawn Cemetery. Mike Blakert of Woodlawn High School grabs a rebound from Patapsco, as his teammates Daryl Webster and Jim English block out.

145

Catonsville's Fritz Maisel (1889-1967) was a famous baseball player. He played for the International League Orioles, the New York Yankees, and the St. Louis Browns. He generally played third base, although occasionally he was at second base or in the outfield. While with the Yankees Maisel created a record of seventy-four stolen bases, which stood for years. He managed the old Orioles between 1929 and 1932. Maisel then joined the county fire department, of which he was chief from 1938 to 1951.

146

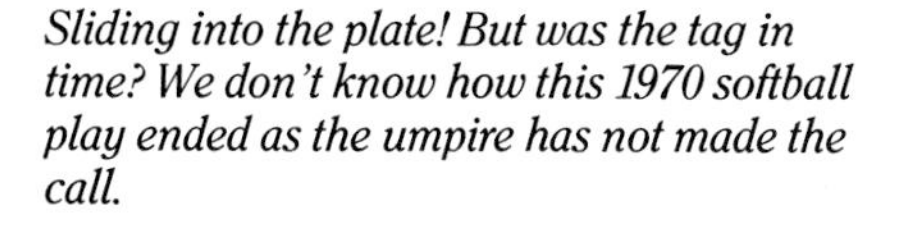

Sliding into the plate! But was the tag in time? We don't know how this 1970 softball play ended as the umpire has not made the call.

147

148

This girls' basketball game of the 1970s is caught the moment after a two-pointer, as the opposing team tries to control the rebound.

149

Towson Senior High School's 1963 basketball team was not only unbeaten in eighteen straight county competitions (including the best private school and Catholic League teams), but went on to become state champions by beating Bladensburg 75-60. From left to right, front row are Bill Thomas, Rich Hunt, Ralph Lee, Lou Frazier; in the middle row are Scott Fosler (co-captain), Steve Pfeifer, Billy Jones (co-captain), Ed Crowding; and in the back row are Coach Randy Walker, Ron Albrecht, Ralph Lee, Jim Hall, and Rich Fosler (manager). Missing from the photo is Jack DiBenedetto.

The 1977 Varsity Soccer team at Patapsco Senior High School sat for a picture. Row 1, from left to right, includes Dean Ward, Steve Grglewski, Coach Bartos, Mike Hammond, Glen Lesnick. Row 2—Nick Pietrowski, Dennis Perry, Vince Lozzi, Mike Ignatowski, Butch Houseknecht, Butch Flamm, and George Hammon. Row 3—Donny Sizemore, Mike Zalowski, Cecil Elliot, Mark Malozi, and Pat Wiatrowski. Row 4—Rick Buckel, Danny Casteel, Greg Baker, David Houseknecht, and Joe White.

151

Charles Weiss took this picture of a YMCA-sponsored Catonsville volleyball block party in the early 1980s.

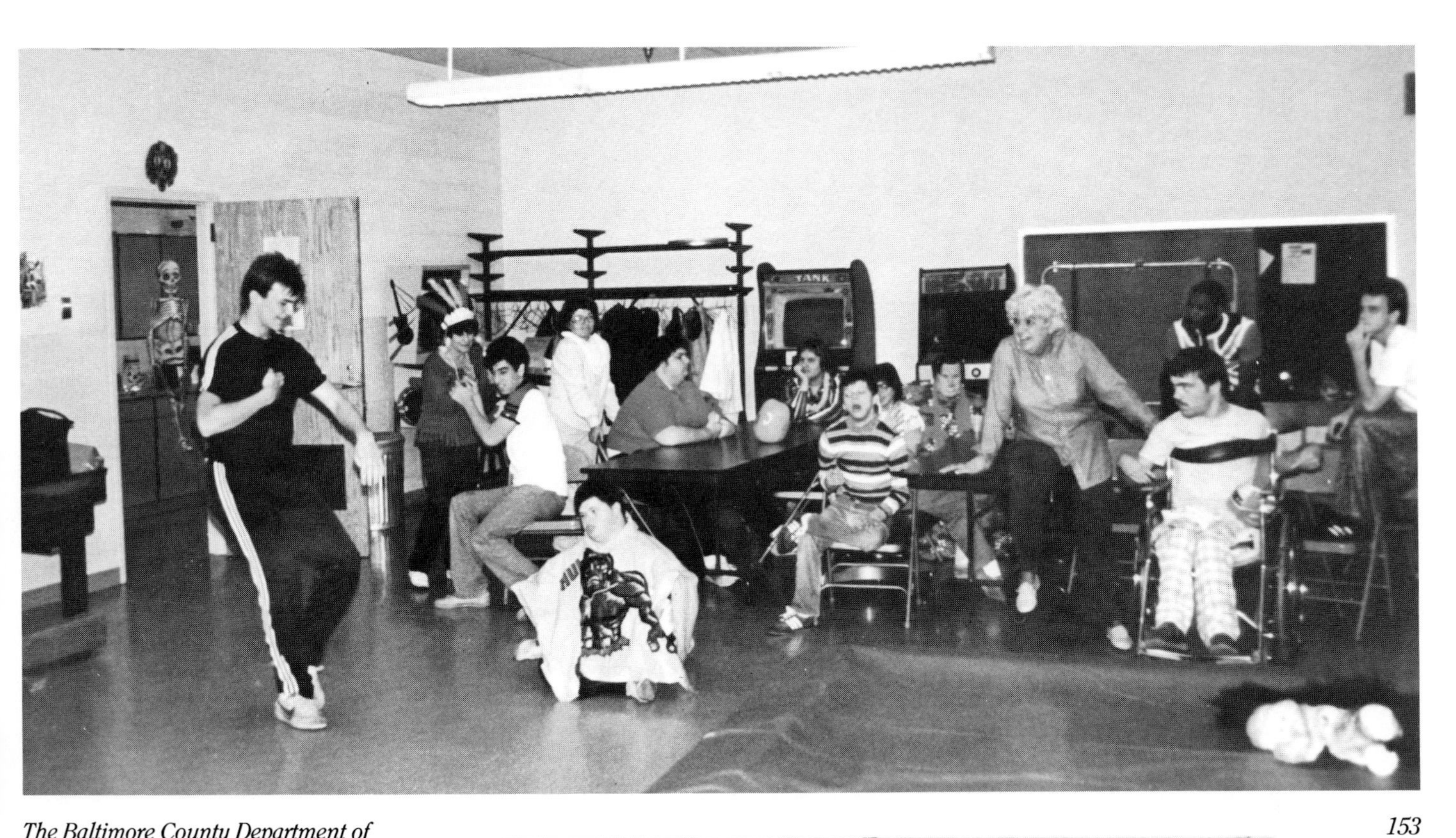

The Baltimore County Department of Recreation and Parks has developed an important program of sports activities for the handicapped.

153

A practice session of jousting, Maryland's strange state sport, a medieval throwback which has been around since the nineteenth century, was photographed by the Baltimore Sunpapers photographer Richard Childress in February 1972. The rider tries to impale a brass ring suspended from the cross pole while charging it at a full gallop.

152

Ron Hill, the 1974 Maryland Marathon winner, charges up the killer Satyr Hill Road ahead of the pack. The marathon, begun in 1973, was run over a twenty-six-mile course starting at Memorial Stadium. There are plans to change the course starting in 1988, centering it near the harbor.

154

The photo shows a Parkville Volunteer Fire Department fund-raising lawn fete in 1922. The fire house is at the left; at center is the Gonce house, at one time a dry-goods establishment. At the right is Kilchenstein's store, at the corner of Taylor Avenue and Harford Road.

156

155

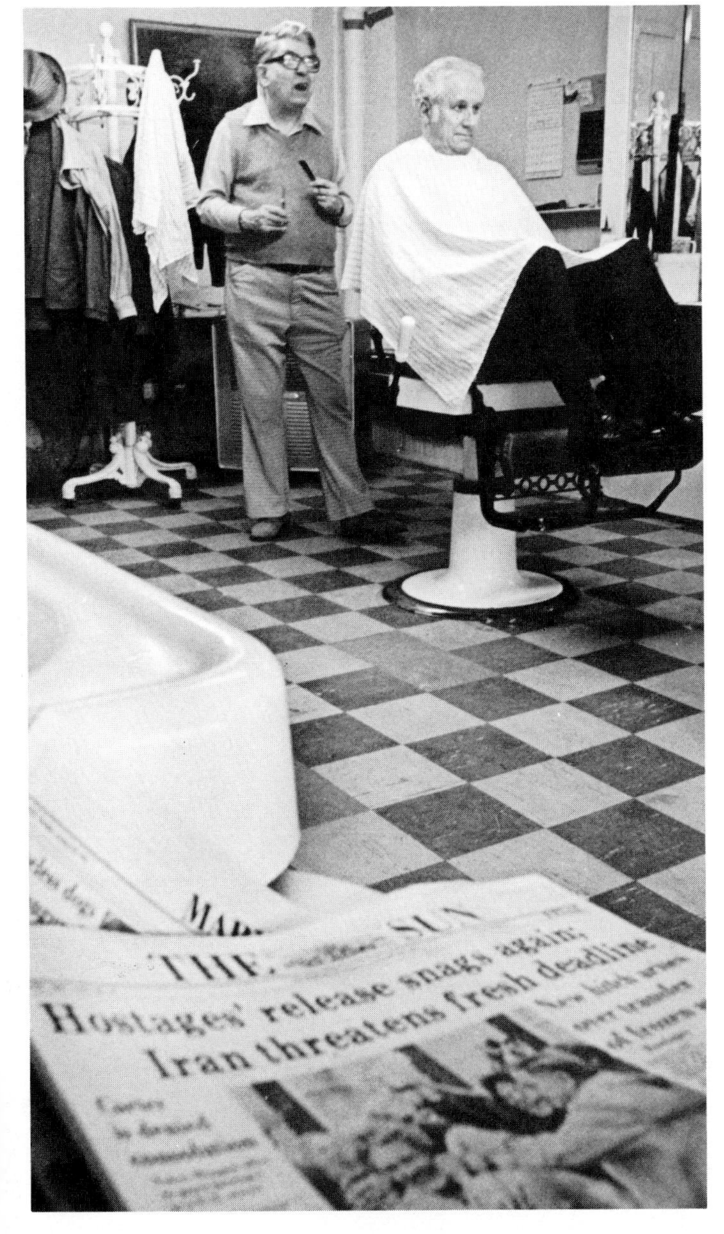

Barber shops have not changed in appearance in sixty years. Here a chatty Catonsville area barber gives his views on the Iran hostage situation in January 1981.

157

Don Crabel and Bill Gayhardt apply barbecue sauce at their charcoal pit at Baltimore Highlands Flower Mart on June 16, 1980.

Mount Zion Lodge, Number 87, IOOF was instituted in Pikesville on April 17, 1853. Costing sixteen hundred dollars, it became a popular place to hold local social functions. Other lodges have used the building, the Jefferson Lodge being the most recent.

In the nineteenth century, lodges of many kinds were formed to serve the functions now covered by insurance companies. They paid members' funeral expenses and took care (as far as was possible) of widows and orphans. When a member was severely injured, the lodge tried to help him with medical attention. As social services became more sophisticated and generally available, the functions of lodges changed to offering general services benefiting the community. The male camaraderie of lodges led them to adopt curious rituals, passwords, and elaborate regalia. Many lodges had a strong tie to religion.

158

The Consolidated Gas Light and Power Company sent demonstration teams around the state to introduce rural communities to the possibilities offered by gas and electricity. In this Hughes Company photo, a group in Boring, Maryland, is meeting on January 28, 1930.

160

Dundalk youngsters at a Gunpowder River youth camp, about 1923. In more than seventy years, thousands of county children have enjoyed camping at these sites under church, YMCA, Salvation Army, or other groups' auspices.

TRANSPORTATION

Cockeysville landowner Zephaniah Poteet and Dr. George A. Thompson (of Phoenix) were two of the many who wrote angry letters to the county commissioners about the bad roads. Said Poteet: "It was necessary to make the road wider. . . .It was not ten feet wide." (*Argus*, April 3, 1890.) He was writing about the road from Warren to Cockeysville, the only route for the six-mule teams which hauled the 500 pound bales of ginned cotton from the Cockeysville railroad station to the Warren Cotton Factory. On the other hand, Dr. Thompson, writing in 1891, complained that on the same stretch of road his buggy had been damaged and he had hurt his head when thrown from it, after his wheels hit a pile of rocks left in the middle of the road, apparently by road repairers.

Throughout the county, and for most of the century, citizens complained about everything: secondary roads, turnpikes, unsafe bridges, washed-out bridges not yet replaced. Early macadamizing improved the highways but did nothing at all for the back roads; it would be decades before some of them were surfaced.

After the turn of the century, streetcars were the most significant means of transportation for many people who lived near the historic roads out of the city—Eastern Avenue, Belair Road, Harford Road, York Road, Reisterstown Road, Liberty Heights Avenue, Edmondson Avenue, Frederick Road, Wilkins Avenue, and Washington Boulevard.

The Good Roads movement of the early twentieth century and the modern superhighways changed everything. Goods and people could move easily; it was possible to go South from New York without having to go through Baltimore. But there were opponents of even these obviously needed improvements.

Twenty-four years ago county executive Spiro T. Agnew spoke at breakfast on a winter morning, when the county had been brought to a standstill by one of the heavy snowfalls of the early 1960s. He recalled a case occurring while he had served on the Zoning Appeals Board in the 1950s. There was a landowner, he said, who bitterly opposed the Beltway, and the condemnation of his fields for the road, because he liked to look out of his window when he got up in the morning and watch the foxes play.

Both the Jesuit Seminary at Woodstock and the adjacent community of Granite, Maryland, were served by the Baltimore and Ohio Railroad. The locomotive, shown here in the early 1900s, is the A. J. Cromwell 1888-type built in the Mt. Clare shops in Baltimore. A chalet-like station house awaited the train.

Baltimore County turnpikes and railroads in the nineteenth century.

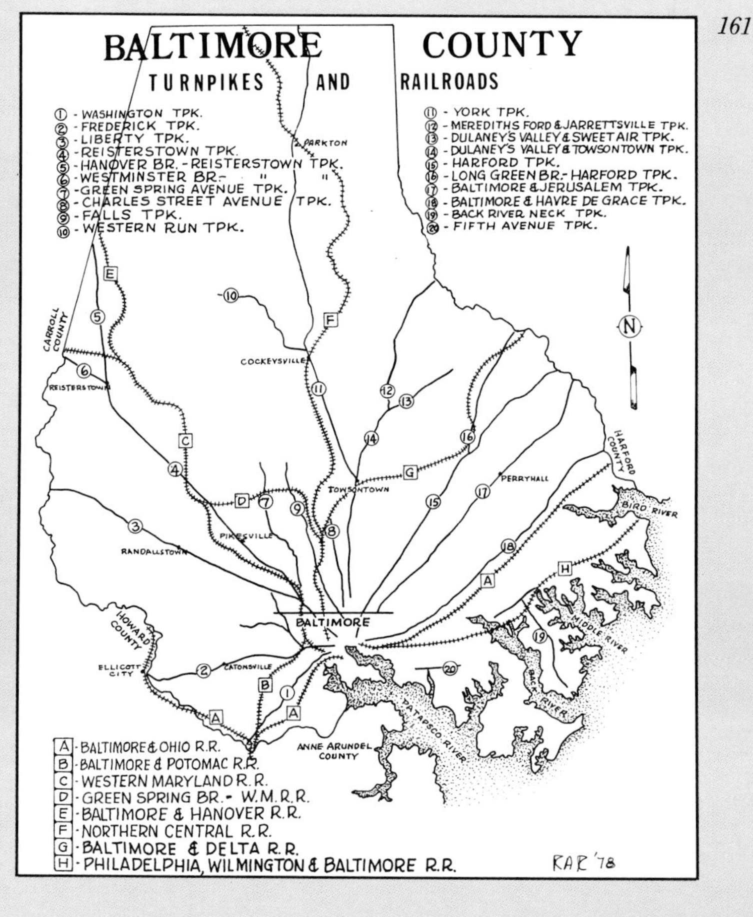

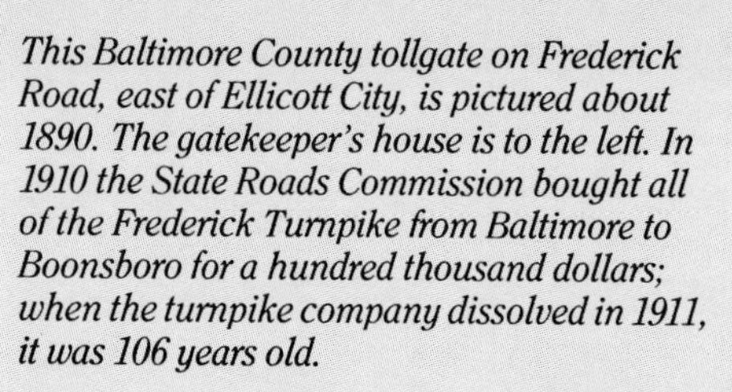
This Baltimore County tollgate on Frederick Road, east of Ellicott City, is pictured about 1890. The gatekeeper's house is to the left. In 1910 the State Roads Commission bought all of the Frederick Turnpike from Baltimore to Boonsboro for a hundred thousand dollars; when the turnpike company dissolved in 1911, it was 106 years old.

162

163

The Greenmount-Carroll County stagecoach was photographed on April 18, 1910.

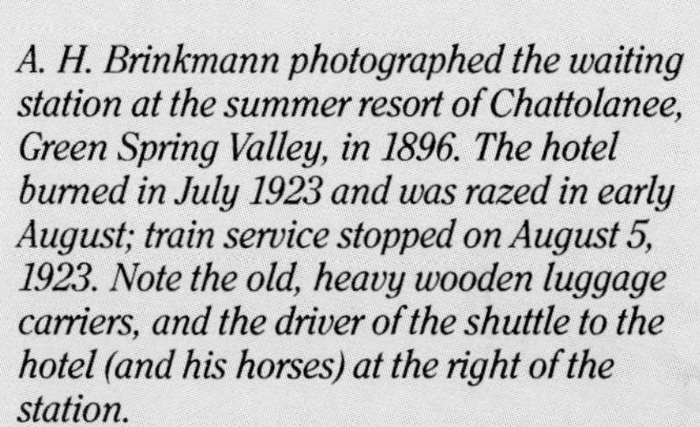

A. H. Brinkmann photographed the waiting station at the summer resort of Chattolanee, Green Spring Valley, in 1896. The hotel burned in July 1923 and was razed in early August; train service stopped on August 5, 1923. Note the old, heavy wooden luggage carriers, and the driver of the shuttle to the hotel (and his horses) at the right of the station.

164

165

A waiting station was built at the Brightside *stop of the Northern Central Railroad in the 1880s, seen here in 1886.* Brightside *was a house converted by the Posey family for use as a summer hotel, catering to selected guests who stayed for months at a time. By 1890, when the Poseys had not met their mortgage payments, the property was acquired by Professor Walter Brooks of Johns Hopkins University and reclaimed for private use.* Brightside, *located at the bend of Bellona Avenue near Lake Roland, burned in the 1930s. Nobody can remember when the waiting station disappeared, but service ended in 1933.*

This ramshackle covered bridge at Cromwell Bridge Road at Club Hill Road dated from December 1877. It lasted until 1924, when a modern concrete span was erected.

166

167

The first covered bridge at Bunker Hill Road over the Gunpowder Falls, 1.1 miles northwest of Hereford, was built in 1880 and survived until 1961, when it was destroyed by fire. Rebuilt by the Baltimore County Department of Public Works using the old methods, it was destroyed again by vandals in August 1971 and was not replaced. The view here dates from the 1920s.

168

The bridge built on York Road at Thornton Mill Road, over the Western Run, is being replaced in this photo from about 1921-1922. The State Roads Commission is constructing the frame for the presently existing concrete bridge. The old wooden bridge is at the right.

169

The State Roads Commission showed the work in progress on the present Warren Road Bridge on October 24, 1922. The view is from the east bank of the Gunpowder River looking west.

In 1857 the Baltimore City Water Department started condemnation proceedings against James Beatty's Bellona Powder Works (once a rival to the Du Pont gunpowder empire) as an impediment in the creation of Lake Roland, the first reservoir in the area. The lake, created by 1861, was a favorite for picnickers, boaters, and wintertime skaters. It had its own truss bridge designed by the Baltimore and Ohio Railroad's bridge engineer Wendel Bollman. It had walkways on each side for pedestrians. The architectural treasure was taken down, possibly for scrap, during World War II. The picture was by A. H. Brinkmann, about 1886.

170

171

In the nineteenth century, Meredith's Ford Bridge was frequently replaced due to floods. This one was not demolished when Loch Raven reservoir was expanded in 1921-1922. Instead, Dulaney Valley Road was rerouted over the Matthews Bridge, and the old bridge was left half submerged in water. Local youth used it as a diving platform until the State Roads Commission, fearing an accident, had it dynamited in the 1930s.

On the 1877 county map in this book, the bridge crossed the Gunpowder River south of Warren, almost where the word "great" appears. At the west end of the bridge was the town of Bosley and Kane's Hotel, all demolished by the reservoir project. In the old days skaters used to glide upriver from the lower dam to Meredith's Ford Bridge in about half an hour.

The staff of a Baltimore and Ohio Railroad dining car line up in front of their work place in the 1930s.

173

174

A Baltimore and Ohio Railroad locomotive and tender moves a Pennsylvania Railroad boxcar beneath the old North Point Road overpass in the 1920s.

175

The Maryland and Pennsylvania Railroad began as the Baltimore and Delta Railroad in 1878, with a line to Towson opening in 1882. The name changed to the Maryland Central in 1882, Baltimore and Lehigh in 1891, and Maryland and Pennsylvania (or Ma and Pa) in 1901. Passenger service stopped on the seventy-seven-mile line in 1954, and all service in 1958. Although the company maintains some service in Pennsylvania, Maryland trackage was removed in late 1958. Young photographer C. W. E. Treadwell caught this picture of a Ma and Pa train near Towson about the time of World War I. The pole on the right carried long distance telephone lines.

176

Charles Mahan took this 1958 photo of the last Ma and Pa train from York to Baltimore, in the Baltimore Yards.

The Glyndon railroad station is actually the fourth structure used by the Western Maryland Railroad. The first, in 1850, was in a building owned by Lawrence Shipley; the second, in 1874, was in Samuel Townsend's store, south of the present site; the third, a handsome structure made of Texas marble with a red tile roof, and set off with fine landscaping, lasted from 1895 until 1903, when it burned. The present building was erected in 1906. Passenger service ended in 1957. Since 1974 the station has housed the Glyndon post office.

177

178

Before macadamizing, Baltimore County's roads looked like this in bad weather. This example was photographed by William C. Kenney on Hydes Road, between Knoebel's Corner and Hyde's Station in the late 1930s. Nothing had changed in two centuries!

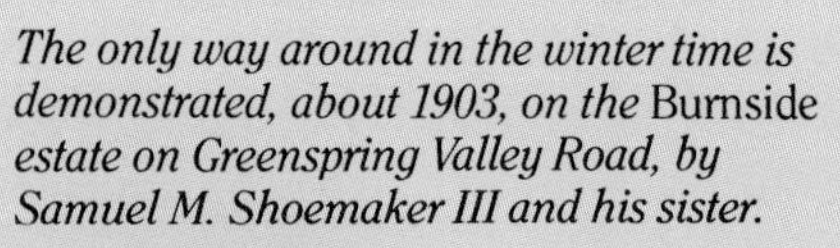

The only way around in the winter time is demonstrated, about 1903, on the Burnside *estate on Greenspring Valley Road, by Samuel M. Shoemaker III and his sister.*

179

180

On Essex Road, the empty streetcar track and a lone car or so were typical of a 1920s road scene.

The change from sleepy rural countryside to urban sprawl is dramatized by this picture. This view shows York Road, Towson, looking south from the middle of the road opposite where the Quality Inn is now. Nothing is to be seen in this pre-World War I view except the Church of the Immaculate Conception on the hill at the right, and the Towson Methodist Episcopal Church on the hill at the left.

181

182

Sunshine Avenue at its intersection with Harford Road in Fork was photographed by the itinerant banker William C. Kenney (1882-1946) in the early 1920s. This was the intersection Confederate colonel Harry Gilmor's 150-man strong cavalry unit clattered through in July 1864 on its way to burn down Ishmael Day's house on Sunshine Avenue.

Kenney traveled all over north central Baltimore County in a Model-T, bringing banking services on a set schedule to rural areas and taking many of the pictures which have contributed to this book. At the time he was vice-president and cashier of the Baltimore County Bank in Towson.

This may not be Mike Mulligan and his magic steam shovel, but it certainly is the State Roads Commission working on Warren Road just west of the present Warren Bridge on October 24, 1922.

183

184

Authorized by the Public Service Commission, "trackless trolleys" on rubber tires ran on regular roads from Gwynn Oak junction to Randallstown. The picture is dated October 23, 1923.

The last trolley leaves Towson on November 2, 1963. Passengers are boarding the No. 8, Towson to Catonsville, at the stop on Washington Avenue in front of the old courthouse. The boys in front were, left to right, Tim LeBrun, Kerry Davis, and Erick F. Davis.

186

The No. 26 Red Rocket *takes on passengers at Fort Howard in 1932. The route included Bay Shore Park, Dundalk, and Sparrows Point. This was the main means of transportation for thousands of workers at Sparrows Point. The United Electric Railways Company attached a second car, a hybrid interurban-like vehicle called an articulated unit, to handle the volume of riders. Service on the line ended on August 31, 1958.*

187

C. T. Luddington founded the Luddington Line, which began flights between Baltimore, Philadelphia, Washington, and New York on November 24, 1930. Amelia Earhart, vice-president of the company, was among the first passengers to be greeted at Martin Field by Glenn L. Martin, with Mayor William F. Broening and his secretary (later governor) Theodore R. McKeldin. The photo shows a last passenger checking aboard a 1931 flight. In 1933 the airline became part of what is now Eastern Airlines.

188

The photo shows an old wooden prop biplane being fueled at Logan Field, Dundalk, in the post-World War I period.

Logan Field, the Baltimore metropolitan area's first airport, appears here in its early active days. Today Logan Village in Dundalk and St. Rita's Parochial School's ball field are all that remain of Logan Field. Built on a hundred acres offered by Bethlehem Steel, it was named for ace stunt pilot Lt. Patrick Logan, who died July 5, 1920, when his controls jammed and he could not level out from a dive at two thousand feet. By 1922 the steel company was charging the city two thousand dollars rent, plus receiving five hundred dollars for operating costs from the state. The U.S. Post Office began airmail service via Logan on May 1, 1929. Municipal Airport nearby was opened in November 1941, a week before Pearl Harbor. World War II kept Logan going for a while.

Looking like oversized beer casks, these are in reality sections of the first Baltimore Harbor Tunnel being constructed and installed by Bethlehem Steel. The tunnel opened on November 30, 1957.

190

The Baltimore Subway opened its extension from Reisterstown Plaza, Pikesville, to Owings Mills on July 20, 1987. It was hoped that eventually commuters would leave their cars in receiving areas and take the train, thereby relieving the roads of traffic and the air of some pollution. The picture shows a train at the Old Court station.

Although portions of the Baltimore Beltway were finished by the middle 1950s, it was not until July 27, 1962, that completion ceremonies were held on the Beltway at the exit site of the future Northwest Expressway near Pikesville. The Northwest Expressway itself was not built for twenty-six more years, and Dundalk was not reached by the Beltway until the building of the Francis Scott Key Bridge.

At left, seated in the front row, is Governor J. Millard Tawes; third from the governor is former county executive Michael J. Birmingham. Next to Birmingham is Dorothy Boone, a county councilwoman (with the child on her lap). Behind the woman to Boone's left is Dale Anderson, a future county executive. A. Gordon Boone, speaker of the House of Delegates, is standing in the back with his head against the diagonal support. At the podium is Congressman (later Senator) Daniel B. Brewster; the two men facing front at Brewster's left are George Fallon, dean of Maryland's congressional delegation, and William Fornoff, county administrative officer in the Kahl and Anderson administrations. (Photo by Fred G. Kraft, Jr.)

194

The Beltway at Route 40, with the Westview Shopping Center with Hutzler's store in the northwest quadrant, was photographed on June 21, 1962, by Lawrence McNally.

193

Towson on the threshold of irrevocable change is shown in this January 17, 1955 aerial view. Architect Lucius White's Harry T. Campbell building of 1951 is to the right of the courthouse with which it harmonized. Still in place is the old Towson fire station at the head of York Road near Hutzlers, and the huge Nimmo house (Democratic party headquarters) just above the Ma and Pa overpass over York Road. The Jefferson Building had not been built, nor had the Loyola Federal Building, the first building to test and break the rule that no building should be higher than the courthouse. (Photo by Lawrence McNally)

195

The fields and forests around the Beltway at Security Boulevard on June 21, 1962, show how much change has come to Baltimore County in twenty-six years.

196

One has to look hard at this May 1962 aerial view of Towson Market Place (then called Eudowood Shopping Center), upper left, and Calvert Hall College, a Catholic high school, center, to recognize the landscape of 1988.

197

The area of Perring Parkway and the Beltway in June 1962 was a far cry from what it is now in 1988. The Korvettes store, then the anchor of the Satyr Hill Shopping Center, is at the center of the picture; Joppa Road is the thin line above it.

The area around Pulaski Highway and the Beltway was still rural on June 21, 1962. All of the June 1962 photos were taken by Lawrence McNally.

198

PUBLIC SERVICE

As early as the seventeenth century there was evidence of significant public service in Baltimore County. In the 1690s the most conspicuous public facility was Fort Garrison. Then, during the War of 1812, the federal government built a powder magazine in Towson (about where the entrance to Hutzler's upper parking lot is), and an arsenal in Pikesville, to disperse munitions in case of invasion.

The Civil War put Baltimore under martial law and its mayor in Fort McHenry. It was encircled by a ring of federal troop encampments not least of which, and certainly the most objectionable, was the one on Federal Hill, with cannon pointed right at Baltimore. City residents needed passes to get through federal lines in order to reach their farms and country properties.

The county had federal troops guarding all the significant bridges, especially the vital Thomas Viaduct at Relay. The only Civil War actions in the county were a couple of Confederate cavalry forays that were really rather minor footnotes to history.

In politics, the patronage system was in full flower; it was whom you knew among the good old boys of the courthouse gang, and how useful you might be, that determined the success of your dealings with the county. All county jobs were political patronage gifts; when Joseph Miller became the first paid policeman to serve Parkville, and had a beat from the city line to Gunpowder River (by himself, but with a car, of course), it was through the influence of Howard Milling, an influential political boss.

When he retired in the late 1940s, he did so because he was tired of having politicians lean on him for "contributions" and being unable to rebuff the shakedown. It would be the mid-1970s before this system was hung out to dry.

From Fort Howard in 1895 to the Nike missile silos of the 1950s, from the Fort Howard Veterans Hospital to the national headquarters of the Social Security Administration, the federal government has had a distinct presence in the county. From customs workers at the Dundalk Marine Terminal, to IRS offices, to the National Guard armory in Towson, the citizen is always aware of the national government's presence.

Engine No. 5, an American La France rotary pumper with a capacity of seven hundred gallons a minute, is shown outside the Catonsville Police-Firehouse, about 1911 or 1912. The driver was Phil Priester, later a Baltimore County fire marshal. Standing from left to right, were Mr. Armacost (first name unknown), Gideon Smith, and William Stevens. The driver's companion is unidentified.

State agencies are everywhere too: state police, state parks (Patapsco, Gunpowder) state hospitals (Mt. Wilson, now closed, and Spring Grove), state licensing (cars, boats, fishing, hunting, business, and professional.) An army of generally agreeable people also worry about the environment, run state universities (Towson State and the University of Maryland, Baltimore County), force everyone to have their auto emissions tested, sit as the judiciary, and perform as state's attorneys.

The county, particularly since charter government was adopted in 1958, is involved in every facet of its citizens' lives: schools, libraries, health, legal, "safety net" and other social services, and on and on. The county builds everything from ball fields to parking garages, from schools to courthouses. It oversees three excellent community colleges, has an immense, highly lauded parks and recreation program, and runs a staggering array of programs countywide for the increasing numbers of senior citizens. There are signs that the county, already boasting such strict fire and building codes that developers claim they are onerous and a hindrance to growth, may actually be about to enact a housing code after twenty-four years of mulling it over.

A few words need to be said about the enormous impact that electricity made on the lives of county residents. In 1910 electricity was available only along Reisterstown Road to Glyndon and Harford Road to Parkville, and at Sparrows Point, the Catonsville area, Mt. Washington, and Towson. In the same year only Towson and Catonsville had natural gas. By 1929 the rural electrification program of the Baltimore Gas and Electric Company had taken lines up the full length of every main road and up a vast number of secondary ones. By 1929 gas had also reached Carney, Parkville, Putty Hill, Essex, Middle River, Dundalk, St. Helena, Edgemere, Sparrows Point, Lansdowne, Arbutus, Halethorpe, Woodlawn, Sudbrook Park, Ruxton, Riderwood, and Lutherville.

Gas and electric appliances brought about a major social revolution, liberating women from the drudgery of the scrubbing board, increasing the health and cleanliness of the rural population through the easy access to hot water for bathing, and, through radio, creating a wider awareness of concern about events outside local communities.

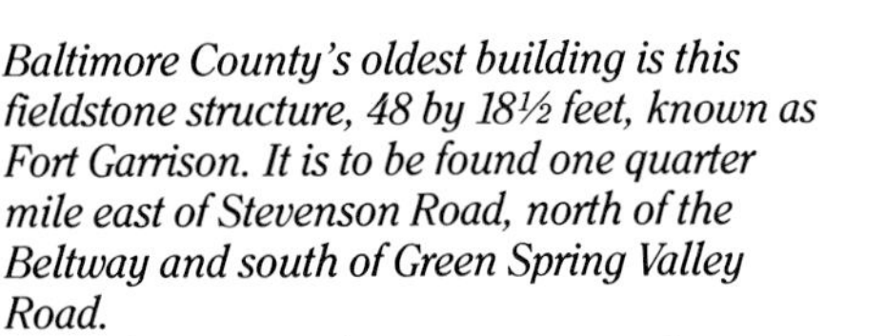

Baltimore County's oldest building is this fieldstone structure, 48 by 18½ feet, known as Fort Garrison. It is to be found one quarter mile east of Stevenson Road, north of the Beltway and south of Green Spring Valley Road.

In the nineteenth century a second story loft with a wood shingle roof was installed. The fort is currently in its original state, with the second story removed.

The structure served as a lookout point for possible Indian attack. As such it housed six rangers and their captain. No attacks ever came. It is doubtful if the fort was used after 1698.

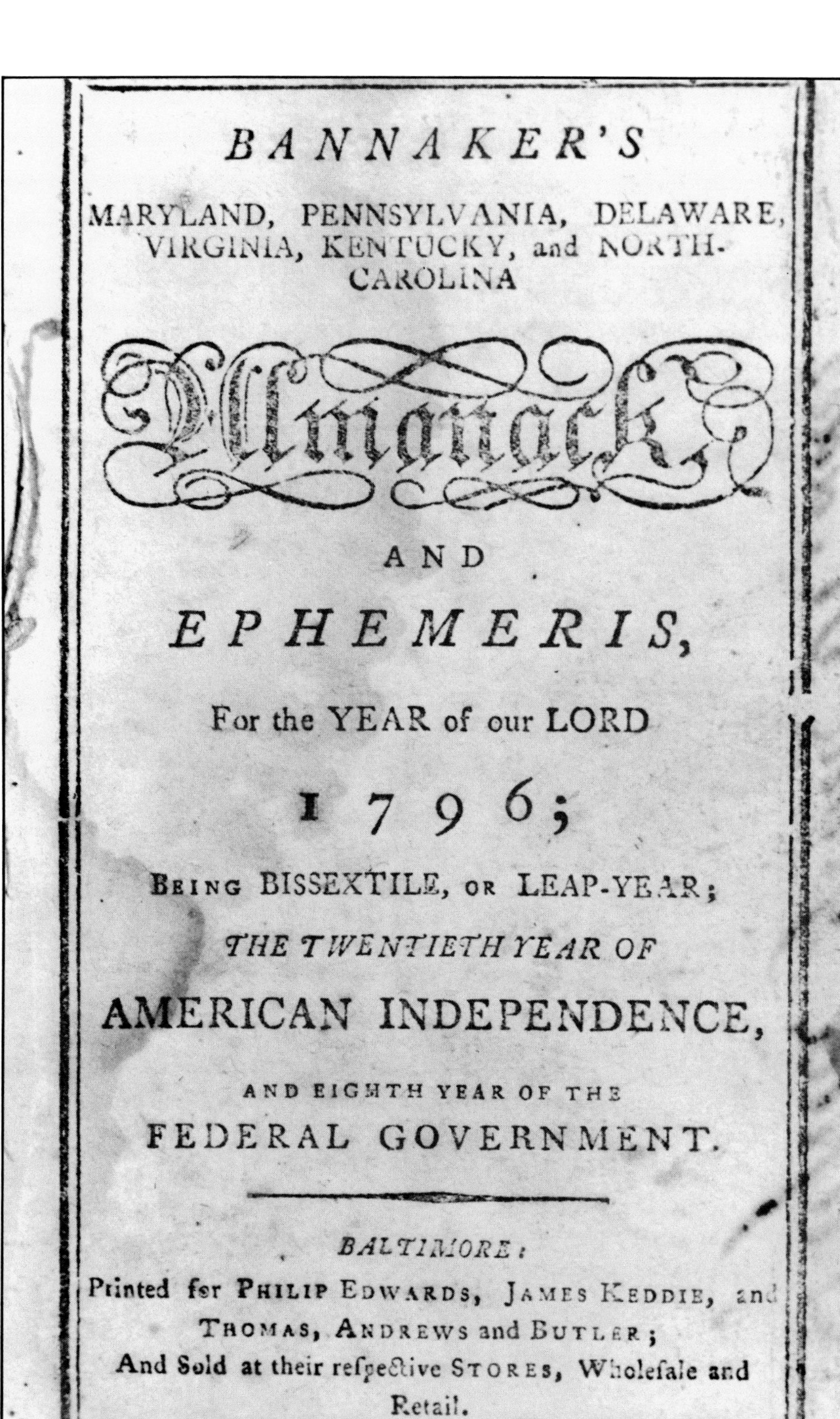
BANNAKER'S
MARYLAND, PENNSYLVANIA, DELAWARE, VIRGINIA, KENTUCKY, and NORTH-CAROLINA
Almanack,
AND
EPHEMERIS,
For the YEAR of our LORD
1796;
BEING BISSEXTILE, OR LEAP-YEAR;
THE TWENTIETH YEAR OF
AMERICAN INDEPENDENCE,
AND EIGHTH YEAR OF THE
FEDERAL GOVERNMENT.

BALTIMORE:
Printed for PHILIP EDWARDS, JAMES KEDDIE, and
THOMAS, ANDREWS and BUTLER;
And Sold at their respective STORES, Wholesale and
Retail.

200

The notable Maryland astronomer and mathematician Benjamin Banneker was the first black American man of science. He was born into a free black family on November 9, 1731. He grew up in a one-room log cabin with a loft, on a hundred-acre tobacco farm near today's Catonsville, a mile from the Patapsco River. His father was a farmer and blacksmith whose calls in the area left many of the farm duties to his son, with whom he shared the farm's ownership.

At the age of twenty-two Banneker completed all aspects of construction of a chiming wooden clock, an astounding feat. There is no evidence that there either were any books on clockmaking in the area, or that he had ever seen one. In fact, in his life to that point he had seen only one sundial and one pocket watch.

His abilities came to the attention of the Ellicott brothers, Quakers who emigrated from Bucks County, Pennsylvania, and settled on the Patapsco to start a country store, build a gristmill and construct other necessary buildings. Banneker became a close friend of George Ellicott, who was twenty-nine years younger. George's brother, Major Andrew Ellicott, was appointed to survey the proposed Federal Territory in 1791. Banneker was chosen to assist Andrew Ellicott in this work by making surveying calculations from astronomical instruments.

Annually for seven years, starting in 1791, Banneker brought out a highly regarded almanac. He sent a copy to Thomas Jefferson, as proof of what black people were capable of doing. In his reply Jefferson wrote: "Nobody wishes more than I do to see such proofs as you exhibit, that nature has given to our black brethren, talents equal to those of the other colors of men, and that the appearance of a want of them is owing merely to the degraded condition of their existence, both in Africa and America." The title page of one of the almanacs is shown here; the spelling "Bannaker" is a printer's error.

While Banneker was being buried in 1806, his log house caught fire and was totally destroyed. Lost were the manuscript copies of his almanacs, his famous clock, and his library. Everything else, including his journals, had been given to his two sisters or to George Ellicott. Banneker's journal has recently been received by the Maryland Historical Society.

Baltimore County bought 42.8 acres of the Banneker farm in 1985. The Friends of Benjamin Banneker Historical Park was organized to offer assistance in supporting the park. The Maryland Historical Trust conducted research at the site for three years, locating a number of artifacts dating to Banneker's residence.

Writing in Maryland Historical Prints, 1752 to 1889 *(1975), Lois McCauley said of the British invasion of Baltimore in 1814:*

> *When the route of the British land attack on Baltimore became known, Major General Samuel Smith ordered Brigadier General John Stricker to move his Third Brigade to a predetermined position on the main road from North Point where Bread and Cheese Creek on the north and Bear Creek on the south constricted the peninsula to less than a mile wide. Here they drew up in a line of defense in front of a wooded area to await the British attack. The force of 3,200 militiamen, mostly from Baltimore, included a company from Hagerstown and three volunteer companies from Pennsylvania. Their artillery consisted of six "four-pounders." The British force numbered 4,700 with eight guns as well as rockets. In this view taken from behind the Maryland lines, their ranks are seen through the trees extending across the background. At this critical point in the battle, the Maryland troops on the left have been drawn back to form a right angle in the line for defense against expected attack on the left flank. General Stricker on a white horse in the road near the center foreground points to them with his drawn saber. Beyond him, two of the guns are aimed down the road to North Point. Officers ride on various missions behind the lines of Marylanders standing shoulder to shoulder behind the fence facing the enemy. Those killed or wounded lie on the battlefield shown at the left. The Maryland forces retreated soon after, but were ready to fight again on the 13th. The British, having followed them almost to Baltimore, lacked the resolve to attack again and so retired.*

This view, designed, painted, and published by Thomas Ruckle (1776-1853) after his painting in the Maryland Historical Society, was lithographed by Endicott and Swett.

202

Writing of another view of the 1814 battle, Lois McCauley described it this way in her Maryland Historical Prints:

> *This primitive bird's eye view of the battle telescopes time and space in recording everything significant that happened before the British retreat. The death of General Robert Ross which occurred out of sight and hours before is represented in the upper right background.*

203

The 1816 Pikesville Arsenal was depicted in an ink and wash sketch (possibly by Francis B. Mayer) about 1845. Unused for military purposes after 1878, the old complex became the Confederate Soldiers Home from 1888 to 1932. The Maryland State Police then acquired it for its headquarters in 1950.

Maj. Gen. Nathan Towson (1784-1854) was the grandson of Ezekiel Towson, whose inn at the York Road and Joppa Road intersection was the genesis of the town named for him. As a seventeen-year-old Nathan had joined a volunteer company in Natchez which had been formed in case the French inhabitants of Louisiana gave any trouble after the Louisiana Purchase. He returned home to farm, only to sign on as a captain in the War of 1812. Promoted to lieutenant colonel for extreme bravery during that war, he became the paymaster general of the U.S. Army. He served throughout the Mexican War, being breveted a major general in 1849. Shown here is his grave in Oak Hill Cemetery, Georgetown.

204

BALTIMORE COUNTY LEVY.
COUNTY TAXES for 1853 & 1854—JOHN L. STANSBURY, *Receiver*
Wm E Stansbury
(NINTH ELECTION DISTRICT.)
To the Commissioners of Baltimore County, Dr.
Amount of Assessment, $ 13.760 COUNTY TAXES, and SCHOOL TAX, at 30 Cents on the $100, $ 41.13
Account 9 per Cent on County & State $61.70 5.55
State $35.58
19.55
April 27 1854 $55.13
RECEIVED PAYMENT.
Wm E Stansbury

If this Bill is Paid on or before the 30th day of April, 1854, a Discount of 9 per cent will be allowed.
On or before the 31st day of May, 1854, 8 per cent.
On or before the 30th day of June, 1854, 7 per cent.
On or before the 31st day of July, 1854, 6 per cent.
On or before the 31st day of August, 1854, 5 per cent.
On or before the 30th day of September, 1854, 4 per cent.
On or before the 31st day of October, 1854, 3 per cent.
On or before the 30th day of November, 1854, 2 per cent.
On or before the 31st day of December, 1854, 1 per cent.
James Lucas, print., Balto.

BALTIMORE COUNTY LEVY.
COUNTY TAXES for 1853 & 1854—JOHN L. STANSBURY, *Receiver*
Wm E Stansbury Trustee
(NINTH ELECTION DISTRICT.)
To the Commissioners of Baltimore County, Dr.
Stock
Amount of Assessment, $ 2400 COUNTY TAXES, and SCHOOL TAX, at 30 Cents on the $100, $ 7.20
Account 9 per Cent on County $7.20 64
$6.56
April 27 1854
RECEIVED PAYMENT.
Wm E Stansbury

If this Bill is Paid on or before the 30th day of April, 1854, a Discount of 9 per cent will be allowed.
On or before the 31st day of May, 1854, 8 per cent.
On or before the 30th day of June, 1854, 7 per cent.
On or before the 31st day of July, 1854, 6 per cent.
On or before the 31st day of August, 1854, 5 per cent.
On or before the 30th day of September, 1854, 4 per cent.
On or before the 31st day of October, 1854, 3 per cent.
On or before the 30th day of November, 1854, 2 per cent.
On or before the 31st day of December, 1854, 1 per cent.
James Lucas, print., Balto.

Stansbury's receipts for his county taxes for 1853-1854 seem modest 130 years later, even considering that the dollar's value was about fourteen times higher then.

205

206

During the Civil War, troops guarded the vital Baltimore and Ohio rail head at the Thomas Viaduct at Relay. The building at the right is the original inn, replaced in 1872 by the Viaduct Hotel, shown in Picture 455.

Cook's Boston Light Artillery was assigned the task of protecting the important viaduct. Here they are at Elkridge on the Howard County side, looking toward the Baltimore County end.

207

208

From reading the Baltimore and Ohio's poster one would not know that the minor inconvenience of a civil war was what had closed the road.

When Thomas and James Dixon, with Thomas Balbirnie, designed the original part of the Towson Court House in 1854, they (or the contractor William H. Allen) failed with the cupola. By 1859 the structure swayed in the wind and leaked, and plaster fell in one of the courtrooms. Rival architect Rudolf Niernsee, called in by the county commissioners as a consultant, suggested taking the cupola down to its present size, which was done. This is the only known view of the cupola's original appearance.

The specifications for the courthouse called for "two patent water closets, with China bowls, pans and fixtures complete." Water was delivered by a gravity flow system from the roof to a holding tank activated by a pull chain. This was Towson's first exposure to inside plumbing.

Five Confederate veterans sit around a pot-bellied stove in the Confederate Soldiers Home, Pikesville, on January 22, 1920. At that time there were only twenty-seven of the old men left in the home.

209

210

Members of the Baltimore County Bar Association sat for a group portrait in Courtroom 5 in 1926. In the back row, from left to right, are Laban Sparks, John Mays Little, W. Gill Smith, Elmer R. Haile, and William P. Cole Jr. In the third row are David G. McIntosh, Jr., Judge C. Gus Grason, Judge Frank I. Duncan, Judge T. Scott Offutt, Judge Walter W. Preston, and Judge J. Fletcher H. Gorsuch. The second row includes Noah E. Offutt, Ernest C. Hatch, George G. Wheeler, James C. L. Anderson, John D. C. Duncan, H. Courtenay Jenifer, T. Lyde Mason, James P. Kelley, Frank Hays Jacobs, Cornelius Roe, Milton R. Smith, Harry L. Smith, R. Moore Jenifer, and James P. Offutt. In the first row are T. Wilbur Meads, Judge William H. Lawrence, Judge J. Howard Murray, Gwynn Nelson, Lawrence E. Ensor, and George B. Marley.

211

212

George B. Marley, chief deputy sheriff of Baltimore County, is seen in his office on December 11, 1929.

The state was still using chain gangs in striped clothes when main roads were being macadamized early in the century. The old steam equipment forms a contrast to the horse-drawn gravel carts.

213

214

The lower dam of Loch Raven was completed in 1883, after some drought years terrified the Baltimore City planners with the possibility of a waterless future. By 1908, when it was clear that an expansion of the reservoir was needed to meet burgeoning needs a semisecret deal was struck to buy the town of Warren for $725,000. The Baltimore Sun *blew the whistle; there were endless hearings, and the deal was called off. When the town was finally bought on February 23, 1922, it and parts of Phoenix together cost a million dollars, plus an additional hundred thousand for so-called rental of the property prior to the actual transfer of ownership. In the meantime a compromise reservoir expansion program had to be agreed upon; between 1912 and 1914 the first level of the upper dam was built. In 1921, the final phase, as shown, was nearing completion according to the original plan. In both stages of the upper dam a temporary railroad spur had been built to bring in materials.*

215

Liberty Dam, opened in 1956, is impressive when seen from the air. The Melville Woolen Company on the North Branch of the Patapsco at Oakland Mills, Carroll County, was in the way of the impounded waters and was bought by the city for $1,574,100. After its equipment and component parts were auctioned, it was demolished. The mill site had been part of a larger Baltimore County when it was built in 1826, but was in Carroll County after 1837.

The Lansdowne Volunteer Fire Department sat for its portrait in 1902. In the front row are August Klapproth; Mr. Housely; William Sinkenbring, Sr.; Mr. Nevins; Mr. Reinhardt; and Adam Rieman (three first names are unknown). Second row: Elmer Wagner; August Reitmiller, Sr.; Charles Hull; William Sinkenbring, Jr.; Otto Haberkorn, Sr.; John Lehner; William Habberkorn; Henry Hoffman; August Reitmiller, Jr.; and Edward Hoffman. Both the Relay and St. Denis Volunteer Fire departments did yeoman work during the Baltimore Fire of 1904, the Relay team getting a signed testimonial from Mayor E. Clay Timanus, praising their efforts.

The Vigilant Volunteer Fire Department at 518 Eastern Avenue, was founded in 1915 and erected a building for twenty-five hundred dollars. As the 1917 photo shows, an early purchase was a 1914 Bessemer motorized chassis with two pumps, fire hoses, and a forty-foot ladder. In 1921 the county built a combined police-fire department building (designed by G. Walter Tovell) next door to Vigilant, which turned over its business to them and converted itself to the still-flourishing Vigilant Building Association. Upon completion of a new station on Myrth Avenue, the county gave the 1921 station to the Heritage Society of Essex and Middle River in 1970 for use as a museum. It remains a cultural gem not generally known or appreciated by county residents.

219

The combined Fullerton police-fire station, opened in 1920, was one of five built by Reisterstown contractor G. Walter Tovell. Besides building what is now the Franklin Middle School (formerly the 1930 high school), Tovell erected local community police-fire station landmarks in Halethorpe, Essex, Pikesville, and Dundalk.

220

The employees in the Lansdowne office of the telephone company, in the early 1900s, have not been identified except for a Mr. Fellers, far right.

The boys of the Pikesville Fire Department clowned around on June 26, 1934, in their 1921 six-cylinder American La France combination pumper, which had a capacity of pumping 750 gallons per minute.

221

222

Bill McCluskey is on water patrol for the Baltimore County Police in the 1960s.

Officer Eleanor Mitchell radios in her report in this 1960s photo.

223

224

As well known to Marylanders as the familiar State Highway Patrol cars are the helicopters of the Aviation Division of the Maryland State Police. Here the Airborne Ambulance hurries an injured person to the emergency room of the nearest available hospital.

225

Seated on the porch on a summer's day in the early 1900s were, from left to right, an unknown person, Samuel Moor Shoemaker II, J. Fred C. Talbott, Redmond C. Stewart, and Frank Hoen. Shoemaker (1861-1933) was master of Burnside, *a self-contained estate at the northwest corner of Greenspring Valley Road and Park Heights Avenue. He was a dairyman, president of the school board for seventeen years, a regent of the University of Maryland, president of the State Farm Board, and, as a member of the State Roads Commission, a champion of good roads. Congressman Talbott (1843-1918), first of the county's Democratic party bosses, ruled more or less benignly from his Lutherville home or his Washington office for nearly forty years. Stewart (1874-1936), who was the lawyer son of importer C. Morton Stewart, dabbled in cotton mill ownership and was Master of Fox Hounds at the Greenspring Valley Hunt Club. As a member of the House of Delegates in 1900 he was as intensely interested as Shoemaker in the good roads program. On the staff of the Judge Advocate General in World War I, Stewart was awarded both the Distinguished Service Medal and the Croix de Guerre. Stewart was president of the Kernan Hospital for Crippled Children for the last four years of his life. Hoen was a member of the A. Hoen lithography firm.*

226

Real estate speculator Harrison Rider (1865-1943) was the heir to the mantle of Democratic party boss when J. F. C. Talbott died in 1918. A large man with an imposing presence, Rider, son of Edward Rider (after whom Riderwood was named) was called "Rolling Thunder." He ran the party and its patronage with an iron fist until rival factions began to challenge his authority. Chief beneficiary of the in-fighting was Rider's young protege, H. Streett Baldwin.

227

Harry Streett Baldwin (1894-1952) grew up on the family farm in Baldwin. He was the fourth in the succession of Baltimore County's Democratic bosses, being preceded by J. Fred C. Talbott, Harrison Rider, and James P. Kelley. While president of the Board of County Commissioners, Streett Baldwin initiated the county's first zoning ordinance. He improved finances by reassessing all property, by stepping up collection of back taxes, and by instituting property sales in default of taxes. Baldwin also served in both the House of Delegates and the U.S. Congress.

Baldwin started as a dairyman but switched to growing snap beans. He organized a successful revolt of county farmers against the percent of profit being skimmed off by Baltimore commission houses. This action encouraged him to go into politics.

Congress decided to build a series of coast artillery forts (Fort Howard, Fort Armistead, and Fort Smallwood) to protect Baltimore. Land was acquired from a member of the Gunther brewing family in 1895 to start Fort Howard. Before construction was completed, many troops had to live in tents, as did "A" Company, in this early view. By 1904 many buildings and five batteries, one of which is shown, were built; a sixth named for Dr. Lazar, a discoverer of the source of yellow fever, was not completed. A parade scene is also shown. No longer useful as a defense, part of the fort's grounds and buildings were acquired by the Veterans Administration for use as a hospital. The county utilizes the rest as an attractive park. The swimming scene off Fort Howard, taken by a WPA photographer in the 1930s, shows the possibilities of this attractive place.

229

230

231

232

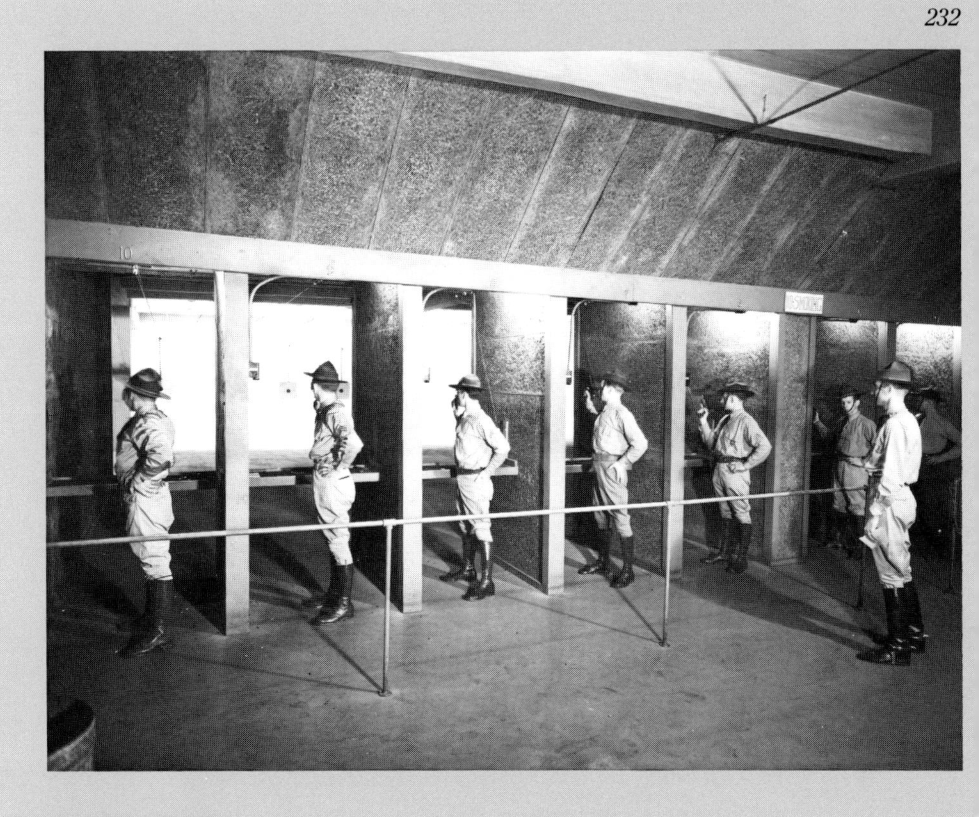

Members of the 110th Field Artillery, Maryland National Guard, make use of their pistol range in the Pikesville Armory on June 6, 1940.

233

Present at an installation of the Ladies Democratic Club of Essex in the late 1950s, are from left to right, in the front row Evelyn Krs, Evelyn Oaks, Jen Mohr, Elsie Stretka, Gertrude Carter, and Kay Wolfe. In the back row are Clara Davis, Catherine Kronnewetter, Elaine Albrecht, Emma Mock, Delores Collins, Gertrude Cowen, Jean Buskirk, Mary Ford, Thelma Jednoralski, Violet Brooks, and Bill Peters.

Construction started on the Social Security Administration's Woodlawn complex in 1957, with occupancy in 1960. This is a recent aerial view.

234

235

Maryland Public Television, then called the Maryland Center for Public Broadcasting, opened in Owings Mills on September 28, 1969. Its award-winning, nationally distributed program Wall $treet Week, *hosted by Louis Rukeyser (left), began on November 20, 1970, and still continues. Raymond K. K. Ho (right) became the third president on October 1, 1986*

★ DEMOCRAT ★

CLARENCE D.

LONG

Vote the "B" LINE

Pull Lever

6B

and leave it down

FOR

CONGRESS

2nd CONGRESSIONAL DISTRICT

Clarence D. Long, Democrat, has since 1963 represented Harford County and most of Baltimore County in Congress. Rep. Long is on the powerful House Appropriations Committee and serves on the Military Construction Subcommittee — important to Aberdeen, Edgewood and Bainbridge. Rep Long has fought in Congress for important issues: Tax reform, help for the elderly and anti-pollution measures are high on his list. Rep Long keeps in close touch with his constituents. He tours his district on Saturdays in his "Office on Wheels" and maintains a local telephone line to his Washington office. Rep. Long served as a lieutenant in the Navy during World War II. A Ph.D. from Princeton and professor at Johns Hopkins University before going to Congress, he has written seven books on economics and has served with the Council of Economic Advisors to President Eisenhower. Married to the former Susanna Larter, they have two children.

VOTE FOR COMMON SENSE GOVERNMENT

236

Clarence D. Long of Towson represented the Second Congressional District from 1964 to 1984. He had a Ph.D. from Princeton and had taught economics at Johns Hopkins for years. In an era of sleazy politicians, Long's integrity was never in question. His obdurate support of the increasingly unpopular Vietnam War, his obstructiveness in preventing the Baltimore harbor from being dredged for ten years, and his opposition to construction of the second bay bridge (which, as a result, cost additional millions when it was finally built), caused him to lose business support, and to have the Baltimore Sun *editorialize against him at election time. After three tries, Republican Helen Delich Bentley, a former Baltimore* Sun *maritime reporter and President Nixon's maritime commissioner, unseated him in 1984.*

No police lineup here, but a group of determined Essex reformers, out to clean up government in 1974; from left to right, Michael H. Weir, Dennis F. Rasmussen, Donald P. Hutchinson, Norman W. Lauenstein, Terry Conley, Quentin Eckenrode, Mae Tuchton Matarozza, and James Hart.

237

State senator James A. Pine, a long-established county political power, is shown at a last hurrah in the summer of 1974, shortly before his defeat in the September primary by an up-and-coming Essex man, Donald P. Hutchinson.

In 1972 the League of Women Voters had successfully lobbied for the passage of a charter amendment mandating that county council candidates would run only in their own districts, and not at large, thus effectively ending the grip the powerful and well-organized eastern Baltimore County political clubs had on county politics. In 1966, following Supreme Court rulings, the number of state senators had been raised from one to eight, greatly reducing Pine's influence.

With the breakup of the old Democratic machine came the rise of reformist political clubs and citizen activist groups, especially the well-informed, influential community councils, which were formed in almost every part of the county.

238

239

The League of Women Voters supported charter government vigorously in 1956.

Vote FOR
HOME RULE CHARTER
NOVEMBER 6, 1956
Let's Make Laws
for Baltimore County
IN
BALTIMORE COUNTY!
LEAGUE OF WOMEN VOTERS
OF BALTIMORE COUNTY
A non-partisan organization devoted to the promotion
of political responsibility through informed and
active participation of citizens in government.
Telephone: Valley 3-8188

THE PROPOSED CHARTER PROVIDES

A COUNTY COUNCIL—the lawmaking body for the County will consist of 1 resident from each of the 7 districts elected by the people of the county as a whole.

A COUNTY EXECUTIVE—the official head of the county government, elected by the people and responsible to them for the administration of county affairs.

AN ADMINISTRATOR—appointed by the County Executive, confirmed by the Council. He will appoint the heads of most of the offices and departments of the County government, with the approval of the County Executive and will supervise their activities. He will prepare the budget for submission to the Executive and Council.

MODERN BUDGETARY AND FISCAL PROCEDURES —a complete financial plan for the County will include long-range planning for capital projects, a balanced annual budget, public budget hearings, an annual audit by the County auditor and a bienniel audit by an independent firm of certified public accountants.

THE CHARTER GIVES YOU

HOME RULE—Baltimore County's laws will be made IN Baltimore County, not in Annapolis, as at present.

BETTER REPRESENTATION—7 Councilmen, one of whom will live in your district, and the County Executive will be elected by YOU to run your County government.

STREAMLINED GOVERNMENT—a consolidation of boards and agencies will make possible more efficient and responsible government. The recent improvements in fiscal and administrative procedures in the County government will be made permanent under the Charter.

VOTE FOR THE HOME RULE CHARTER!

241

Sandra A. O'Connor, a Republican, was elected as Baltimore County's state's attorney in 1975, in the wake of scandal which saw Samuel Greene, a predecessor, jailed for accepting a "carnal bribe." She worked effectively to restore the public's confidence in the department.

240

The 1957-1958 County Council, first after the Charter was adopted, was, from left to right John K. Davis, Republican, First District; Judge William C. Coleman, Republican, Second District; J. Cavendish Darrell, Democrat, Fourth District; Gordon G. Power, Republican, Third District; John E. Lassahn, Republican, Fifth District; Joseph L. Schield, Democrat, Sixth District, and James M. Barry, Democrat, Seventh District.

242

The Towson Branch of the Baltimore County Public Library was started by the Women's Club of Towson in 1938. Mary Osborn Odell, the first Towson librarian, began service in a rented house, using orange crates for shelves and the bathtub for storage. By 1974 the Towson Library served as administrative offices for a countywide library system as well as its Towson patrons, and required a three-floor innovative building designed by Tatar and Kelly. By 1987 this was one of the most heavily used branch libraries in the United States. County executive Theodore Venetoulis spoke to the library staff on staff day in the Towson Branch, in October 1976. Library director Charles W. Robinson is at the far right.

243

244

The Baltimore County Public Library's Cockeysville Branch, 9833 Greenside Drive, designed by Jewell, Downing and Associates, opened for business on February 14, 1982. Among its many innovations were a creative use of cheerful neon signage to guide people to the material they need, and open-face display of books in their jackets on specially designed shelving.

245

The opening of the White Marsh Branch of the Baltimore County Public Library, 8133 Sandpiper Road, took place on January 25, 1988. The attractive building, designed by Lapicki-Smith and Associates, was leased from Nottingham Properties, Inc. who built the mall and the library and were developing the community of White Marsh. Shown from left to right are Charles W. Robinson, director of the library; Michael R. Amann, member of the Board of Library Trustees; Norman Lauenstein, chairman of the County Council; Dennis F. Rasmussen, county executive; Carol McEvoy, aide to Councilman William R. Evans; and P. Douglas Dollenberg, president of Nottingham Properties, Inc.

246

247

The ninth all-Democratic county council, spanning the 1986-1990 term, included, from left to right (standing): Melvin B. Mintz, Second District; Dale T. Volz, Seventh District; Charles A. (Dutch) Ruppersberger, Third District; Ronald B. Hickernell, First District. Seated from left to right are Barbara F. Bachur, Fourth District; Norman W. Lauenstein, Fifth District; William R. Evans, Sixth District.

Helen Delich Bentley unseated incumbent Clarence Long in the Second Congressional District in 1984. Bentley continued to show great interest in matters concerning the port and the jobs it supports. The photographer found her enjoying friendly constituents at Essex Community College's Ethnic Festival in the fall of 1987.

SCHOOLS

Pictures of students show many of the changes which have occurred in the last ninety years. Dress codes and uniforms have gone. Boys no longer wear heavy woolen clothing in hot weather. Girls look more mature and are allowed to let themselves look attractive. Even hair length is a matter of personal preference.

The barefoot boys at the Warren School in May 1921, had more in common with their equally barefoot counterparts in Winslow Homer's *Crack the Whip* of half a century earlier than they do with their counterparts of today. School curriculum changed slowly; rural one- or two-room schools remained largely unchanged in many respects from the nineteenth century until the school consolidation process of the 1920s. Many of the old schools were then recycled as private homes. Eklo, Ashland, and the former black school at Sparks are three examples of such recycling.

The uneven quality of public education, which was maintained in a miserly way by penny-pinching county commissioners, led to an astonishing proliferation of private schools (often church-affiliated) between the early 1800s and the 1930s. Examples include St. James Academy, Monkton; the Milton Academy (now the Milton Inn); the Long Green Academy; St. Timothy's Hall; St. Timothy's School (formerly in Catonsville, now relocated in Stevenson), McDonogh; Oldfields; Hannah More; Garrison Forest School; Roberts-Beach School and the Crosby School, both in Catonsville; the Overlea School and Mount de Sales Academy of the Visitation in Catonsville; Lutherville Female Seminary; and various schools attached to Catholic parish churches all over the county. Some institutions arose to meet needs not being addressed by society at large, such as St. Vincent's Male Orphan Asylum, where WMAR-TV now is on York Road in Rodgers Forge, and St. George's Industrial School for Destitute Children on the Western Maryland Railway line in Glyndon. This last was once known as St. George's School for Boys. It thrived between 1870 and the 1920s, and, incredibly, actually sponsored an integrated picnic on September 10, 1916.

The Baltimore City Water Department's appraisers had a photographer in tow when they surveyed the properties in the Loch Raven watershed which the city would have to condemn and purchase, to allow room for the expansion of the impounded waters. He photographed the children outside the Warren school on May 27, 1921, one year before the school closed forever.

Graduates of Hannah More Academy line up for their picture in the late 1920s. The academy, which had begun in 1829, first accepted students in 1832. It merged with St. Timothy's, Stevenson, in 1974.

A chromolithograph of St. Timothy's Hall, a military school, was printed on an 1868 graduation certificate. St. Timothy's Hall was started in 1845 by the Reverend Dr. Libertus Van Bokkelen, the rector of St. Timothy's Episcopal Church, to the left in the picture. Well-known men such as Gen. Fitzhugh Lee and John Wilkes Booth attended this school as boys.

250

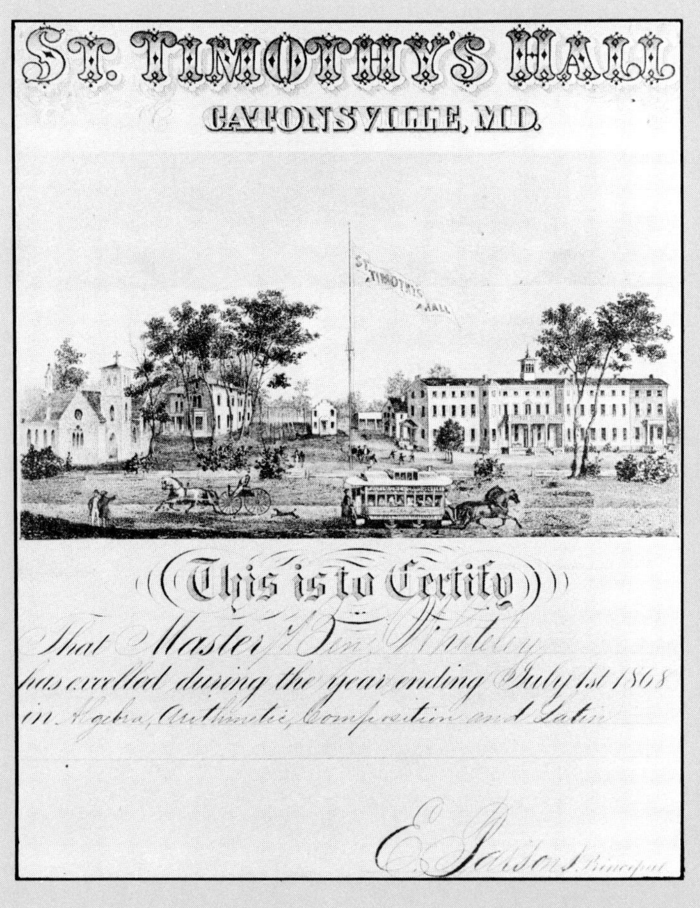
ST. TIMOTHY'S HALL
CATONSVILLE, MD.

This is to Certify
That Master J. Benj. Whiteley
has excelled during the year ending July 1st 1868
in Algebra, Arithmetic, Composition and Latin

E. Jackson Principal

249

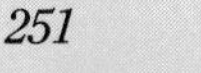

251

Mount de Sales Academy was founded in the summer of 1852 by nuns from the Visitation Order, headquartered in a Georgetown Convent. Because of the violent Know-Nothing, anti-Roman Catholic agitation in Baltimore at that time, the Mother Superior found it advisable to arrive in lay clothes when she came to take over the property. The school opened with 21 students; the number increased to 51 by the end of the first year. A century later there were 215 pupils receiving the excellent education offered by the school. After 1971 the school became a private Catholic high school.

Beginning in 1916, the cupola and cross of this notable building were used as a triangulation marker by both state and county surveyors.

The Reverend Dr. Libertus Van Bokkelen (1815-1898), pictured as an inset in a memorial window at St. Timothy's, established the first church-sponsored military school for boys in the nation. The Civil War was divisive; in spite of their headmaster's support of the Union, most of the students withdrew to fight for the Confederacy. The school closed. Van Bokkelen was appointed the first state superintendent of education and served from 1864 to 1867. He established what is now Towson State University, among other progressive acts. A vindictive, Southern-sympathizing legislature fired him, at which point he resumed his rectorship of St. Timothy's Church. In 1871 he rented the school buildings to the Misses Carter who used them for a girl's boarding school. The main structure burned on June 29, 1872. The grounds and the few remaining buildings were sold in 1881 to the renters, who then started what is now known as St. Timothy's School. This school moved to Stevenson in 1951.

In 1869 Van Bokkelen became president of the National Education Association. From 1874 to 1886 he was rector of Trinity Episcopal Church in Buffalo, New York. (Photo by James D. Officer)

252

The Dulaney Valley School, built to accommodate sixty children, opened for the school year 1877-1878 six miles from Towson on land mostly donated by the heirs of Joshua Jessop. It cost $1,695. Because it lay in the path of water impounded by the expanded Loch Raven Reservoir, the school board accepted Baltimore City's offer of twenty-five hundred dollars for the building and a hundred dollars an acre for adjacent land. The photo is dated June 1921. The site is now under water near Peerce's Plantation, Dulaney Valley Road.

John McDonogh was born in 1779 of Scotch-Irish parents. Apprenticed to a mercantile house, he left for New Orleans when he was twenty-one to deal in sugar, land, and slaves. By 1817, having had a spiritual conversion, he renounced his dealings in slaves, freed or planned the freedom of those he owned, and became a chief member of the American Colonization Society. When he died, John McDonogh left several major benefactions: one started the public school system of New Orleans; another funded the farm school for destitute children in Baltimore, which evolved into the McDonogh School.

The McDonogh School started in 1873 and was headed by Col. William Allen, a former Confederate ordnance officer and professor of applied mathematics at Washington and Lee University.

On October 23, 1928, the old main building (shown in a Hughes Company photo) burned. People in the Green Spring Valley housed the boys; other schools offered books; businesses lent equipment; and banks offered unlimited credit for an unlimited period. When it reopened, the school had larger and more modern facilities.

Gradually the farm orientation of the school changed; by 1963 the school had sold its dairy herd. The school discontinued the military program beginning with the 1972 school year. A 1909-1910 school year photo shows earnest (and glum?) looking children in their uniforms, identified as (front row) Thomas B. Benson, Wilson Eugene Gary, Myers Grissenger, Herbert C. Diedeman, Rausch, and Richard E. Charlton. In the second row are Howard E. Townsend, Percy Brown, Boring, Moran, E. Jones, Andrew Zeller, and George W. Dimpsey. The third row includes Walter A. Trautmann, Frederick G. Vetra, James M. Catiton, William B. Ruark, Boyrle (Boyle?), William C. Lewis. In the top row are Reardon, Walter H. Kincannon, H. Beale Rollins, William J. Higgins, Kones, and Harry C. Slater. Which boys are not identified in the third and fourth rows is unknown. Rollins became wealthy in operating a bus line and was a generous supporter and long-time member of the school board.

Equestrian skill is demonstrated by these exuberant boys at the school in 1957. A few years later, in the 1970s, the school became coeducational; an early woman graduate was Pam Shriver, the internationally recognized tennis champion.

253

254

255

Principal Zachariah C. Ebaugh, principal of Franklin High School, Reisterstown, is pictured with his boys of the years 1892-1893. After decades of careless use, the old brick building, originally the 1820 Franklin Academy, was recycled in the 1960s into the Reisterstown Branch of the Baltimore County Public Library.

Ebaugh served as county superintendent of schools from 1898 to 1900, but returned to Franklin because of his desire to teach and be around children. He died in 1906.

From 1885 until the early 1900s, Franklin was the only high school in the county. Under state law at that time, a school had to offer three grades above the sixth to be deemed a high school. Until 1939 only seven grades of school were available for black children in Baltimore County. The only black high school in either Baltimore City or Baltimore County was Frederick Douglass High School in Baltimore City. This one school was to serve the black children located throughout an area of no less than 655 square miles.

In 1939 the Benjamin Banneker, George Washington Carver, and George S. Bragg high schools were opened for blacks in Catonsville, Towson, and Sparrows Point, respectively. Bragg had been converted from an elementary school. Carver became the Towsontown Junior High School after the 1954 Brown vs. Board of Education of Topeka, Kansas *Supreme Court decision. Still later, Carver was converted to the Central Vocational-Technical Center in Towson. The three new black high schools offered four additional grades and graduated their first (eleventh-grade) classes in 1943.*

257

The 1883 Eklo School in Middletown, which was closed as a result of consolidation, was sold in 1933 and is now a residence. At the time of the photo, about 1917, principal John H. Hale was conducting Rural Life Education classes for farmers, and showing exhibits in the tent at the back.

The 1918 Baltimore County Eklo School bus. The school was closed in 1931 and the pupils transferred to the new sixth district school.

The girls in the home economics class at Towson High School in 1910 may or may not have been headed for a life in service. Their clean, starched uniforms and caps correctly in place were in keeping with the no-nonsense approach to mixing they carried out under a stern-eyed teacher.

260

The Crosby School on Beaumont Avenue, Catonsville, closed in 1960. Children in pressed, freshly washed summer clothes were photographed on June 10, 1914. In the back row, from left to right, are Mary Macgill, Nellie Biays, and Billy Davis. In the middle row are George Kimberly, Charlotte Riggs, Martha Gundry, Herbert Preston, and Louis Bresee West. Seated in front is Eugene de Bullet.

261

The 1918 graduating class of Catonsville High School lined up for its picture in the 1917 yearbook. The five in front, from left to right, are Paul I. Bauman (on the first step), Albert F. Metzger, Hilda M. Dumler, Jack Helfrich, and Mazie E. Robinson. In the rear are Randolph Burbank, Margaret D. Blake, Edith T. Morsberger, William T. Ritter, Ernest de Kalb, Vernon L. Piel, and Eva F. Hildebrandt.

The teachers at Essex Elementary School in 1919 included one fourteen-year-old boy. When Miss Morgan, the third and fourth grade teacher, became ill, the principal, Miss Gist, said to eighth-grader Joseph Ornson: "Joseph, you go and teach Miss Morgan's class. I don't want to show any partiality among the girls!" Joseph did, for twenty days, at two dollars a day substitute's pay.

Henry D. Perky, of Swiss-German descent, was born on a Mount Hope, Ohio farm in 1843. After college he taught school, tried business, and studied law. In Denver by 1879, he organized or built several railroads, founded the Steel Car Company of St. Louis, and organized a mining and industrial exposition in 1882.

Doctors ordered Perky, a severe dyspepsia sufferer, to maintain a diet of easily digested foods. He experimented with cooked wheat as a breakfast cereal, and established two factories for a shredded wheat cookie in Massachusetts. He formed the Natural Food Company at Niagara Falls in 1900. Fortified by a successful experiment in education in Worcester, Massachusetts, Perky got the idea of so grand an agricultural high school that he purchased the 1,293-acre Filston Farm, *and took out options on some adjacent acres, including the disused Phoenix Cotton Mill. He built elaborate school buildings and an auditorium. He called all this (as he had his Worcester School) Oread, after the Greek nymph of the foothills.*

Financially overextended, facing cash flow problems, embroiled in a lawsuit with his contractor for not meeting specifications (the county inspector said that one of his buildings was unsafe for human habitation), Perky went into his bathroom on June 26, 1906, and killed himself.

264

Only the administration building, photographed here in 1906 and now a private home, remains. But Perky's dream was realized, in a way, when Baltimore County opened the Sparks Agricultural High School in 1909.

265

266

The combined faculty of Franklin Elementary and High schools, Reisterstown, sat for a 1929 picture. In the back row are Miss Gray, Miss Hanna, Miss Huttenhauer, Miss Shipley, Miss Jones, Miss Tipton, Mr. Vogtman and Mr. Wheeler. In the middle row are Mr. Hyson, Mr. Hall, Miss Gorsuch, and Miss Frantz. In the front row are Louise B. Goodwin, Miss Russell, Miss Saffell, Miss Parsons, Miss Sterling, Miss Grimes, Miss Lauder, and an unidentified person.

The second grade of Perry Hall Elementary School visits the Baltimore County police headquarters on Washington Avenue in Towson on March 19, 1954, with their teacher, Marjorie Miller. In the first row are Linda Brewer, George Brewer, Lingard Dietz, Donna Erhardt, George Kloiber, Darileen Finn, Alvin King (partly hidden), Albert Thorpe, Robert Zahn, Gwen Cloman, and Danny Brockmeyer. In the second and third rows, left to right are, Mrs. Brewer, Charles Garland, Roger Bickford, Ethel Cadle, Holbrook Whitney, Dennis McLemore, Nancy Zink, Eileen Pfeiffer, Virginia Betz, Marjorie Wolf, Linda Howard, and Mrs. Cloman. The fourth row includes Karl Schmidt, John Jordan, Mary Letke, and Robert Heubeck. In the fifth row are Lucille Lintz, Brenda Neuhauser, Robert Southard, and Joyce Snyder. The top row shows Mrs. Betz, Mrs. Whitney, Mrs. King, Miss M. E. Miller, Mrs. Southard, and Mrs. Kloiber.

267

The 1938 Christmas pageant at the Cockeysville School is the prototype of all such pageants anywhere, anytime.

268

The agricultural instructional services of the University of Maryland hired steamboats—called Corn Boats—to take teams of instructors to rural areas. They also chartered "Good Corn Lecture Trains," as shown here on the Ma and Pa Railroad in 1905. Seated in front, from left to right, are William A. Amoss, director of the Farmer's Institute; Dr. H. J. Patterson, director of the Maryland Agricultural Experimental Station; and Dr. Joseph R. Owens, Maryland Agricultural College. Two students of the college, Walter B. Harris (left) and Edward Ingram Oswald, are holding up a box. Behind the box and barely visible is Dr. R. W. Silvester, president of the college. A. D. Shamel of the University of Illinois is standing between Patterson and Owens. Behind Shamel, from left to right, are Charles A. Councilman of Bloomfield, *the Glyndon tract now known as* Sagamore Farms; *W. T. L. Taliaferro of the college, behind Councilman; E. Gittings Merryman of* Gerar, *a farm on Shawan Road (a brother of Nicholas Bosley Merryman of* Hayfields*); and, behind Merryman, a Dr. Webber.*

A school for black children was started in 1873 at 417 Schwartz Avenue, west of York Road, south of St. Pius X Church. About 1905 it moved to 437 Schwartz Avenue. There is evidence that the city took on the education of these county children after 1918 and sent them four miles away to 155 East Arlington Street.

The black community initially had to find the money to start the school on its own, including rental of space (417 Schwartz was a private house). All county black schools were consistently denied a fair proportion of money for salaries, books, repairs, and fuel, and had to struggle with this inequity even beyond the end of segregation in 1954. A science supervisor recalled encountering labs in black schools that had no materials! There was an unusual amount of time spent instructing black children in skills such as drawing, which would be of little use to them in the market place.

The building at 437 Schwartz Avenue was constructed by the Grand United Order of the Nazarites, who used the second floor for lodge meetings. Subsequently both former school buildings reverted to private ownership and have been restored as private residences.

Jesse Nicholas (1873-19?), pictured here with his charges, was principal from 1894 to 1905. He was then posted to the black school on Hillen Road in Towson, a long-vanished structure built by the Freedmen's Bureau after the Civil War.

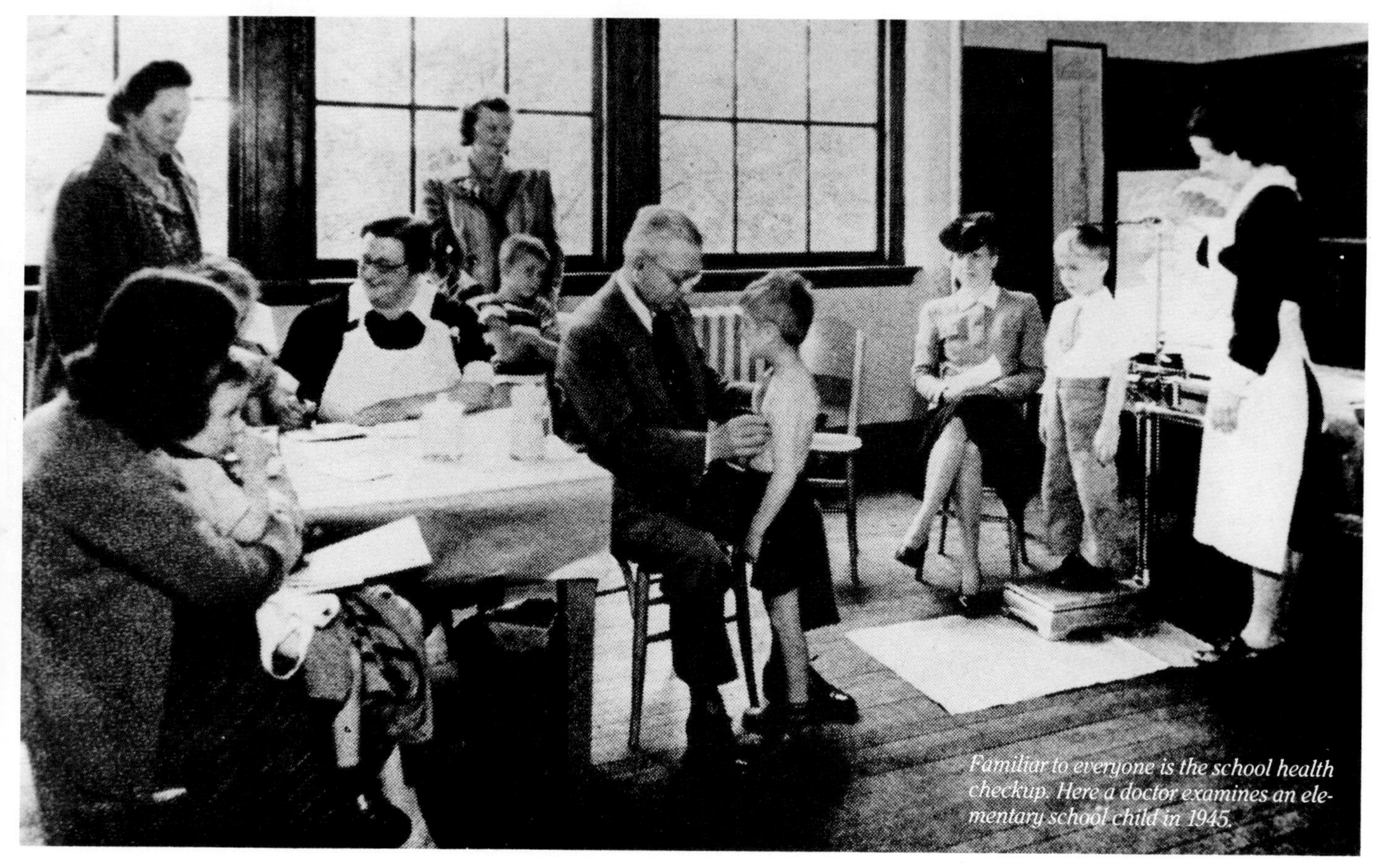

Familiar to everyone is the school health checkup. Here a doctor examines an elementary school child in 1945.

271

The sixth grade in the Fullerton School listens to its teacher in the 1950s. (Photo by Pete Rowe)

These students at Hereford High School were intent on studying India in a social studies class on February 2, 1966. (Photo by James Lally)

272

273

Some scenes of school life which hardly change from decade to decade: the 1952 Harvest Dance at Catonsville High School; majorettes at Sparrows Point High School in 1954. From left to right they are M. Hafer, C. Donet. C. Stall, C. Strasbaugh, and B. Hayes. Chesapeake Senior High's Ron Dillman pins a Towson opponent in 1984.*

275

274

276

Photographer Hal Schmulowitz caught an impressive Walter G. Amprey, the principal of Woodlawn Senior High School, at a graduation ceremony in the early 1980s. By the late 1980s Amprey was an assistant superintendent in the county school system.

277

These Catonsville-area nursery school children register a variety of comments on the proceedings at their graduation exercises in the early 1980s.

The State Normal School, now Towson State University, moved to Towson from Lafayette Square, Baltimore, in 1914-1915. A prime example of the Jacobean Revival, designed by Parker, Thomas and Rice, Stephens Hall served as a combined classroom, office, and administration building until 1971. It was named for Morse Bates Stephens, a state superintendent of education.

278

When Jay Lyston graduated from Towson State Teacher's College in June 1954, he received his diploma from Governor Theodore R. McKeldin at the outdoor ceremony. Insects were a problem at these affairs; at the 1953 commencement exercises the cicadas, the seventeen-year locusts, dropped in swarms on the guests and graduates, causing panic. His uncle, Fred Feder, who ran a Towson photographic studio, took the picture.

Robert Steiner, a chemistry professor at Catonsville Community College, demonstrated a nanosecond fluorometer in May 1980. The students were all attention.

280

287

286

The original St. Charles College, a seminary, had been built in Howard County, opposite Charles Carroll of Carrollton's Doughoregan Manor. *After it burned in 1911, the seminary reopened with new buildings in Catonsville. The complex was used as a Sulpician high school from 1911 to 1969. It then became the new campus of St. Mary's Seminary College, which vacated its Paca Street headquarters.*

The beautiful chapel was a gift from members of the Jenkins family, who were related to the first president of the original St. Charles College. The designers were Murphy and Olmsted of Washington, D.C.

When the preseminary students were moved to St. Mary's Seminary on Roland Avenue in Baltimore, the Catonsville property was sold for a retirement community, Charlestown, where architecturally compatible buildings are being constructed.

James, Cardinal Gibbons, seen here with the seminarians and faculty at Woodstock College in 1919, had come to celebrate the fiftieth anniversary of the school.

The Jesuit Fathers started building Woodstock College in 1869. By the time it closed in the early 1970s, the large campus was a self-contained world with a parish church (St. Alphonsus Rodriguez); its own bakery and power plant; a library of three hundred thousand volumes; science laboratories; classrooms; beautifully executed chapels; a refectory; an observatory; a delightful greenhouse with a Victorian gingerbread roofline; formal gardens; delicate wrought-iron gazebos on a promontory overlooking the Patapsco; a Victorian train station; and, at one time, a footbridge over the river. There was even a volunteer fire department, manned by seminarians, as well as a modest orchestra.

The refectory is shown decorated for the fiftieth anniversary celebrations at the college in 1919.

281

282

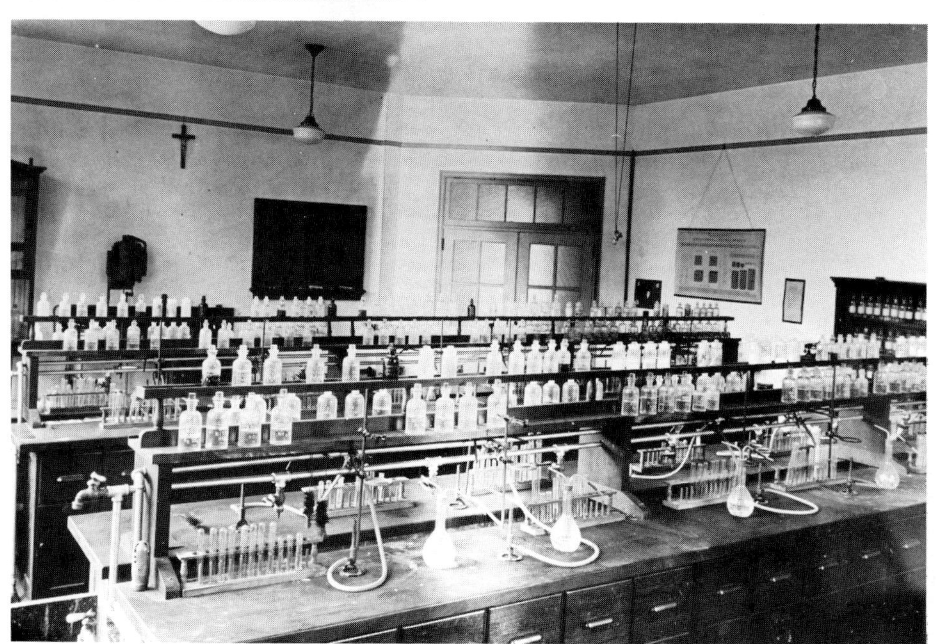

284

283

The library contained many incunabula (books printed before 1500). The whole collection was moved to Georgetown University when Woodstock closed.

285

EVENTS

Most of the events shown here speak for themselves: Fourth of July celebrations, electioneering, cornerstone-laying or turning over ground for a new public building, award giving, special events of a one-time nature, and natural or man-made disasters. Such activities take place everywhere; Baltimore County is no different from any other area.

Blacks are noticeably absent in many of the pictures in this collection. As invisible, second-class participants in the American dream, they were not supposed to be in evidence unless back-breaking or undesirable work needed to be done. Until 1954 blacks had to sit in the gallery at movie houses (to which they often had their own entrance), went to their own beaches (in Anne Arundel County), were not invited to join in the fun at swimming holes, baseball fields, bowling alleys, and pool rooms, and went to saloons only if there was a high divider between the white and "colored" sections (as there was in Charles Bosley's Bosley Hotel in Towson). Blacks could not shop at many of the stores whites went to or be served in the better restaurants, and had to sit in the backs of streetcars and railway coaches. There were always separate drinking fountains and restroom facilities. Interracial socializing was out of the question. A story from Phoenix in the *Baltimore County Union*, January 15, 1881, shows how such limits were brutally enforced, with smug and unquestioning white public approval.

> On Friday night, 7th inst., a number of boys were engaged in coasting when a colored man employed by Mrs. Patterson came out to take part. This the boys did not like and for revenge stretched a rope across the track which caught the colored man under the chin and spread him out in the snow in the most approved fashion. A little difficulty followed but the colored man did not engage in any more coasting that evening.

With all this in mind, the reader may see why the picture of the Towson Fourth of July Parade turning the corner at York Road and Pennsylvania Avenue is so poignant. The black boy standing in the middle of the street would dearly love to join the white boys from Hamilton carrying the American flag. But it could not be in 1908.

The Lutherville Female Seminary opened on October 4, 1854, under the aegis of Dr. John Morris, founder of Lutherville. The school burned in January 1911, apparently the result of a student's defying a ban on smoking. Rebuilt, the school lasted until 1952. It is now College Manor, a nursing home. Banker-photographer William C. Kenney was on hand in 1911 as the ruins still smoked.

314

Also generally absent in many pictures from the collection are women in roles other than companions to men, or doing anything other than what society had decreed they could do: that is, raise families, learn domestic science, teach, run church socials, sing in choirs, or elegantly perform their role in the long boring days of Victorian social ritual. However, behind the scenes women's lives were changing. While drudgery at home was decreasing, due to the availability of electrical and gas appliances, wage-earning possibilities were expanding beyond the traditional jobs of teaching, being a counter clerk, domestic service, or standing at a textile loom. The experience of women in factory jobs during both world wars especially exposed women to new opportunities.

One local breakthrough for women occurred when Dorothy Boone became the first county councilwoman in 1958. It was twenty years, however, before another woman followed her into the county council chamber.

---

100 Dollars

REWARD.

RAN AWAY from the Subscriber, living ten miles from Baltimore, on the Reister's Town road, on Friday night the 10th inst. Negro

FREDERICK,

Calling himself Frederick Merryman, about five feet seven or eight inches high, thirty-five or thirty-six years of age, remarkably stout built and well set, has a scar on one of his cheeks from a burn, also a considerable white scar on his shoulder, commencing from the lower part of his neck, occasioned by a scald, has small red eyes. He took with him a country cloth short coat, grey color, a tow shirt, a white ruffled one, and a white cravat marked F. Merryman with durable ink, he has other cloths that cannot well be described. Frederick is supposed to have a mother and sisters residing near the Baltimore seminary, where it is very likely he may be harbored. It appears that he has for some time thrown out hints of his intended elopement, and talked frequently of his intention of getting on board a vessel. Masters of vessels and others are cautioned against harboring or aiding said runaway. The above reward, will be paid if apprehended out of the state, or fifty dollars if within, and secured in any jail, so that I get him again, or if brought home all reasonable charges allowed.

ROBERT LYON,

Reister's Town Road.

Baltimore County, July 12th, 1819.

POSTPONED

Sheriff's Sale of a Negro Boy.

IN accordance with the judgment and sentence of the Circuit Court for Baltimore county, and by virtue of the order of said Court, I will offer for sale, on *Wednesday, the 16th day of July, A. D.* 1862, at the hour of 12 o'clock M., at the Court House door, in Towsontown, a NEGRO BOY, named *Benjamin Lewis Simms,* aged about twenty years, of medium size, &c.; sentenced by the Court to be sold to serve as a slave out of the State of Maryland, for a term of TEN YEARS from day of sale. He will be sold at private sale if applied for previous to the day of sale.

Terms cash in bankable money.

And notice is hereby given to any party suffering by the offence for which said negro was convicted, or other party who may legally claim a portion of the proceeds of said sale, under Article 30, Section 189, of the revised laws of Maryland, to file the same with the Clerk of the Circuit Court for Baltimore county, within three weeks of the date of the first insertion of this advertisement.

JOSEPH WALKER,

June 21.—4t Sheriff of Baltimore county.

PUBLIC SALE OF

"RISTEAU'S FANCY."

These grim reminders of slavery date from 1819 and 1862.

290

The great flood on the Patapsco River of 1868 is shown in this Harper's Weekly *engraving of August 8, 1868, where the waters are shown overtaking the Gambrill's flour mill. The rampaging river destroyed the Granite Cotton Factory upstream from Ellicott City, greatly damaged Gray's Factory, obliterated the Avalon Iron and Nail Works (just upstream from the Relay Viaduct), damaged in one degree or another every other mill on the river, took out all the bridges, and claimed fifty lives. Twenty houses were washed away; the total property loss in the valley was estimated to exceed a million dollars. Thirty years after the flood, relics of it were still being uncovered in different parts of the valley.*

Flash floods have been frequent, unwelcome summer events throughout Baltimore County's history. This one overtook a grand assemblage of classic cars at Chesaco Avenue and Philadelphia Road on July 20, 1931.

291

292

In the late summer of 1971, fire chief Austin Dietz met with the bereaved families of four volunteer firemen. The men drowned while trying to help others during a freshet which on August 1 had turned Bean Creek at Philadelphia Road into a raging torrent. In the front row, from left to right, are Mrs. John Mueller, Mrs. Rip K. Shaffer, Mrs. Charles Ruck, Chief Dietz, Mrs. Charles Hopwood, and Mrs. Milton de Sombre. In the second row, are John Mueller, Rip Shaffer, Martin de Sombre, William Barton, and Robert Carr. The third row includes Norman Baumgart, Lawrence Sugars, and Charles Polesne.

293

The worst flood to hit the Patapsco River since the disaster of 1868 was tropical storm Agnes in the week of June 21, 1972. Damaging many buildings in and near Ellicott City, the flood piled up debris around the Daniels railroad piers, rerouting the river. The result was the total flooding of the factory, which never reopened at the site. A fire in the mid-seventies finished the job; the site is now a collection of ruins sealed off by a chain link fence. The effects of this dreadful storm were countywide; a man, stalled in his Cadillac in the Cockeysville underpass, drowned when the electrically controlled windows could not be opened.

294

More trouble from the 1971 summer storm, this time on Belair Road.

295

Col. Jerome Joyce was the owner of a hotel near Camden Station, Baltimore, An ebullient self-promoter and local area booster, he masterminded the November 2-8, 1910 Halethorpe Air Show. The Baltimore County Union, *October 22, reported on Joyce's negotiations at an international air meet at Belmont Park, New York, where he recruited a stable of French, English and American aviation acrobats. At Halethorpe these pioneers did amazing maneuvers in their erector-set vehicles of canvas, visible struts, glorified bicycle wheels, and fifty-horsepower motors—like staying aloft for all of fifty-four minutes. The weather did not always cooperate, and wind did fifty thousand dollars worth of damage to a hangar tent and its planes. The show lost twenty-five thousand dollars for its backers. Admission ranged from $1.00 to $2.50 with automobiles being charged $2.00 per passenger. Attendance was low.*

The Schneider Cup airplane race was started in 1913 by Jean Schneider, a French arms manufacturer. By winning the race at the Solent in 1923, the U.S. team won the right to choose the venue of the October 1925 race, which was off Bay Shore Park. Jimmy Doolittle, famed later for his raid over Tokyo during World War II, won the race for the U.S. Team. A surprising upset was that of Henri C. Biard, in the British Team's Supermarine S-4, shown here, then the fastest plane in the world. It developed aileron difficulties and crashed, although the pilot escaped.

Cpl. Ned Martini, with pilot D. F. A. Joyce and postal employee J. Cameron Coleman prepare to meet the first mail plane from the South at Logan Field on February 19, 1934.

297

298

The Towson Volunteer Fire Parade, about July 4, 1908, is moving up York Road, making its turn west from York onto Pennsylvania Avenue, a route still followed by present day Fourth of July parades. A group of children from Hamilton is carrying a large American flag at the right, while volunteers, behind them, pull a heavy piece of fire equipment. In the background can be seen a horse and carriage, a streetcar, and the Ma and Pa Railroad bridge, which stood to the south of the present Towson Library. The boy at the left would evidently like to join the parade.

299

The Towson Elk's Lodge on Pennsylvania Avenue was built in 1905. It is shown after the Volunteer Fireman's Parade of 1909 or 1910 has just passed. The expression and activities of the bystanders merit close examination with a magnifying glass. We speculate that some women are watching a mother who has just boxed her son's ears, that some nosey women are trying to see what the man is looking at, that the dandies, standing at the curb's edge, are bored. Perhaps the heavy man striding purposefully ahead, oblivious to everything, is in search of the nearest food.

The Towson Volunteer Fire Department parade of July 4, 1910, went up York Road to the fire station, which stood in the area of Joppa Road between York Road and Dulaney Valley Road. The fire house was built in 1879 as Mary Shealey's new store. The Volunteer Fire Department moved in in August 1892. The building was demolished on July 6, 1955. The second floor had served as a meeting place for the Towson Guards and other groups, and was the meeting place for Roman Catholics until St. Francis Assisi Church was opened in 1882 on a site now occupied by the Towson water tower. The Church of the Immaculate Conception was built in 1903 to accommodate the growing congregation.

When a new police station was built on Washington Avenue in 1926, it became headquarters and the Towson precinct was lodged above the old fire house.

Albert Weis's store (later called Corbin's) is to the left of the fire hall. Bosley's Hotel can be seen to the left of the tree at the right. A corner of the stone Towson Hotel is at the extreme right. A horse's head partially obscures the well-known pump which stood in front of the hotel. The fire equipment is a Holloway chemical fire engine.

301

The signing of the Declaration of Independence was the theme of this 1920s Dundalk Fourth of July horse-drawn float.

302

The National Brewing Company's beloved Shires move in their purposeful way at an Essex Fourth of July celebration of the 1970s.

303

304

Train wrecks have occurred from time to time on all of Baltimore County's lines. The head-on view of an early wreck of the Western Maryland near Boring, Hanover Pike, may be compared with the side view of the wreck of Northern Central's Express 5062, south of Blue Mount (near Monkton) on August 18, 1913.

It is possible that the Western Maryland crash was one that occurred at Fowblesburg in September 1915 when the Reisterstown Volunteer Fire Department assisted that of Boring in controlling a blaze. On the map (page 19), Boring is northeast of Reisterstown and is marked C[olored] M[eeting] H[ouse]. Fowblesburg is marked Upperco, north of Woodensburg.

On September 27 to October 16, 1927, the Baltimore and Ohio Railroad staged a huge extravaganza in Halethorpe, which attracted thousands of spectators. The Fair of the Iron Horse celebrated the advances in transportation from the Conestoga wagon up to the largest locomotive then on the rails. Three engines are shown as they appeared before the grandstand in this spectacular event.

305

306

307

308

The immense crowds attracted by the Fair may be gauged in this picture, as hundreds are seen milling about some of the rolling stock.

309

The Fullerton Hotel, advertised in 1926 as being "six miles from Baltimore on the Belair Road," is now an Elks Lodge. On May 18, 1929, it was the setting for a testimonial dinner for W. Howard Milling (1882-1941). Milling was born on the Stemmers Run farm of James and Ida Milling. A Middle River farmer, he was also president of the Cowenton Permanent Building Association.

Among the many political offices Milling held were delegate, Essex magistrate, clerk of the circuit court, and county commissioner for nine years (1929-1938). His affiliation was with that faction of the local Democratic party controlled by James P. Kelley. One of his daughters married Carville Akehurst, the well-known Fullerton florist.

310

1

312

During the Depression, under the auspices of the Works Progress Administration, McDonogh's campus and facilities benefited from the labor of hundreds of men. Numerous maintenance and repair projects in every part of the McDonogh campus were funded. Hugh F. Burgess, Jr., and Robert C. Smoott III wrote in their McDonogh School: An Interpretive Chronology *(1973):*

> *The government contributed over $100,000 in materials as well as all labor costs in these projects.*
>
> *Under the auspices of the Public Works Administration, several major campus construction projects were completed. The Finney building was constructed with the government contributing forty-five percent of the cost. The boiler room was constructed at the same time on the same basis, forty-five percent from the government, fifty-five percent from the school. The John McDonogh stadium was constructed with the government contributing seventy-seven percent and the Patrons Club the remainder.*
>
> *The total expenditure in all the WPA and PWA projects is almost impossible to estimate, but an average figure of $100,000 per year for the seven years during which the school participated would seem a minimum figure.*

Three photos illustrate aspects of this program. In one, workers are constructing an Imhoff tank for the school's septic system.

313

President Franklin D. Roosevelt tours the Glenn L. Martin plant in Middle River on October 1, 1940.

The great Reisterstown fire of February 11, 1928 was discovered at 3:45 A.M. in Sander's meat market on Main Street. Near-freezing weather and the lack of a public water supply amplified the disaster. Water was pumped from a pond two miles west of town, and neighboring fire departments lumbered through snow and mud to get to the scene. Lost were a lunch room, the meat market, a confectionery store, a bowling alley, the A & P store, a pharmacy, two groceries, and several second-level apartments. Eighteen fire companies were at the scene. Fortunately there was no loss of life.

315

Essex Avenue suffered a ten-alarm fire on August 3-4, 1957 that wiped out seven businesses and a branch bank. Also lost were both the Acme and the A & P supermarkets, a Read's Drugstore, the Ben Franklin variety store, a Chesapeake and Potomac Telephone office, a furniture and bedding storage warehouse, and an Arnold's Men's and Women's shop. The hundred-foot-high flames caused a million dollars worth of damage.

BALTIMORE COUNTY POLICE DEPARTMENT

January 3, 1942

GENERAL ORDER # 31

Pertaining to the surrender of Radio Transmitters, Short Wave Radio Receiving Sets, and Cameras by German, Italian, and Japanese aliens.
also: weapons, ammunition + explosives

A telegram received from Bernard J. Flynn, U. S. District Attorney states: "All German, Italian, and Japanese aliens are required to surrender to local police authorities, by 11 P. M. Monday, January 5, 1942, all Radio Transmitters, Short Wave Radio Receiving Sets, and Cameras."

In view of the above, the designated articles will be received at all Station Houses. The person surrendering said articles will be given a receipt for same, also all property received will be tagged with persons name and address, and forwarded to these Headquarters.

BY ORDER OF

Oscar M. Grimes

OSCAR M. GRIMES
CHIEF OF POLICE

317

A month after Pearl Harbor, Police Chief Oscar Grimes (1940-1951) took action against enemy aliens. The property was returned at the end of the war.

In mid-May 1968, the so-called Catonsville Nine, protesting the U.S. involvement in Vietnam, invaded the local draft board (No. 33) offices housed in the Knights of Columbus building, 1010 Frederick Road, Catonsville. They seized and burned six hundred files of those classified most eligible for drafting. Center, standing, from left to right: Rev. Philip F. Berrigan, S. S. J.; Rev. Daniel Berrigan, S. J. Left, seated, Br. James McGinnis (not one of those charged for the protest), Mary Assumpta Moylan; David Darst; at the right, Marjorie and Thomas R. Melville of Washington, D. C. The others are George Joseph Mischle, John Joseph Hogan, and Thomas Pohl Lewis. The nine, none from Catonsville, received sentences ranging from two to more than three years. Over the next twenty years Philip Berrigan would be arrested some twenty times for one demonstration or another.

319

318

The Essex Vietnam War-Korean War Memorial, adjacent to the Heritage Society of Essex and Middle River at 510 Eastern Boulevard, was dedicated in 1985.

320

The bitterness of the Vietnam War and an echo of the demonstrations of the 1960s surfaced in November 1975. Towson State University students protested the appearance of Nguyen Cao Ky, former vice-president of South Vietnam, as a speaker.

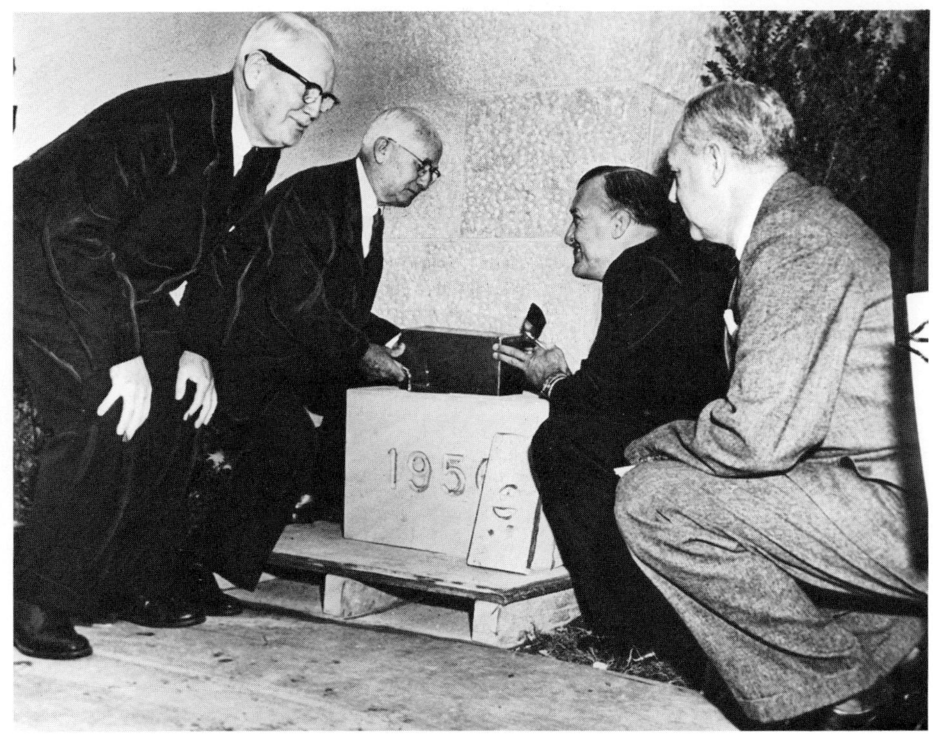

321

On October 25, 1958, county executive Michael J. Birmingham (second from the left) and John Gontrum, chief judge of the Circuit Court, left, were joined by Governor Theodore R. McKeldin (second from right) and Hall Hammond, chief judge of the Court of Appeals, as a time capsule was buried in the cornerstone of the annex to the old courthouse.

Senator John F. Kennedy, Democratic nominee for president, electioneered in Towson Plaza on September 16, 1960. He is gesturing to Congressman (later Senator) Daniel Brewster. Behind Brewster is A. Gordon Boone, Speaker of the House of Delegates. Two seats to Boone's left is Michael J. Birmingham, former county executive. In the front row, arms folded, is Christian H. Kahl, then the incumbent county executive. The Plaza was altered extensively in the 1980s into a covered mall, and renamed the Towsontown Centre.

323

Officials present at the ground-breaking for the new police headquarters on Kenilworth Drive, Towson, in 1961, were, from left to right, Captain Damon P. Gerber, Inspector J. Gordon Holmes, Chief Gilbert Deyle and County Executive Christian Kahl.

Born in Baltimore, Kahl (1905-1985) trained to be an accountant and a real estate broker. He was appointed clerk of the Circuit Court in 1941 and was elected a county commissioner the next year. He served three terms as a commissioner, two of them as president. In 1958 he became the first county executive elected under charter government. A split in the Democratic party in 1962 enabled a Republican, Spiro T. Agnew, to be elected.

Agnew became governor in 1966, defeating Baltimore County Democrat George P. Mahoney, who ran a thinly veiled campaign based on prejudice. Dale Anderson then won the first of two elections for the county executive's position.

Kahl managed a private real estate business until 1969, when he became the state manpower administrator. In 1971 he was appointed executive director of the Employment Security Administration, from which he retired in 1975.

324

325

This group from left to right, includes Brig. Gen. James P. S. Devereux, director of Public Safety; fire chief Winfield Wineholt; county executive Spiro Agnew; and police chief Robert Lally. They are testing a fire box telephone on November 12, 1963, across from the old courthouse. Never brought to trial, Agnew filed a plea of Nolo Contendere *in October 1973 and resigned as Vice-President of the United States, after the United States Attorney's office in Baltimore, examining the practices of Dale Anderson, discovered that Agnew had been on the take from contractors and developers as county executive 1962-1966, governor of Maryland 1966-1968, and vice-president of the United States, 1968-1973.*

Wielding mean shovels at the March 1, 1971 ground-breaking of the County Courts Building were (left) Lester L. Barrett, chief judge; (center) Dale Anderson, county executive; and (right) Francis Barrett, chairman of the county council. Watching were Orville T. Gosnell, clerk of the court (behind Judge Barrett); Vernon Smith (Anderson's bodyguard); Gary Huddles, Second District councilman; Francis X. Bossle, First District councilman; R. Bruce Alderman, county solicitor; Daniel L. Colosino (aide to Anderson); and Stanley Guild, Jr., budget director.

326

This 1971 demonstration in front of the County Office Building in Towson is protesting zoning adjacent to Interstate 83, which Councilman Walter Tyrie (Third District) proposed to give a developer, during the first Comprehensive Zoning Maps, Four-Year Cycle hearings in 1971. Although these raucous and disorderly public hearings went on into the early morning hours, the zoning was not approved by the County Council. Tyrie was replaced by C. E. (Bud) Ritter, a Republican, at the next election.

For much of the twentieth century, land use in Baltimore County has been a source of contention and corruption. As with appointments to certain county jobs in the old days, getting preferential zoning was merely a case of whom one knew and how much one was willing to slip under the table for it.

Police officers who helped raise money for Muscular Dystrophy are shown in this 1972 photo. From left to right are: Frank Messina, Donald Shriver, Tom Doyle, Mike Fuller, Stu Guise, Bill Turner, an unidentified representative from the Muscular Dystrophy Association; and three patients.

327

328

Austin Dietz, fire chief; Frederick Dewberry, county executive; and Donald T. Warren, deputy chief, at an award ceremony in 1973. Dewberry, a former county councilman, succeeded William Fornoff as county administrative officer in the spring of 1973. He was appointed by the County Council to replace Dale Anderson when the latter was convicted in Federal District Court on four counts of income tax evasion, one count of conspiracy, and twenty-seven counts of extortion, many in connection with the contracts for the County Courts Building. Dewberry lost the Democratic primary to Ted Venetoulis in 1974. He later became the executive director of the Regional Planning Council.

CHURCHES

Following the Glorious Revolution of 1688, religion played an important role in both Maryland and Baltimore County life. The Calverts, proprietors of Maryland, were Catholics. They did, however, permit other denominations to exist. After 1691 the Anglican Church became the established church, a role it held until the American Revolution. This led to the creation of such parishes as St. Thomas, Garrison Forest; St. John's, Joppa (later moved to Kingsville), and St. James on the Manor. Later, the growth of Methodism and the great migrations from Europe created a need for religious diversity. Other denominations serving the new arrivals prospered. Many of the newcomers worked in the mills, or in the stores and businesses which grew up around crossroads towns.

Churches and schools performed a recognized, if unspoken, role in keeping the work force in a peaceful and tractable frame of mind. Mill owners and community leaders knew a good thing when they found it. They served on church boards; they frequently donated land to a denomination to erect its building; and, not infrequently, quietly gave regular financial support, including the pastor's modest salary. Churches receiving such direct underwriting included some in the company towns of Warren, Alberton, Sparrows Point, Franklinville, and Paper Mills (later called Hoffmanville).

Churches and schools, too, were the social focal points of company towns and rural communities. The small amount of entertainment available occurred in connection with one or the other of those institutions: typical were Christmas pageants or church suppers, oyster roasts and raffles to support the local church or volunteer fire department, school graduation exercises, and the support of sports teams. Cornet and brass bands often met in the church or school hall to practice. And almost every community had a band: Rayville, Western Run, Sparrows Point, Oella, Relay, Lansdowne, Pikesville, Warren, Phoenix, Towson, Catonsville, to mention a few. Only the 109-year-old Daniels band remains from the once-crowded field of town bands, and only the talented boys and girls who perform in the county's high school bands on parade days today are the cultural successors to community people who marched and paraded eighty or ninety years ago.

The names found in old lists of church boards and vestries, and the testimony left by memorial windows and

The cornerstone of St. John's in the Valley Episcopal Church, Butler Road, Glyndon, was laid in 1816, on land donated by Charles Walker. Walker and members of the Worthington and Johns families covered the major expenses of the construction. The original structure was destroyed by fire on Christmas 1867. The present church, shown here, was built in 1869 by the Westminster, Maryland, firm of Short and Leister.

plaques, are evidence of the close relationship of the churches to the successful people in their parishes. Further clues may be found in every adjacent churchyard, where the headstones read like a roll call of the decades of each community's history.

Baltimore County's churches and synagogues are beautiful, spirit-lifting places. They vary from simple, unadorned but very moving structures, to buildings designed by famous architects, with interiors enhanced by skilled artisans. Such buildings match similar buildings anywhere; the magnificent chapels in Woodstock and St. Charles colleges might easily be mistaken for ones in Europe. Not grand at all but reassuringly simple were three churches whose original buildings were log structures: St. John's African Union Methodist Protestant Church on Bellona Avenue, built in 1833, which burned and was replaced in 1886; the 1854 St. John's Evangelical Lutheran Church on Dance Mill Road, Blenheim, replaced in 1873, by one designed by the Amrein brothers; and the High German Lutheran church on Cockey's Mill Road, Reisterstown, used from 1754 to 1854, of which only the brick-walled cemetery remains.

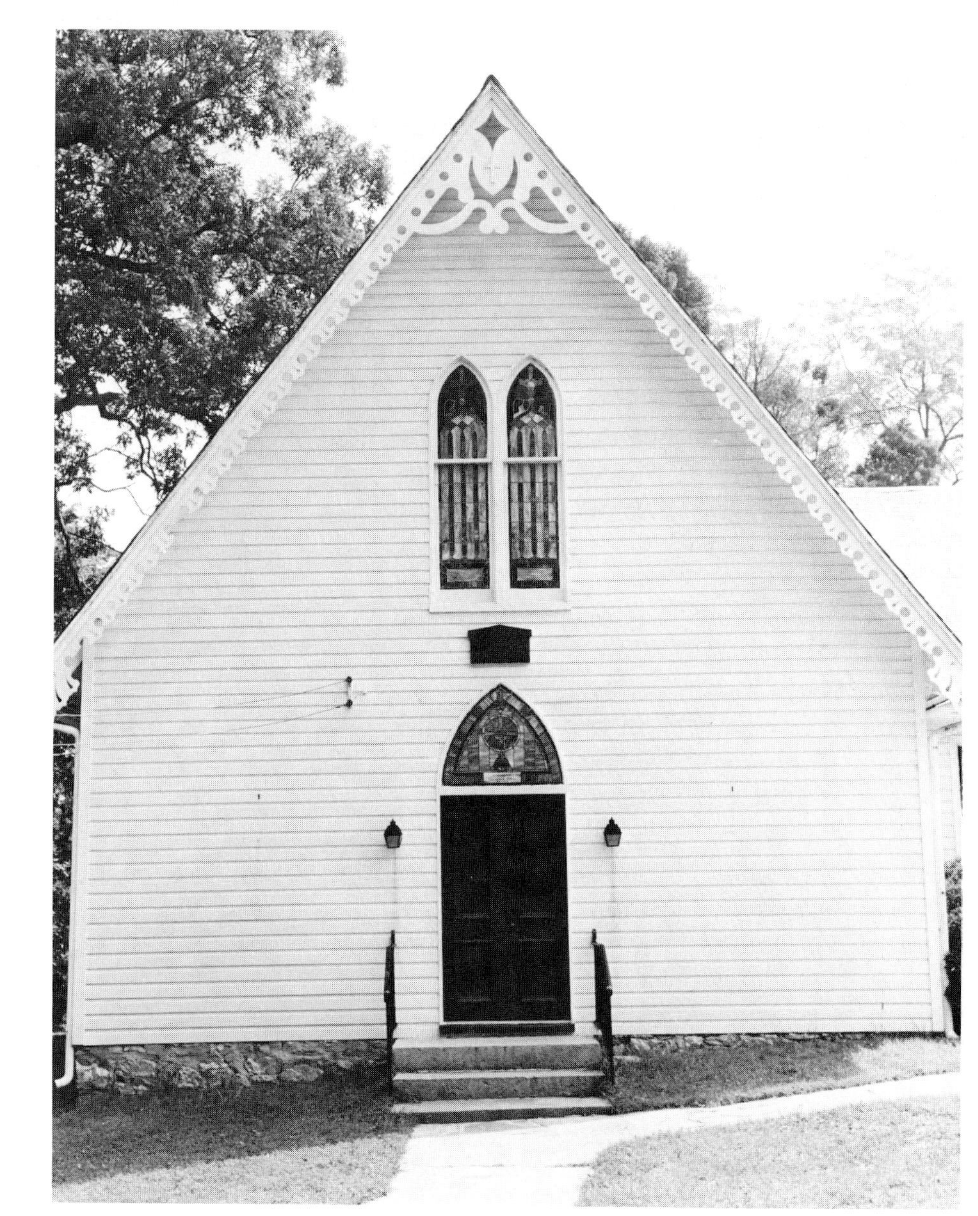

Mt. Paran Presbyterian Church, 10308 Liberty Road at Lyon's Mill Road, Harrisonville, began with a title to three-quarters of an acre in May 1784. The name is Biblical, the original Mt. Paran being located in the Sinai.

Mt. Paran was renovated and substantially Victorianized in 1883, but much of the simple construction of the eighteenth-century church, including random-width floorboards and the old pews, remain. The vestibule was added at that time. Further work was done in 1924.

331

329

The parish of St. John's, Kingsville, actually dates to a vanished church built at Elk Neck, Cecil County, in 1697. By 1724 the church had moved to Joppa, and by 1817 it was in a building on Belair Road, in Kingsville, which had been constructed by Edward Day, who also gave the land. It was enlarged in 1850, and the tower shown here was added in 1870. By 1896 a new stone church had been erected elsewhere on the property. The bell tower of the old church was unsound by 1905 and was removed; the McShane Foundry recast the cracked bell.

330

Sater's Baptist Church, Sater's Lane off Falls Road, Lutherville, has segments which date from 1742. It is regarded as the Mother Church of Maryland Baptists, and in the 1980s still has an active membership of approximately eighty. Sater's was named for Henry Sater, an English immigrant who deeded an acre to the Baptists for a house of worship.

The chapel was rescued from ruin in 1864; it was altered during the restorations. It was restored again in 1952 after a low-flying plane had buzzed the church during Sunday service, causing a beam to become dislodged. Fortuitously, the heavy timber was caught by a cross beam and did not land on the startled congregation.

The 1755 60-by-30-foot transept of St. James Episcopal Church, Monkton, was first called a "Chapel of Ease." It was made of brick cast in English molds and laid in Flemish bond. Additions were made in 1791 and 1871. In 1884 the tower was built with bricks from the adjacent St. James Academy, which was no longer used. As the photo shows, the tower burned after being hit by lightning on June 2, 1941. The McShane Foundry bell crashed and had to be recast, losing three hundred pounds and changing its pitch and resonance in the process.

John Emory (1789-1835), a Methodist bishop and an important figure in the early history of that church, was born in Queen Anne's County, Maryland. A graduate of Washington College at the age of nineteen, he was accepted into the bar and opened an office in Centerville. When Emory joined the ministry in 1810, he became estranged from his father, who had fantasized over a successful legal career for the young man.

Emory joined the Baltimore Conference in 1818 and became editor in 1830 of the Methodist Magazine and Quarterly Review. *He had a hand in the establishment of Wesleyan University. In 1832 he was ordained a bishop, successively headquartered in Baltimore, the Eastern Shore, and Reisterstown. While at Reisterstown he suffered a throw from his buggy on the turnpike and died from his injuries. He is buried in Mt. Olivet Cemetery in Baltimore.*

333

334

335

The first meeting at Emory Grove, Glyndon, was held at the old Waters Camp Ground in August 1868. Incorporated in 1871 and named for Bishop John Emory of the Methodist Church, Emory Grove was reincorporated in 1884 as the Emory Grove Association of Baltimore City.

At first the Methodists stayed in tents laid over wooden platforms, shown here in 1886. The association rented the tents each season in Baltimore, had them shipped to Glyndon and erected, and then dismantled them at the end of the summer.

By 1900 there were two hundred tents, a forty-bed hotel (built in 1887), and a main meeting tent set over rough pineboard seats. In 1900, to replace the tent, an old market building was bought in Hanover, Pennsylvania, and installed by Benjamin Franklin Bennett. This building was referred to as the Tabernacle and is still in place.

A shuttle bus took people from the Glyndon railroad station to the campsite, where cottages had been built.

336

Stephanie Raphel's house, Fontenai, *was designated a mission chapel in 1841 so that Catholics in the Upper Falls area could celebrate Mass. St. Stephen's Roman Catholic Church, 8030 Bradshaw Road, actually began as a parish in 1863 with the purchase of the Sons of Temperance Hall. The site of the present church and cemetery was donated by the Franklinville Cotton Factory owner, Hugh Simms, not himself a Catholic. The cornerstone was laid on May 25, 1889; Cardinal Gibbons came to the dedication a year later. In this picture the rectory is to the left of the church. The house of the teaching Sisters is behind the church, and the school is behind that.*

337

The earliest extant meeting house for the Society of Friends in the county was a stone building of 1773, still on Beaver Dam Road. A newer structure, built in 1821 on the present Quaker Bottom hillside, burned and was replaced in 1866. A defective chimney flue was the culprit, but the church furniture and a library of five hundred books were saved. After falling into near desuetude by 1940, and subjected to only occasional use, the New Gunpowder Meeting House has been brought back by renovations and restorations which started in the 1950s. The picture dates from 1903.

338

The Primitive Baptists built this simple stone building, the Black Rock Baptist Church in 1826-1827. The church was located on an acre of land donated by Richard Johns, a miller. Additional ground for burials was given by plow manufacturer Evan Davis. Both men were prominent in the neighborhood of the intersection of Butler and Falls roads. It is seen here about 1976.

339

Chestnut Grove Presbyterian Church, Sweetair Road, Phoenix, began in 1825 in the Long Green Academy. The present church was built between 1842 and 1843. The appalling condition of the county's roads is shown in this winter of 1921 photo. Even a Model T with its high road clearance would have had a hard time.

340

The first services for the Hiss Methodist Church congregation were held in the home of physician Dr. William Hiss. A stone "Hysse's Chapel," built in 1839, was replaced in 1895 by this building, pictured in a photo from about 1904. A growing congregation required yet another expansion to the present Parkville church in September 1954.

341

Salem United Methodist Church, Upper Falls, on the Franklinville Road south of Chapman Road, began with the gift of a lot by William McCubbin and the erection of this stone chapel in 1847. A 1926 renovation enlarged the church with a bell tower and vestibule. However, by 1954 the need for a larger building was apparent; the congregation moved to new quarters at 7901 Bradshaw Road in 1956. Photographer William C. Kenney's picture dates from the World War I era.

343

Designed by Robert Carey Long, Jr., in 1844, St. Timothy's Episcopal Church, Catonsville, has a restrained, well-balanced interior.

Another stone chapel is located on the south side of Old Court Road and the north side of Sudbrook Lane, two blocks east of Reisterstown Road. Originally called the Pikesville Church when it was built in 1834-1835, it was subsequently named for its first pastor, Joseph Mettam. Mettam Memorial Baptist Church is the oldest religious structure in Pikesville.

Born in England, Mettam came to Maryland by way of Virginia. A fall from a horse led to a convalescence in Pikesville. He became a member of the Religious Society of Regular, or Particular, Baptists who were given a plot of land for a church by a local doctor, James White. Other neighboring property owners gave stone from their quarries or timber from their parks. Mettam joined with five other congregations to found the Maryland Baptist Union Association, which in turn became the Baptist Mission Board of Maryland. Although the Mettam congregation was out of existence by 1830, the structure's connection to early Baptist history in Maryland is significant. The Lion's Club of Pikesville restored the building in 1966; its board meets where, as does the Stevens Garden Club, which maintains the grounds.

German-speaking Lutheran immigrants started building Old Salem Evangelical Lutheran Church on the west side of Ingleside Avenue, just south of today's Route 40, Catonsville, on September 12, 1849, and had finished it by January 23, 1850. The 1849 Seraphin organ is operable again and is played at annual services. A foundation now maintains the church and cemetery; the congregation moved to a new building in 1903. The picture dates from 1900.

St. John's African Union Methodist Protestant Church on Bellona Avenue in Ruxton started in 1833 as a log building constructed by the Reverend Aquilla Scott, a Falls Road blacksmith, and other free blacks. That building burned in 1886 and was replaced. St. John's was restored in the 1970s and placed on the National Register of Historic Places in 1980.

345

346

The main chapel at Woodstock College, shown in the late 1950s, is a dignified and impressive setting for a Mass.

St. Alphonsus Rodriguez parish church, attached to the Jesuit seminary at Woodstock, had a Sunday school called St. Peter Claver's for black children in the community. The picture shows black altar boys from St. Peter Claver's leading a procession in the 1920s.

347

348

The musical tradition of the minstrel show with all its connotations died hard. For at least twenty-five years, starting in 1903, St. Alphonsus Rodriquez Parish Church hosted such shows, and may have continued doing so into the 1930s and 1940s. Notwithstanding this ethnic stereotyping, however, both the Woodstock seminarians and faculty were providing spiritual services to the all-black tuberculosis hospital upstream at Henryton, Carroll County. There are pictures in the Woodstock College collection of the priests playing Santa Claus for sick black children in their wards, and leading the ambulatory convalescents to Sunday services.

349

The first building of St. Stephen's African Methodist Episcopal Church, 1600 Eastern Avenue, was built in 1870 of logs covered with siding. It is seen here, around the 1890s, with the congregation. It was replaced in 1907 and again in 1972.

The cornerstone for Mt. Gilboa African Methodist Episcopal Church on Westchester Avenue at Oella Avenue, Oella, was laid on May 27, 1860. The church was photographed after a post-Easter, April 1977 fire. The Reverend H. R. Curtis is in the foreground. Mt. Gilboa was built by free blacks.

352

Our Lady of Mt. Carmel Roman Catholic Church, 1704 Eastern Avenue, Essex, marked its first baptism in 1893 and its first wedding a year later. The original building, pictured, was replaced in the 1920s. German Catholics made up the original congregation.

353

Lansdowne Christian Church on Clyde Avenue is shown early in the twentieth century, with some of its now-lost gothic eccentricities still intact. The church was organized on March 1, 1903, after Charles Wesley Hull, a Union Army veteran, gave both the land and the construction money for a memorial church to the Grand Army of the Republic. By June 12, 1904, the building was finished. Starting in 1905 and continuing until the death of the last Union Army veteran of the Civil War in 1956, there was a memorial service for the GAR held here on the second Sunday in May. The stained glass windows show the GAR badge rather than religious scenes. The church basement is now a museum of Lansdowne history.

354

These brushed and scrubbed boys were in the Lansdowne Christian Church choir in 1940.

The church shown in this early 1900s picture of Relay still stands at 5025 Cedar Avenue, at the corner of Arlington. Although now known as the Catholic Center of Relay, this little gem began as Arlington Presbyterian Church. The Sun *in April 1880 reported that Thomas Dixon and Charles L. Carson were the architects.*

355

356

The children who formed the first confirmation class of St. Timothy's Evangelical Lutheran Church, 2120 Dundalk Avenue, looked a little tense in 1929. From left to right are William Beer, Oscar Suttka, Ruth McDonaugh, Margaret Norris, Delia Inauniemi, Pastor Walter Merz, Lorraine Diekman, Anio Raukko, Kenora Klemm, Lalia Inauniemi, John Marshall, and Blaine Deem.

358

B. E. von Paris at his first communion in 1919 looks like countless boys before and since at such a benchmark event.

357

The restrained interior of Sparrows Point Methodist Church, which stood from 1889 to 1972, is dominated by the organ.

359

The Towson Methodist Episcopal Congregation and that of the Methodist Protestant Church in Towson, divided since 1861 over the cost of installing an organ, merged to form the Towson United Methodist Church in 1958, and moved to this building on Hampton Lane. The 1871 Methodist Episcopal Church on York Road was sold to a funeral director; later it was razed for the Investment Building. The 1908 Methodist Protestant Church on Allegheny Avenue at Bosley was sold to the Women's Club of Towson. (Photo by Harold Spicer)

360

Baltimore Hebrew Congregation's Reform Temple is at Slade and Park Heights avenues. The state gave Baltimore Hebrew its charter in 1830, at which time a handful of Jews were worshipping in a rented room over a grocery store at the corner of Bond and Fleet streets. By 1845 they had moved to Robert Cary Long Jr.'s splendid Greek revival Lloyd Street Synagogue (third oldest in the United States). Following its move to Madison Avenue and Robert Street, during the latter part of the nineteenth century, the congregation adopted reform practices.

361

Starting out in Exeter Hall, Exeter Street, in 1871, and using such places as the Eutaw Place Temple, Chizuk Amuno's Conservative Congregation moved three times in Baltimore City before locating at 8100 Stevenson Road in 1953. Kann and Ammon, Inc., designed the structure.

362

Beth El Congregation began in 1947 with a small group of progressive thinkers within the conservative movement. The congregation first met in a community hall on Liberty Road, then built at Hilton Avenue and Dorithan Road. H. Bruce Finkelstein and Benjamin Brotman designed the present temple at 8101 Park Heights Avenue in 1960.

363

Beth Tfiloh's charter was granted in 1921. Practicing Orthodox Judaism, the congregation started out at 3200 Garrison Boulevard before moving out to 3300 Old Court Road in Baltimore County in 1960.

AGRICULTURE, BUSINESS, AND INDUSTRY

Before the Revolution and extending well beyond the federal period, industry in Baltimore County was generally confined to iron furnaces, forges, paper mills, some fulling mills, and gristmills. There was the Lancashire Furnace in the Stemmers Run area, later recycled as the Locust Grove Furnace. The Carrolls and Dulaneys owned the Baltimore Company; Charles Carroll the Barrister (so known to distinguish him from his cousin Charles Carroll the Signer) built his mansion *Mt. Clare* near the ironworks in order to better supervise it. The company owned a lot of land; generally it was in the vicinity of Montgomery Ward's Monroe Street store in west Baltimore. The Ridgelys started to work their Northhampton furnace holdings (with the help of slaves) in 1760, and continued to operate them until 1829.

There were gristmills everywhere. Any location where there was, or could be induced to be, a fall of water, sooner or later attracted a miller. The roads to these long-vanished or recycled mills still carry the names: Trenton Mill, Painter's Mill, Hunter's Mill, Dance Mill, Hartley's Mill, Cockey's Mill, Merryman's Mill, Keeney Mill, Gore's Mill, and Lyon's Mill. Much of their output was for local area consumption. When the Ellicotts arrived at the Patapsco, utilizing the brilliant advances of the inventor Oliver Evans, consolidation began and big business was under way. By mid-century, Charles Gambrill, successor to the Ellicotts, was virtually the czar of Maryland flour milling. The successor to his firm, the Wilkins-Rogers Company, is actually still in business at the same site.

The advent of railroads in 1828 meant that goods could now be moved independently of the generally wretched roads and the expensive string of toll gates. By the time the Civil War was at hand, the Industrial Revolution was in full swing in selected areas of Baltimore County. There were cotton factories in Oella, Alberton, Grays, and Granite on the Patapsco; Franklinville, Phoenix, and Warren on the Gunpowder; Woodberry and Hampden on the Jones Falls (still part of the county until 1888).

About World War I, C. W. E. Treadwell took this photograph at the farm of his uncle, William S. Treadwell, who rented the property from the Ridgelys of Hampton.

There were other cotton factories on the Gwynn's Falls at Powhatan (Woodlawn) and Wetheredville (the old name for Dickeyville, then, too, still in the county). There were iron furnaces at Oregon, now the site of the Baltimore Symphony Orchestra's summer concerts, and at Ashland, which is now an upscale, revivified collection of attached and detached mill workers' housing which sell for big prices.

There were massive copper rolling mills and bridge-building works in Canton (also still part of the county until 1918). It was hardly surprising that when the county police force was unified under the command of one person in 1882, headquarters would be at the center of the action—not Towson, the county seat—but Canton, where all the laborers, bars, brawls, and general disturbances were. There were fertilizer works at Canton, perfuming the inner harbor air and depositing a film over everything around. Later, Henry Reckord opened a similar plant at Reckord in the upper part of the county.

There were paper mills all over the upper part of the county (Hoffmanville, Beckleysville, Rockdale, and Marble Vale, on Paper Mill Road), adding their contribution to bad air and polluted streams. Philip H. Glatfelter, founder of the Pennsylvania paper company which is still in existence, started out in Baltimore County. He lost a significant case before the Court of Appeals in Annapolis, described by John McGrain in *From Pig Iron to Cotton Duck* (page 291):

> Joseph Walker, a downstream farmer and gristmiller, sued the papermaker for blackening the waters of Little Gunpowder Falls with sulfuric acid, soda ash, lime, and bleaching powder: the residue of paper manufacturing from straw. Walker charged that his livestock had been killed by drinking the contaminated water. His attorney argued that a person's shoes would be dissolved by wading into the stream, and that an attempt to wash clothing in the effluent would bring blood to the fingers in minutes.

Although Walker won his case, the court awarded him only one cent in damages.

Most of these busy hamlets developed into true company towns, as did Sparrows Point when it was started by the Pennsylvania Steel Company in 1889.

All the while there were local blacksmiths and carriage makers (both doubling as undertakers), country storekeepers, stone masons, well diggers, doctors (but not many), saloon keepers, livery stable operators, hotel owners, and many other business people in every post office village in the county. Turnpikes and railroads were kept busy with both the agrarian and the industrial output.

By the end of the century, however, the bloom was off the rose for Baltimore County. Perhaps it was the post-Civil War depression of the 1870s, or maybe it was the depression in 1893 which was the watershed. No matter, for by the end of the century, city annexation had absorbed the Hampden-Woodberry industrial complex, part of Canton, and Dickeyville, in fact, much of the county's population and tax base. The victory was Pyrrhic, as the Mid-Atlantic region lost out to the cheaper production capabilities of the South, just as it had beaten New England at its own game earlier. There are now no textile mills in the metropolitan Baltimore region; the last cotton mill in Baltimore County shut down in 1928; Alberton, mostly in Howard County, moved to higher ground and deeper into Howard County after tropical storm Agnes in 1972; and the last woolen mill in the county closed in the spring of 1972. There are no copper rolling mills, no fertilizer plants. Big Steel hangs on, somewhat tenuously, playing on what it perceives to be an uneven field in world trade. There are no paper mills.

There are, though, exciting new businesses, many in high technology, many providing services, others closely identified with the Defense Department. There are internationally famous spice and cosmetic companies. Computer and electronics research and development companies abound.

The developer has been part of this changeover, recycling disused industrial villages, buying up farmer's acreage for housing at a variety of income levels for the workers in the new industries. Special industrial parks have been created for these new enterprises: Hunt Valley, Owings Mills, Rutherford, Loveton, Chesapeake, and White Marsh.

Although the employer now provides for pensions, paid vacations, company-paid health plans, sick time, maternity leave, substance abuse counseling, use of a company car and other perquisites, no company owns (or wants to own) a town, with all the paternalistic responsibilities and headaches that implies.

As small towns and hamlets were swallowed by megalopolis, and the Beltway since 1962 has made one part of the county accessible to every other part, small scale enterprises have faded and large operations have taken their place. There are a number of reasons for this: children often did not want to carry on the family business; or, inadequate provision was made to provide for a viable managerial succession; or, firms were undercapitalized; or, firms took their profits (such as they were) and ran, did not reinvest in modern technology, and became noncompetitive. Thus a Giant or a Super Fresh replaces scores of family businesses; a Hutzlers or a Hechts, a Hechingers or a Stebbins makes obsolete a whole group of trades plied by individuals only half a century ago.

The pictures in this book reflect the changing patterns of employment.

365

Baltimore iron-founder Peter Mowell built his remarkable farm complex at Glencoe between 1851 and 1856. A curious horse ponders the carriage house and stables in 1976.

367

Ida Clayton Schreefer feeds a turkey on the East family farm near Parkton in the 1920s.

366

A cattle sale is announced for Monday, April 7, 1842.

Making apple butter was the order of this November day in 1938. Mrs. Hess, Mrs. Sewell, Mrs. Isennock, and Rebecca Sewell Hess are simmering apple pulp on the J. A. Isennock farm in the Long Green Valley.

368

369

Two boys bring home a wagonload of wood, about 1903.

370

371

A field of grain, cut and tied in sheaves, was photographed near Hereford in the 1920s. Another 1920s photo shows grain sheaves covered with grain sacks or tarpaulins, to keep out moisture and prevent rot from setting in before the thresher arrived. Often the sheaves of oats, rye, wheat, or barley were stacked and simply covered with the other sheaves laid across the top of the pile. The location of the second field is unknown. Both pictures were taken by William C. Kenney. The Burnside farm covered its heaps of alfalfa with canvas about 1911.

372

Photographer Emma K. Wood found this field of corn shocks in the Lutherville area about the time of World War I.

Haying was a predictable seasonal farm activity for at least 150 years. Here a wagon moves down Front Street in Lutherville, about 1911.

373

374

Francis B. Mayer (1827-1899) sketched this Pikesville-area farmer sharpening his scythe with a whetstone, dated 1845. Mayer, later a well-known nineteenth century genre and portrait painter, came from a distinguished Baltimore family. His uncle was Brantz Mayer, a founder of the Maryland Historical Society. Francis was the son of Charles Frederick Mayer, a Baltimore lawyer, and Eliza Caldwell Blackwell. A bequest in Dr. James Smith's will in 1841 left the Mayer family some property in Pikesville. It was on visits to this property that the talented teenager found many interesting subjects to sketch, including two other pictures in this book, Pictures 409 and 415.

375

The barn at Meadowdale Farm, *still standing on the south side of Belfast Road and west of Tanyard Road, Butler, was built in 1893 by Lewis M. Bacon, third owner of the farm. The large three-section house was probably started between 1825 and 1841 by Abraham Cole, Jr., who left it to his son, Lewis R. Cole, who in turn sold to Bacon in 1877. This photo of the barn was taken in 1976.*

376

377

A steam tractor was often used to provide power for threshing. This one was contracted out to others by Thomas Jessop and is threshing on the Dance Farm, Blenheim (near Sweetair), in the early twentieth century. Threshing could be a social event. The "My Lady's Manor Items" of the Union News, September 5, 1914, had this.

> *The familiar toot and chug of the traction engine is heard on our roads now and the farmers wives are planning the menu for the threshing season which is on them. Formerly when threshers came to a farm house a dinner of ham and cabbage with potatoes and apple pies was served, but today the threshers revive memories of the old story of the preachers who, when they visited their flock in their homes, were surfeited with chicken. The men who follow threshing as a vocation get so much cabbage that they do not enjoy or eat cabbage any longer, and the farmer's wives have to plan some other kind of dinner and in a large quantity.*

Professional threshermen owned self-moving steam tractors or horse-drawn steam engines that continued in service until the 1930s and sometimes later, and wealthy farmers also had steam engines, usually of the stationary or donkey engine type. Gas engines were first used in the 1890s, to power water pumps, before showing up in this century in tractors used for threshing or the spraying of fruit trees. In 1975 photographer John McGrain found this 1923 tractor at a farm steam days show in Arcadia, in northwest Baltimore County.

The Meadows, *a stone house in the Red Run area, Owings Mills, was built by Thomas Owings between 1722 and 1798. It stood on a tract given to him by his father, the miller Samuel Owings I. The log barn or stable, seen here about 1977, dates from the earliest years of the house.*

378

379

Photographed in 1917 at Trump Mill Farm, *Stemmers Run, Eastern Baltimore County, are, in the hayloft Willy Jones and B. E. von Paris; standing, from left to right, are Margaret von Paris, Bonaventure von Paris, and Marie von Paris.*

380

The cattle herd at Burnside, *the Samuel M. Shoemaker estate in the Greenspring Valley had been started in the late 1860s. By the turn of the century the Guernsey herd was well known. In 1932 Samuel Shoemaker II, active in agriculture, public education and the good roads movement, started a dairy on the estate which lasted until World War II. The dairy transported milk to an outlet called the Walker-Gordon Laboratory, where it could be bought by customers. The inventive Shoemaker devised many ingenious labor-saving devices around his farm, such as an astonishing automatic cable system for moving loaded containers of milk around safely and slowly. Shown in the photo is a bottling machine and some old glass milk bottles.*

381

The Henry J. Reich farm in Catonsville, 1895. The horse-drawn equipment in the foreground looks like a sickle-bar mower (left) and a cornplanter (right). Wheaton Place Apartments on Old Ingleside Avenue are now on the farm site.

Few photos of black families in the 1800s were taken, and even fewer have survived. This one, from about 1893, shows a young family standing in front of their home, a tenant farmhouse on the Ball property in Catonsville. The windows lack glass, a door is not visible, and the roof looks worn—but the little house appears to have a wooden floor, which most such tenant houses lacked. The littlest member of the family, who did not quite manage to stand still for the photo, has a possessive grip on a wagon, in which we can guess both children enjoyed many rides. The members of the family have not been identified.

382

383

A typical nineteenth-century farm scene. This is at Wester Ogle, *Owings Mills.*

384

Wilton Farm Dairy, Catonsville, opened in 1888 and closed a little short of its hundredth year. Shown are a delivery wagon and the approved method of snow removal.

In this picture the horses John and Pete (raised by Louis F. Zaiser at the Wilton Farm) are joined by Wilbur Unglesbar and Benny Scheufele on January 31, 1928.

385

386

A. H. Brinkmann of Catonsville photographed this farm family on the Powhatan Road, Woodlawn, in the mid-1880s. The children are enjoying the shade of tall trees on what looks like a hot and sunny day. The modest but pleasant home behind them is solidly set on a stone foundation and is equipped with roof gutters supplying a rain barrel at the right corner of the house. The yard is busy with paraphernalia of mostly unknown purpose, although a grindstone and wooden bucket can be identified at right.

387

Typical of early ice houses in Baltimore County was this one at Drumquhazel, *photographed early in the century. The mansion, dating from about 1856, and estate on the east side of York Road, south of Anneslie, had been acquired by Elisha H. Walker in 1901. Farm owners cut blocks of ice from their ponds and stored them for year-long use in these structures. A Caldor store, other shops, and the Drumcastle Apartments now occupy the site of this working farm, which was broken up about 1946.*

388

Life for many in the good old days was lived in crude structures like this log cabin or barn photographed on the Ball estate, Windsor, *on the Old Frederick Road in Catonsville in 1893. The primitive log and wattle construction, over a dirt floor, kept out neither cold, nor insects, nor snakes.*

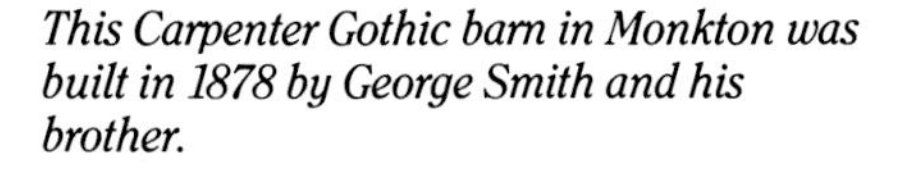

This Carpenter Gothic barn in Monkton was built in 1878 by George Smith and his brother.

389

An interesting feature in this picture of a young groom, named Walters, and his horse is the tripod behind them, which was used for hanging slaughtered hogs and draining them. Joshua Fitze took this Reisterstown scene on April 23, 1905.

390

391

392

Dr. A. C. McCurdy, an 1878 University of Maryland Dental School graduate, in addition to being a well-known Towson dentist and prize tomato raiser, was also a game warden and the long-time president of the State Fair. It is believed that he is in the middle of picture 391, holding the prize ribbons as others judge cattle at the Timonium State Fair, about 1909. McCurdy's Towson house and garden and the street named for him disappeared when the Investment Building was erected. The other picture shows the dentist tending his tomatoes.

393

A routine hoof cleaning seems to be in progress at the Mount de Sales Academy barn.

394

It seems to be nearly unbelievable that this was Dulaney Valley Road near Towson in the World War I era.

395

Alvah Merritt and his nephews, Enoch and Alonzo Merritt, are standing on their pig farm in the Merritt Point area in 1898. This was later the site of the Merritt Point Elementary School, which is now closed.

Someone, somewhere in the Patapsco Neck-Sparrows Point area, raised an incredible stand of corn around the beginning of the century, and a photographer asked some men to pose as a human scale to show off the height of the stalks. The result for modern viewers is a rare study, not of tall corn, but of three black men at the turn of the century. Their names, homes, and occupations are unknown, but most likely they were local farm people. The man at left looks weary, whether from hard work or worry or both we can only guess. The man in the center looks somewhat retiring, or perhaps only felt shy about being photographed. The pride and upright dignity of the third man suggests that the astounding crop behind him might in fact be his own—or perhaps he was a man who brought dignity to everything he did, even so simple a deed as helping a photographer create an interesting picture.

397

Sagamore Farms, *Glyndon, is part of a larger tract which was variously called* Welshe's Cradle *and* Bloomsbury, *a Worthington family holding. The farm was acquired in December 1885 by Charles A. Councilman, the "alfalfa king," who called it* Bloomfield. *Alfred Gwynne Vanderbilt bought it in the 1930s and turned it into a horse-breeding showplace. Shown is the indoor exercise ring. Vanderbilt sold the stabling facilities and acreage to James Ward in the 1980s.*

Now gone, this interesting stone silo once existed on the Bloomfield *estate in Glyndon. The picture dates form the early 1900s.*

Emma K. Woods of Lutherville, about 1912, found plowing being done the way it had been for centuries.

399

400

A reaper is shown on the Mt. Pleasant *farm of Zephaniah Poteet, off the Sherwood Road, between Cockeysville and Warren in 1901*

401

402

These structures—a two-seater stone privy and two corn cribs—stood at Vauxhall, *a Jessop family estate on the Gunpowder River north of the Warren factory and south of Paper Mill Road. In 1921, when the property was condemned and bought by the city for the Loch Raven expansion project, the estate was owned by Lewis R. Keizer, a Lutherville businessman. The property was not destroyed and by the mid-twenties became part of a pre-sale photographic survey of surviving watershed buildings. At an auction then-mayor William F. Broening bought the estate for a low price for himself, creating such a furor that he was compelled to sell it back to the city. When the city did nothing with it, it fell into neglect and was ultimately destroyed.*

Other vanished buildings from this working farm included corn cribs, a butcher shop, a wagon shed, a smokehouse, a hay barrack, a dairy house, chicken houses, a stable, a springhouse, an ice house, and a pump house. There were also barns for cattle.

403

A. Aubrey Bodine photographed these agricultural implements on the wall of Elmer Schmidt's blacksmith's shop, at the intersection of Long Green Road and Manor Road in June 1958.

John H. Hale, principal of the Eklo School in Middletown, ran the Rural Life Education Club between 1914 and 1918 to help residents improve their agricultural output. Pictures from club events include a tractor demonstration, a lecture, and a demonstration on canning; and a group of farmers decked out in their Sunday best in an orchard.

404

405

406

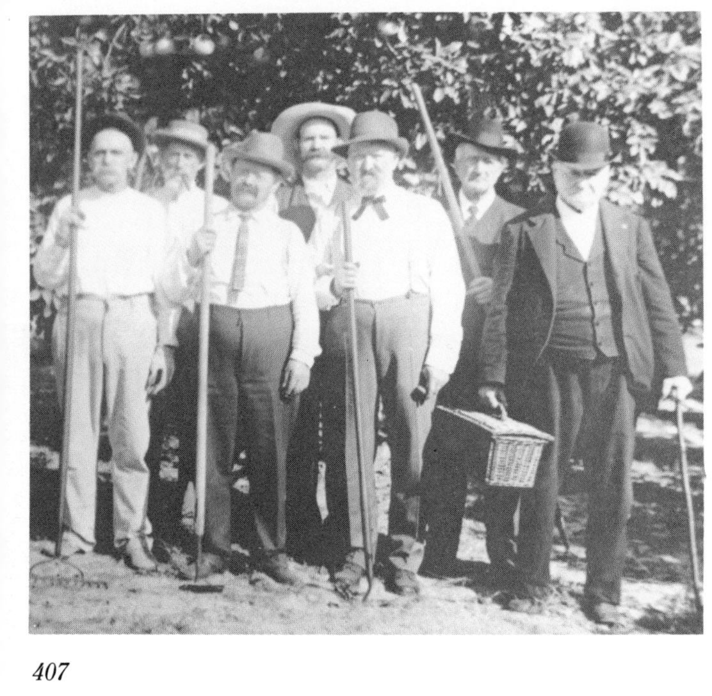

407

408

The Maryland State Grange was founded in 1874, seven years after the National Grange of the Patrons of Husbandry, America's first national organization of farmers. The Grange movement was an outgrowth of a sense of helplessness felt by farmers as a result of the disruption of the Civil War and its financially unstable aftermath. The advent of mechanization impressed on them, also, the need to seek help in adjusting to growing cash crops instead of merely being self-sufficient.

Centennial Grange No. 161 was organized on March 13, 1876, under the direction of C. Lyon Rogers of Owings Mills. Rogers started six Granges in the county in the 1870s, and evidently developed a useful working relationship on the side with the courthouse regulars; by 1907 his son, C. Lyon Rogers, Jr., was county treasurer and tax collector. Centennial No. 161 built this meeting hall on Allegheny Avenue, Towson, at the southeast corner of the alley running from Joppa Road to Allegheny Avenue, now part of the site of the five-story Bosley Building. The building was open by June 1890, received its deed a year later, and was dedicated in 1892. By 1903 Centennial No. 161 had folded.

The property was sold to Edward B. Passano, manager of the Williams and Wilkins Publishing Company. Passano took down the old Grange to make room for a garage in February 1912.

409

Flour milling on the Gwynn's Falls, south of present-day Milford Mill Road, started in 1728. Milford Mill ground away under a large number of owners, the last one of whom made cider there, from 1928 to 1937. After the county took the mill for taxes in 1937, it fell into decay and had disappeared by 1950.

Lyon's gristmill, Owings Mills, began in 1761. It closed when its water was cut off by the Western Maryland Railway in 1873. Teenage artist Francis B. Mayer did one of his meticulous drawings of it in 1845. Shown here is the hopper, suspended above the millstones, and an arrangement of wooden gears.

410

Rockland Mill, shown here in 1905, has had a remarkable parade of owners and adaptive reuses. The original mill building, still at the southeast corner of Falls and Old Court roads, was probably designed by John Davis in 1813 as the hub of a mill village for William Fell Johnson. Johnson's family owned parts of the village off and on for the next 160 years. The mill first manufactured calico and then switched to flour production from 1864 to 1922. In the 1950s, movie actress Dorothy Lamour ran a cosmetics factory there. In 1979 the mill was converted by Martin P. Azola into offices, and two years later the village houses were renovated and sold. Pro-Confederate, pre-Civil-War-era sheriff Richard Hook owned the mill at one point. It was seriously flooded during both tropical storm Agnes, June 1972, and hurricane David, September 1979.

411

Samuel Owings's Upper Mill, the last and largest of his three mills, dates from the last quarter of the eighteenth century. Subsequently called Eureka Mill, it has been known since 1848 as Groff's Mill, named for the Lancaster County, Pennsylvania family which bought it. Since a realignment of the railroad cut off the water supply in 1907, it has been used for a fuel and feed business. The photograph was taken in 1975.

412

413

Dance's gristmill and sawmill on Dance Mill Road, west of Dulaney Valley Road, really dates from about 1842, when Joseph G. Dance acquired and rebuilt the earlier Edwards Mill. The 1850 census reported that he was grinding 550 barrels of flour annually. By the 1880 census, Alexander Dance held title and had added two circular saws to cut lumber. The mill was sold to J. W. Isennock in 1919 by E. Scott Dance, a Confederate veteran by then seventy-six years old. The mill closed in 1922 and was mostly razed by 1931. What has survived is a stable today. The photograph dates from about the turn of the century.

414

The basics of cider pressing have not changed much in 140 years. Francis B. Mayer sketched this hand-operated press near Pikesville in the 1840s. Interested people still watch cider being squeezed from apples at Weber's Cider Mill Farm, Proctor Lane, north of Carney, or Maple Hill Farm in Glen Arm.

Orange Grove Mill had been going for four years when Charles A. Gambrill, flour king of the Patapsco, bought it in 1860. Low-lying River Road in the background of this October 1899 photo actually ran through the middle of the building. Seen are, from left to right, Richard Benton, Mabel Elwood Phillips, Corliss Clayton, and Thomas L. Phillips. Clayton, son of the day engineer, was named after the well-known Corliss steam engine; the Phillips children belonged to the plant superintendent. The end came when the mill burned on May 1, 1905.

415

The 1809 cotton mill at Oella, incorporated as the Union Manufacturing Company, was designed by renowned French architect Maximilian Godefroy, designer of the First Unitarian Church on Franklin Street. It was the largest cotton mill in the country when it was built. The mill burned in 1815 and was replaced.

Although the company suffered relatively minor damage during the 1868 flood, the owners were hard-pressed financially by the aftermath of the Civil War, and were out of money when they auctioned the village in February 1887. The purchaser, William J. Dickey, who also had mills in what is now Dickeyville, switched from cotton to wool. The firm stayed with wool until it closed in the spring of 1972, the fashion for double knits and informal clothing having killed the market for worsteds and woolens.

In the 1980s sewer and water lines were introduced into the nineteenth-century mill-town for the first time. The mill buildings in this picture replaced nineteenth-century buildings in 1918—after an exploding light bulb in the volatile atmosphere of a textile factory necessitated a total reconstruction. The buildings are now used for such purposes as storage and boutiques. The workers' old homes have been attractively rehabilitated for modern living. A worker checks out the threads on the loom in a 1960s photo.

417

The ad read "Walter Johnson—the Big Train—wears a Dickey Tweed." Walter Perry Johnson (1887-1946), was a pitcher with the Washington Senators from 1907 to 1927. He was one of the first five players elected to the Hall of Fame in 1935, based on the 414 wins of his career. Johnson served as president of the Association of Professional Baseball players. He made an unsuccessful run for Congress in 1940, after which he did some radio broadcasting.

418

The Warren school's last class graduated in June 1922. By November 1922, much of the century-old cotton milling town had been demolished. In this picture, at the left, is the shell of the old stone band practice building; earlier it had been a damp, dangerous, despised school building. Next is the "Double House," before 1864 a tavern. Next to that, with its bell tower, is the public school, with an addition built at the expense of the mill owner. On the other side of the Gunpowder River is the shell of the old stone gristmill, and, on the other side of the mill race, a group of workers' stone houses. The road is being regraded to follow the route of present-day Warren Road. Paper Mill Road bridge is in the upper center of the picture. Although the town was destroyed and its ruins flooded, the flag pole was not removed. It remained visible above the waters of Loch Raven until it rotted in the mid-1940s.

419

Powhatan Cotton Mill, known originally as the "Baltimore Manufacturing Company-Gwinn's Falls," is pictured in the foreground in the early 1880s. Built in 1810, the mill was designed by Robert Mills, the architect of Baltimore's Washington Monument. By 1820 there were seven men, fifteen women, and fifty-nine boys and girls spinning and another twenty-three girls on the power looms. There were no child labor laws in Maryland until 1873, and widespread use was still made of children in the mills in the early twentieth century.

Never a great money maker, Powhatan went through a variety of ownerships, including William Lorman, Ross Campbell, George Slothower and numerous Leverings. The panics and crashes of the nineteenth century, and the uncertainty of power when the river was low, affected profitability. A number of fires culminated in an all-consuming terminal one, on December 7, 1895. In 1902 the Woodlawn Cemetery Company bought the property for another use. A Methodist church was moved across the frozen Gwynns Falls on whiskey kegs; remaining residents were forced to move, and the old tract became the present-day cemetery.

421

Alberton, a cotton mill town on the Patapsco, was mostly in Howard County, although some of the workers' houses and St. Stanislaus Roman Catholic Church were on the Baltimore County side. This post-1871 view shows Upper Brick Row, at the extreme left; Guilford (two houses behind the owner's mansion, which has a tower and is to the left of the mill); three houses on "the green"; the company store; a Bollman truss bridge and Lower Brick Row, extreme right. Alberton was started in 1845 by the Elys, a family with a flair for bankruptcy and lawsuits. By 1859 James S. Gary owned the mill village. Although damaged by the disastrous 1868 flood, the old town survived to prosper in the nineteenth century but barely made it in the twentieth. On November 23, 1940, the village was auctioned to the C. R. Daniels Company of New Jersey for sixty-four thousand dollars. Daniels specialized in cotton duck manufacturing, and this is what the Romanesque churchlike mill was manufacturing when tropical storm Agnes in 1972 ended production. The C. R. Daniels Company now operates from higher ground in Howard County.

James Albert Gary (1838-1920), the mustached man seated in the center, is shown with his family at his estate, the Summit, *in Catonsville. Gary was the son of James S. Gary, who had bought the cotton mill at Alberton. In the manner of the time, the father started the boy in the business as a child in the picker room which often left him too tired to eat at the end of a mill boy's day. He worked in every department of the mill, which he ran after his father's death in 1870.*

Gary was a Republican in a Democratic state. He was unsuccessful in a bid for the governorship, but as dean of the party in the state, he controlled federal patronage in Maryland for most of the last quarter of the nineteenth century. He served briefly as McKinley's Postmaster General, but resigned over the Spanish-American War. He was president of the Merchants and Manufacturers Association and the Citizens National Bank, and vice-president of the Consolidated Gas Company. Gary received praise for the way he ran his town and for his support of schools, cultural opportunities, and churches. He was, however, a strong opponent of child labor laws.

423

Rodgers Forge stood at the corner of the east side of York Road and Stevenson Lane for 102 years until it was razed for a service station in 1947. Built by George Rodgers and held in the family until 1931, the landmark served also as the tiny post office for the rural community around the neighboring estates of Stoneleigh, Anneslie, *and* Dumbarton.

424

The Baltimore Sun's *photographer flew over the cotton manufacturing villages of Warren and Phoenix in December 1921, before both were eliminated or much altered by the Loch Raven dam expansion. The Phoenix mill, which was built of Texas marble, and its power plant straddling the millrace, are in the foreground. In the center is the superintendent's house. On the other side of the road, between two boarding houses, was Frazier Episcopal Church. Sparks from its wood stove burned it down during the service one Sunday in 1928. At the left of the mill is Frames Methodist Episcopal Church, which was moved to Mount Avenue, Phoenix, and still exists.*

Milling activity in Phoenix seems to date from 1839 but ended after the mill was purchased at an auction in 1916 by Summerfield Baldwin (owner of Warren) and his son, who used the property as a chip in their bargaining with Baltimore City over the condemnation price for Warren.

425

The town of Reckord, on Harford Road at the Little Gunpowder Falls, started in 1848 as a sawmill and gristmill site. Bought by Henry Reckord in 1860, the mill processed sorghum during the Civil War. In 1867 Reckord switched to fertilizer, using bone dust and rendered animal carcasses. At its peak the factory employed over forty and had a branch in Bel Air, five miles away. The firm became noncompetitive, and by 1902 was in receivership. This view was taken in the 1880s or 1890s.

426

427

Aubrey Bodine's photos of June 1958 found Elmer Schmidt still working in Slade's 1854 shop at the intersection of Long Green and Manor roads, the same blacksmith's shop his father had bought in 1891. The shop closed a few years after this, when the State Roads Commission widened the road.

428

A photo from early in the century shows the Whitney-Gardner butcher shop in the 700 block of Frederick Road, Catonsville, with the staff at their posts. From left to right are Toddie Whitney, Louis Poehlmann, and Mr. Gardner.

The John S. Wilson Lumber Company, Catonsville, was founded in 1881, at which time it was called Wilson and Poehlman. It is still there, located at 741 Frederick Road, having survived a major fire in August 1974.

429

William Foley opened a general store in Pikesville before 1890. He ran a sideline in feed, coal, wood, cement, and bricks. Inside the store in the early 1900s is Timothy Foley, son of the founder, and a young assistant, John McGurie. Note the pressed tin ceiling.

430

431

Henry Guttenberger opened his store at the corner of Eastern and Mace avenues, Essex, in 1910. Shown in its pre-World War II days, it is still in operation in 1988.

432

Albert M. Weis's store stood on the east side of York Road, Towson, between the present-day Hutzler's intersection and Investment Plaza. Left to right in 1914 were Albert M. Weis, Henry Weis, and Madeline G. Weis. Weis sold his store (built in 1886) to Goucher College in 1921, although he ran it for two more years. Elmer Corbin then operated it from 1923 until the 1950s, when the college demolished the building. Weis's delivery wagon, in the early 1900s, has the wall of the old Towson Methodist Episcopal Church in the background. Nelson Hutchins, left, son of a saloon keeper, and Henry Weis stand by the wagon. The boy in the back is not identified.

433

William Butt, was a produce man affectionately known as "Mr. Buddy" for fifty years to people on his home delivery route in Hampton, Dulaney Valley, Perry Hall, and Loch Raven Village. He is shown inside his wagon in March 1988, as he prepared to retire. With him is his thirteen-year-old helper, Sean Flaherty, of Loch Raven Village. Butt had started out selling only produce from his family's truck farm. When that was sold, he marketed others' fresh food.

434

The oldest part of Frederick W. Josenhans's store dated from the 1880s and was put together with wooden pegs. In 1907 Josenhans opened his store, which stood on the corner of old Eastern Avenue and Back River Neck Road—a place still known as Josenhans Corner. It was a meeting place for weekend excursionists arriving on the streetcars heading for the beaches. This view was taken in 1913. It was demolished in the 1960s.

435

The store and post office at Bentley Springs is pictured in the early 1900s. William Bentley had turned this remote spot on the Northern Central Railroad into a summer spa in the 1880s.

436

437

Cashiers at the Ben Franklin store in the 500 block of Eastern Avenue waited for customers in early 1957. In August that year fire destroyed the entire block.

Main Street, Reisterstown, is seen about 1950. The recycled Russell's store had then become the Crown Department Store. By 1988 it had gone.

438

After Eudowood Sanitarium closed, its livestock was sold and the farm itself became Eudowood Shopping Center (later renamed Towson Market Place). The crowds gathered in front of Montgomery Ward on opening day, September 22, 1957.

German-born Louis W. Held came to Towson from Washington, D. C., shortly after the Civil War to start a bakery. The present building at 537 York Road replaced one lost in the fire of 1877. The bakery closed in the early 1930s; Souris's Saloon has occupied the building since 1934. Shown from left to right are an unknown patron, Miss Stewart Cole, John Seng Held, Preston Tracey, another unknown customer (seated), and Charles Tracey.

440

441

Dr. Louis Hergenrather opened his York Road, Towson pharmacy in 1904. Dr. Hergenrather, who lived at 401 York Road, built the modern pharmacy-soda fountain extension in 1916, utilizing 403 York Road as well. Shown here in the 1920s are Jessie Cross, clerk; Dr. Hergenrather; and Robert Feast, behind the register. The name of the counter clerk is unknown. Kauffman's took over the pharmacy in 1945 and operated it until the 1980s, when it moved to Kenilworth Park. The building is scheduled for demolition.

442

In 1922 Benjamin and Edna Gorfine opened this hardware store at 414 York Road, Towson. The photograph of them in the store was taken in 1922. They built a store with second-floor living quarters at 416 York Road in 1929 on the site of saddle-maker Henry Dienstbach's garden. When the Gorfines retired in 1968, the store was rented to the Speigel Catalog Company. In 1973 Richard Rudolph opened his Towson Bootery there.

443

The John Beckley House at 202 Main Street near Cockeys Mill Road, Reisterstown, dates from 1779, and was built by John Reister (1715-1804) as part of the holdings of Reister's Desire. *The two-story brick dwelling, plus a brick kitchen, a blacksmith's shop and a milk house were sold in 1786 to Beckley, a blacksmith, who had married a Reister. One of Beckley's sons served as a sergeant in the Baltimore County Regiment of Militia in the War of 1812.*

By 1905 the property was up for auction; Fannie S. Naylor acquired it, and her husband advertised an "ice cream parlor opposite the Central Hotel" in 1906. It remained as such in the family until 1974. Terry Brown opened a ski shop there in 1976.

Mary Shealey moved into her "large and beautiful brick dwelling" in October 1867. It was torn down in 1950 to make way for Hutzler's. Charles Bosley (1822-1894), owned it from 1887 to 1894, when it was known as Bosley's Hotel. Bosley is the figure in the black hat on the left. Note the old-style gas lamp at the extreme left of the picture. Goucher College girls, coming back on the streetcar from a trip to town, waited here for transportation to the new campus (after 1941).

444

The Blakeslee-Lane Studios took this aerial view of the Westview Shopping Center and Route 40 west on January 5, 1959.

445

446

Also by Blakeslee-Lane Studios was this view of the innovative Hutzler's Brothers Store in Towson on January 13, 1953. Designed by James R. Edmunds and opened on November 24, 1952, the store became the flagship of the Hutzler's chain of stores, proving to be the most profitable and the most durable. Its position almost athwart York Road was a disaster and created a nearly insoluble puzzle for state and local traffic engineers.

This store represented one of the first entries by a major Baltimore City retailer into the suburbs. It was an ominous event, as, following the exodus of the middle class, almost every major retailer relocated in the county, often in several locations.

J. Maurice Watkins, Sr., at various times a Baltimore County bailiff, tax collector, and officer of the Orphan's Court, also ran a saloon and oyster house. The public house was at the left and his family's quarters were on the right side of the building. In November 1886 Watkins's parlor was used by the Towson National Bank (Baltimore County's first bank) while its own building (which formerly stood next to the present Towson theater) was being constructed. The Watkins building is now the Crease Restaurant. J. Maurice Watkins, Sr., is the figure leaning against the tree at the left in this photo from about 1889. He died in 1911.

447

Although Highlandtown was annexed by Baltimore City in 1918, David Bohne's saloon at 4100 East Lombard Street was in the county when this early 1900s picture was taken. Note the elaborate juke box at the left. Philip Hock (left) and David Bohne are behind the bar.

448

449

In this 1913 ad David Bohne advertised Sherwood Rye, distilled in Cockeysville by the Wight family.

Bernie Lee's Penn Hotel was fashioned out of the brick house, dating from about 1870, that had been the home of Union veteran and Towson lawyer Maj. John Yellott. The mansard roof of the Yellott house was still apparent in the 1970s. Lee's bar and restaurant, which opened in the late 1940s, was a favored stopping-off place of both the courthouse and County Office Building crowds. Lee (standing at the left) had a remarkable memory for faces. After he died in 1972, a number of enterprises failed in the old building. (Photo by Charles Hart)

450

This inn on Frederick Road, Catonsville, dates to 1866, when it was owned by the rector of St. Timothy's Episcopal Church, the Reverend Dr. Libertus van Bokkelen and his wife. By 1876 Frederick Weber, from Bavaria, owned it and operated it under the name Catonsville Garden. Under the ownership of his daughter-in-law, Dorothea, it was known as Weber's Hotel or Weber's Tavern. One of Dorothea's daughters was Louisa Weber Butsch; when she acquired title after 1943, the inn became Butsch's Gardens. Subsequently it has been known as Mullineaux Toll House, Strawhat (in the 1960s), Wine Warehouse (in the 1970s), and McPatrick's Pub (in the 1980s). A move to put the inn on the Baltimore County Landmarks Preservation List by its current owner was viewed askance by local historians, who saw a building much changed inside and out. The photo dates from about 1904.

451

The Kingsville Inn, 11750 Belair Road, Kingsville, is now a branch of the E. F. Lassahn Funeral Homes. Shown here in 1976, the building may date to 1710, when it was a home for Nicholas Day. By 1742 the Reverend Hugh Deans, a Scot who had been appointed by Governor Benjamin Ogle to St. John's Episcopal Church, Kingsville, was living there. He continued to do so for the next thirty-four years.

In the early era of the automobile, and before 1925, the old house had become a popular restaurant. It was bought by the Lassahn Company in 1971.

452

453

The site of the Lee J. Hobbs Hotel at 151 Main Street, Reisterstown, has been used for a service station since 1948. The brick building, once known as the Yellow Tavern, dated back to Jacob Medairy in 1779. By mid-century it was owned by Daniel Banks, who renamed it for himself. After his death the building passed through many hands, being known in 1898 as the S. B. Vondersmith Central Hotel. It stood across the street from the old Franklin High School (now demolished); north county students got off at the Glyndon railroad station a mile away and walked to the hotel, where they waited until the school opened at 9 AM.

454

The Monkton Hotel, started in 1859 and described as complete in the newspapers of 1860, was the impressive property of Samuel Miller. The 1879 Directory of Baltimore, Carroll and Harford Counties *also notes that Miller was the postmaster, storekeeper, and railroad agent.*

455

The Viaduct Hotel at the Baltimore County end of the Thomas Viaduct at Relay was more a "mealing" station than a true hotel. Built in 1872 to a design by Ephraim Frances Baldwin, it replaced the structure seen in Picture 206. Its days were numbered following the introduction of dining cars. It closed in 1938 and was demolished in 1950.

The hotel is seen here in 1886. At the beginning of the twentieth century, the hillside behind the hotel became the site of the Gundry Sanitarium, a now-vanished facility for a well-heeled clientele afflicted with alcoholism and nervous disorders.

The Avalon Inn near the Eccleston station in the Greenspring Valley, was built in 1898 by the Greenwood Springs Company. In addition to the hundred-room hotel there were four cottages, stables, and other buildings. Defective wiring caused a fire that destroyed the hotel on the morning of October 30, 1912, at a loss of fifty thousand dollars to the one-year owner, Sarah F. Wright. Joseph Hughes, the headwaiter, and Charles Hughes, a bellboy, gave the alarm. No loss of life occurred but there was some panic.

456

457

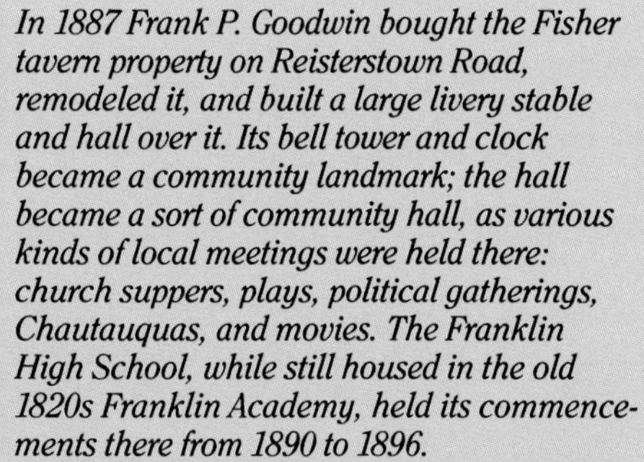

In 1887 Frank P. Goodwin bought the Fisher tavern property on Reisterstown Road, remodeled it, and built a large livery stable and hall over it. Its bell tower and clock became a community landmark; the hall became a sort of community hall, as various kinds of local meetings were held there: church suppers, plays, political gatherings, Chautauquas, and movies. The Franklin High School, while still housed in the old 1820s Franklin Academy, held its commencements there from 1890 to 1896.

The owner in 1940 replaced the house with an Acme market and the stable with a filling station. The hall was turned into apartments. The bell and clock were moved to the Masonic Temple on Main Street. The view here was taken in the 1930s.

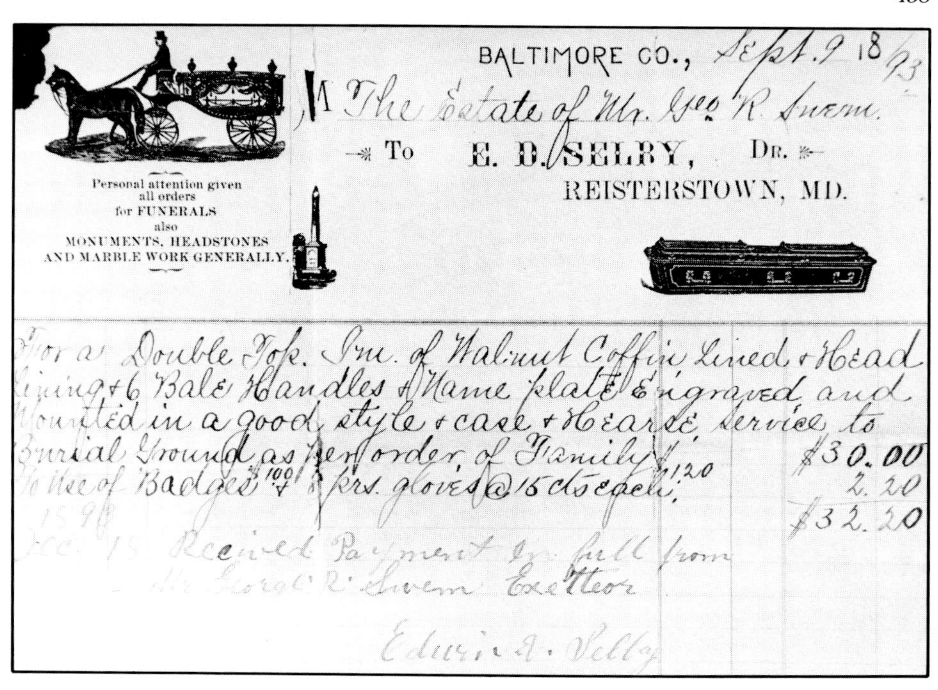
BALTIMORE CO., Sept. 9 1893

M The Estate of Mr. Geo. R. Swem.

To E. D. SELBY, Dr.

REISTERSTOWN, MD.

Personal attention given all orders for FUNERALS also MONUMENTS, HEADSTONES AND MARBLE WORK GENERALLY.

For a Double Top. Im. of Walnut Coffin Lined & Head Lining & 6 Bale Handles & Name plate Engraved and Mounted in a good style & case & Hearse Service to Burial Ground as per order of Family $120	$30.00
To Use of Badges $1.00 & 8 prs. gloves @ 15 cts each. 1.20	2.20
	$32.20

1893 Dec. 15 Received Payment in full from Mr George R. Swem Executor

Edwin A. Selby

The 1890s are recaptured in this billhead for services rendered by Selby's funeral establishment in Reisterstown and in an ad for Rowe's carriage works in Cockeysville.

459

460

Maj. John Ducker, a veteran of the War of 1812, built his store on Main Street, Reisterstown,a bout 1830. His son Ephraim sold it to the Russell brothers in 1867; they built the addition at the right, providing room on the second floor for the Masonic Lodge. William Russell, who lived above the store, was murdered by burglars about 1880. This photograph was taken in the 1930s.

461

Although incorporated in 1891, the National Bank of Cockeysville did not move into this building until 1904. The building is still used for commercial purposes. In this 1920s photo the electric car of John Tyrie, owner of John H. Tyrie & Sons Monument Works, is parked outside.

462

The directors of the Towson National Bank lined up for their picture in 1946 on the sixtieth anniversary of the founding of Baltimore County's first bank. Originally housed in a bell-towered building which stood immediately south of the Towson Theater, the bank moved to the site occupied by the present Mercantile Bank building in 1912. By the 1950s it had merged with Mercantile, and by the late 1960s the classic marble building was demolished and replaced by the present high-rise building. In front, from left to right, are Michael J. Birmingham, C. Franklin Almony (assistant cashier), H. Guy Campbell, Samuel P. Cassen (vice-president and cashier), S. Clayton Seitz, and LeRoy Y. Haile. In the rear are J. Robert M. Davis (assistant cashier), G. Clyde Andrews, Goss L. Stryker (vice-president), Frank I. Wheeler, Milton R. Smith (counsel), Clarence G. Cooper, John W. Crouch (assistant cashier).

Wheeler had been one of the first depositors in the bank in 1886. Birmingham became county executive, while Seitz owned the Towson Ice Company, and Campbell was a member of Harry T. Campbell and Sons, the stone materials company. Haile founded Loyola Federal Savings and Loan Association, Cooper was superintendent of education, and Crouch became a vice-president of Mercantile after the merger.

463

By 1929 Baltimore had several airplane companies. The Berliner-Joyce factory at Turner's Station made wooden pontoons for Navy seaplanes, as well as a two-seater tandem cabin commercial plane. On its twenty-five acres the company even had a wind tunnel, 50 by 100 feet in size. The Doyle Aero Corporation made the Oriole, a small scout plane, at Elm Avenue and Thirty-first Street. The Curtiss-Caproni Company had runways and hangars adjacent to Municipal Airport. The Pitcairn Aviation Company, operating from Logan Field, started airmail service on May 6, 1929, with twenty-three domestic routes, and routes to Canada, Central and South America, and the Caribbean.

The Chesapeake Aircraft Company, then called the Curtiss Flying Service, prepared to move its landing facilities from Logan Field to 94.27 acres on the south side of Smith and west of Greenspring avenues in Mt. Washington in 1929, and had done so by 1930. For tax purposes the new property was held by the "Baltimore Air Terminal of New York." By 1937 the property was held by the Curtiss-Wright Corporation of Garden City, New York. The 265-plus-acre facility closed in 1945.

Smith Avenue shopping center now covers the site.

464

465

Glenn Luther Martin (1894-1957) grew up in Kansas. An early convert to flying—he is holding a model of the plane he flew in 1909—he opened a factory first in California and then in Cleveland in 1917. The need to expand, the difficulty of getting contracts for conventional land-based planes, the desire to be both near Washington, D. C., and a metropolitan area, led to the Milburn farm in Middle River and the building of seaplanes. He surreptitiously purchased the property in 1928 for a "New York sportsman club." A year later he was employing between four hundred and a thousand people.

Shown is an overview of the complex in 1965. Riveters are at work during World War II.

466

467

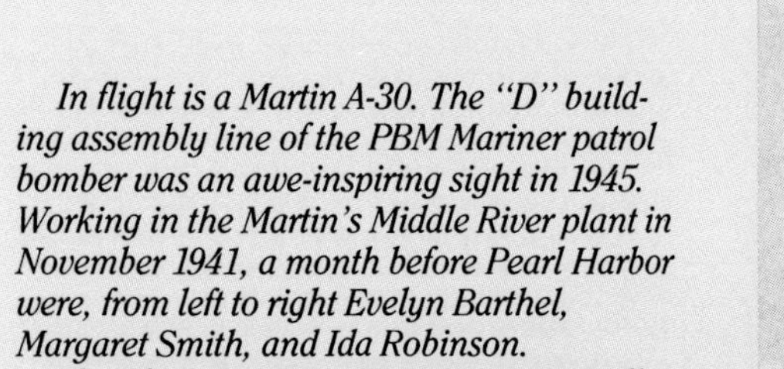

In flight is a Martin A-30. The "D" building assembly line of the PBM Mariner patrol bomber was an awe-inspiring sight in 1945. Working in the Martin's Middle River plant in November 1941, a month before Pearl Harbor were, from left to right Evelyn Barthel, Margaret Smith, and Ida Robinson.

The Glenn L. Martin Company eventually dropped airplane manufacturing; however, the successor firm, Martin Marietta is still a major defense contractor. The Middle River plant has been involved in rocket work.

468

469

470

471

Typical of the handsome flying boats built by Martin's was Pan Am's Bermuda Clipper rolling down a launching ramp in 1931.

When this P5-M2 rolled out of its hangar at the Martin Plant on December 20, 1960, it was the last plane from Martin's and the end of an era. From being the county's biggest employer, Martin's Middle River plant shrank to a vestige of itself, hanging on until contracts in the 1980s gave it a new lease on life.

472

Baltimore ordinances forbade the filling of artillery shells within the city limits. From about 1916 to 1918, the Bartlett-Hayward Co. (later Koppers), at Turner's Station near Dundalk, employed six thousand people doing this. Here workers crimp the nose cones onto shrapnel cases.

473

Ashland Iron Works, shown here about 1871, began in 1844 and ran until 1885. After closing, it was cannibalized by the Pennsylvania Steel Company for the new plant being built at Sparrows Point. Political boss J. F. C. Talbott and two cronies (fertilizer manufacturer Joshua Horner and lawyer Emmanuel Hermann, Jr.) bought the town for thirty-six hundred dollars and used slag heaps for cinders for road surfacing (they had the county contract). They sold the town to the city during the Loch Raven expansion project; the city in turn sold it to Baltimore furrier Mano Swartz. The Swartz family owned the town until the mid-1980s.

474

The Bethlehem Steel Plant and its shipyards dominate this aerial view of Sparrows Point, taken about 1950. In the upper center, near Sparrows Point, is Fort Carroll, a typical 1947 hexagon-shaped casemated Third System Fort. Col. Robert E. Lee, as a young Army engineer, participated in the construction of the fort. Abandoned and sold by the federal government, Fort Carroll is presently owned privately but not used. The Third System Forts were initially designed after 1816 by a French military engineer, Simon Bernard (who had been a brigadier general under Napoleon) and in particular by Joseph G. Totten, who was chief engineer of the U.S. Army from 1838 to 1864.

475

477

478

The Blakeslee-Lane Studios took this harbor view of Sparrows Point in 1937.

Steelmaking at Sparrows Point began with the purchase of the Fitzell farm in 1887. Later, other tracts, including the old excursion amusement park called Tivoli, would be added. Using the Chesapeake Bay as a highway, the company inexpensively moved raw ore from Cuba to the Point, and the finished product, often in the form of rails, to almost every railroad company in the world. A town grew up, with the company supplying almost every need, including seeds for the workers' vegetable gardens. The employer even sponsored contests with prizes for the most attractively maintained property. Blacks were housed in their own section, called North Side, on the far side of Humphrey's Creek (a body of water later filled in, as the company expanded and took more and more land, including its town, to house its blast furnaces and wire mills). Bethlehem Steel built schools for the children; these were later taken over by the Board of County School Commissioners. The education offered in this and other company towns was often superior to that offered by the county, and certainly was housed in better facilities. The company built ball fields, gave land for churches,and took care of the health of its workers and their families. In true company-town style, Bethlehem Steel gave its workers credit at the company store against wages yet to be earned.

In 1916 the Bethlehem Steel Company bought out the Maryland Steel Company, the successor to the Pennsylvania Steel Company.

For years Bethlehem Steel was the county's major employer, and was ultimately surpassed only by the Glenn L. Martin Company in total size of workforce. Over the years there were many dreadful accidents at the Point, as it was only after World War II that workers were required to wear hard hats. From a workforce of over thirty thousand before the long strike of 1959, Sparrows Point was under ten thousand for most of the 1980s. A recent upturn in business at both plant and shipyard gives hope of a better future.

Bethlehem Steel's open hearth furnaces are relics of the past, but in their time they were splendid spectacles. Hot, noisy, and dangerous, one of them is seen here in the 1920s. A man stacks in the tin mill in the 1920s.

A welder works in the shipyards in the 1930s.

479

The collier Vulcan is launched on May 13, 1909.

480

481

Two steelworkers pose with their work place behind them, in a powerful Blakeslee-Lane studio picture of the 1930s.

CONTRACT

The Conference between the Steel Workers Organizing Committee and the Bethlehem Steel Company starts . . . . .

Sept. 16th, 1941

for the purpose of signing an Agreement covering wages, hours and working conditions of the employees of the Bethlehem Steel Company.

"JOIN YOUR UNION NOW!"

100% Union Means 100% Contract

Steel Workers Organizing Committee
C. I. O.

OFFICES
32 Dundalk Ave. 3600 Eastern Ave. 712 N. Bond St.

Vote SWOC-CIO-Sept. 25th VOTE SWOC-CIO-Sept. 25th Vote SWOC-CIO-Sept. 25th

482

The Steelworkers Union drums up membership in advance of contract talks in 1941.

Workers of Local 245, United Steel Workers of America, picket Eastern Stainless Steel on May 3, 1952. Seven years later the entire steel industry was struck for 116 days, a blow so severe that the industry lost market share it never subsequently recovered. Employment in that industry would never again reach the pre-1959 high. Benefits gained by earlier union actions were trimmed in the 1980s as both management and labor, in an uneasy partnership, sought to save jobs and keep plants open by making plant operations "lean and mean." Competition from Germany, Japan, and other sources caused many steelworkers to finish their careers in other lines of work. (Photo by Vernon Price)

483

484

Edward L. Palmer designed Dundalk's Dundalk Building in 1919. It formed part of the community's unique shopping center and park space, which has since been protected with landmark status. Two other segments, the Dunleer and Dunkirk buildings were also put up in 1919.

Both Dundalk and the neighboring community of St. Helena were created by the U.S. Shipping Board Emergency Fleet Corporation to provide homes for Sparrows Point workers during World War I. Both places retain the advanced "Garden City" concept advocated by landscape planners of the time: curving, tree-lined streets, open space and recreation areas, and a self-sufficient community center which brought together public services (police and fire), churches, schools, a motion picture theatre and stores. In the mid-1940s the Bethlehem Steel Corporation turned over its solidly built real estate office building for use as a public library, which still occupies the building.

485

Black and Decker moved manufacturing from its Towson world headquarters to Hampstead, Carroll County, in 1965. In this 1945 picture, a worker monitors an armature coil winder which automatically counts the number of turns in each coil.

486

The Consolidated Gas Company reported in November 1926 that Terminal Stores, at Belair Road and Overlea, in addition to its other activities, served "well prepared hot food" and made syrup and candy.

487

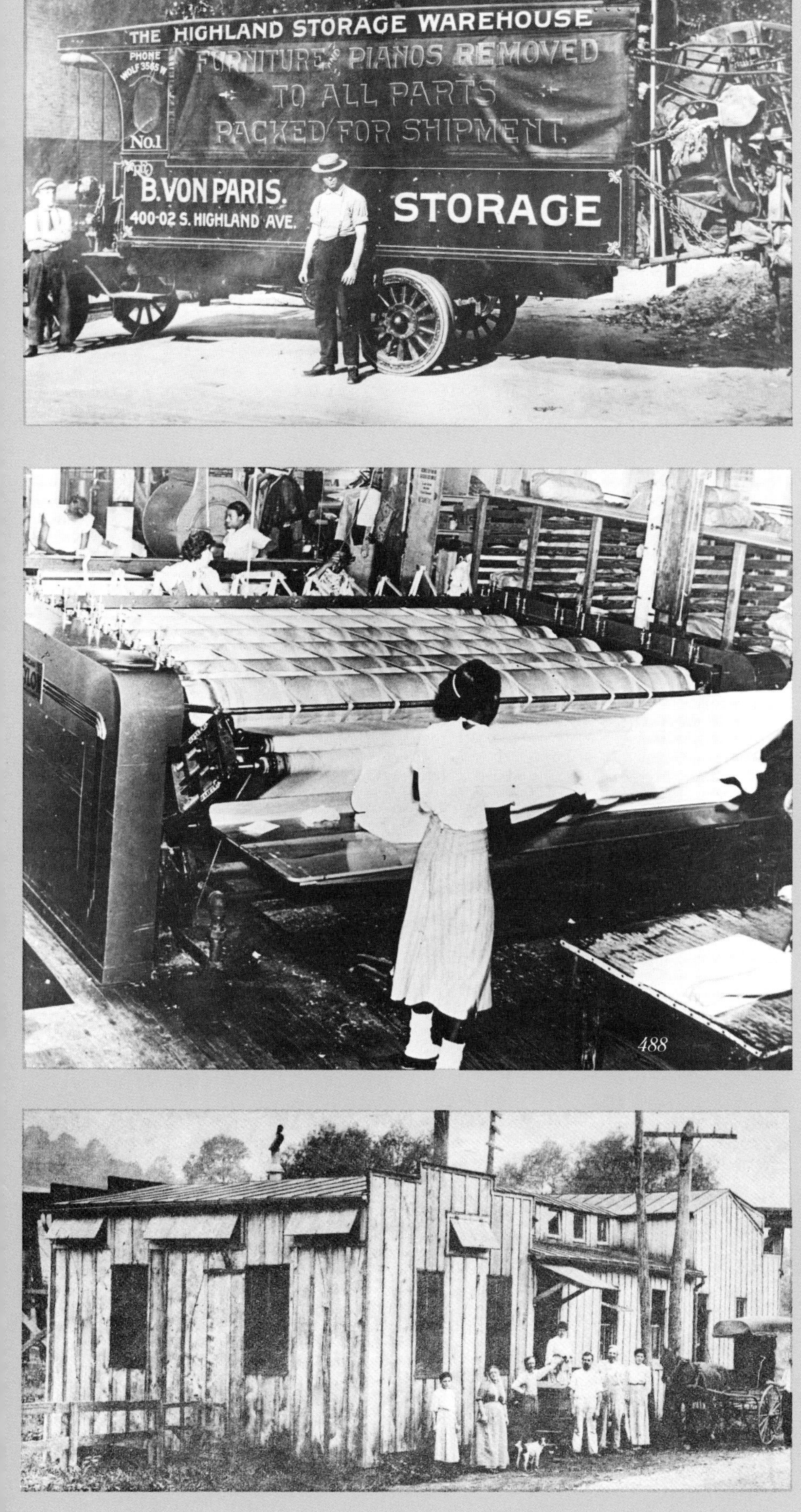

488

489

Things were somewhat more casual in the moving business in 1915 when B. von Paris and Shorty Downs moved six rooms of a family's possessions, including a piano and dog, from Baltimore to Jersey City. A similar though later B. von Paris truck, a 1919 Selden, has been restored and is now on exhibit at the Baltimore Industrial Museum.

At the age of twelve, Bonaventure von Paris (1882-1960) went to work for his father, Eligius, in the draying business in Baltimore City. When twenty-four he went to New York to study modern moving techniques. On his return in 1907 he started the family in the long-distance moving business. By 1908 he had bought out his father, who was in poor health.

At a new business address on Foster (later Highland) Avenue, von Paris started the family in the storage business as well. By 1919 the company had disposed of its horses and wagons. Von Paris's six children became actively involved in the company.

The company moved its warehousing to 1920 York Road, Timonium, in 1965. The company, the local representative of North American Van Lines, has branches in Anne Arundel County and in Potomac, Maryland.

Originally a service offered by Bethlehem Steel to its company town dwellers, the Enterprise Laundry was bought by Don Watson in 1937. It operated until the town was demolished in 1973. Here sheets are being pressed. Another laundry, run by John Mumma near the Long Green station of the Ma & Pa Railroad, is shown early in the century. People up and down the line brought their laundry to the stations, put it on the train for delivery to the laundry by horse-drawn wagon, and picked it up from the train at their own stations when it was done. The laundry was closed during the 1930s; it gradually fell into ruin and was removed.

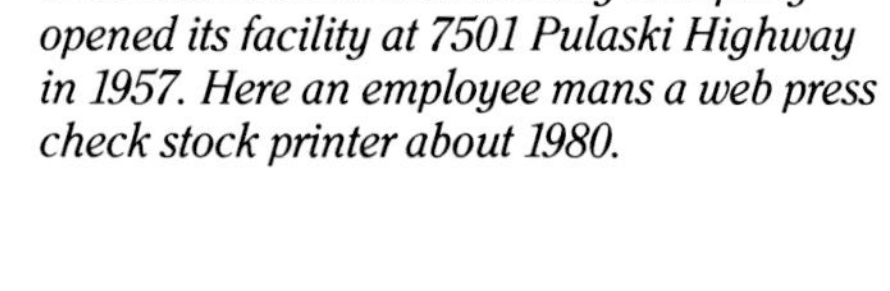

The American Bank Stationery Company opened its facility at 7501 Pulaski Highway in 1957. Here an employee mans a web press check stock printer about 1980.

490

Ken Jackson, a McCormick & Company's Hunt Valley Food Services Department employee, is at a "pre-mix" stand in 1978. Dry mayonnaise ingredients are mixed here before being piped to the filling lines.

491

492

Legum Chevrolet at 7900 Eastern Avenue (across from Eastpoint Shopping Center) changed its name from Park Circle Chevrolet in 1977 and occupies a site used for many years by Charley Irish's Chevrolet. It is one of many prospering car dealerships and repair centers in Baltimore County. Two cars are undergoing diagnostic testing in this mid-1980s photo.

American Totalisator had a manufacturing plant on Hillen Road in Towson from 1953 to 1981. Here ticket-issuing parimutuel machines are being readied. The company is now the Worldwide Wagering Systems Division of General Instrument Corporation, with offices in Hunt Valley.

493

Joseph Merritt, Sr., started his wholesale hydrangea business in Dundalk in 1913; his son, Joseph, Jr., took over in 1955 and ran it for another thirty years before closing the business. Employing twenty to twenty-five people at its peak, Merritt's distributed nationally.

494

495

Bruce S. Campbell (right), son of founder Harry T. Campbell, joined his father in the company around 1908. He became a director of the Timonium State Fair and a breeder of thoroughbred horses. He is at the Campbell booth at the fair with Governor Albert C. Ritchie and an unidentified lady in the 1920s.

496

The Texas, Maryland quarry of Harry T. Campbell and Sons was photographed in the 1960s. Interstate 83 is in the distance at the upper left. The company began when Harry Tyler Campbell (1859-1922) of Lauraville, contracted to furnish crushed rock ballast for the Harford Road horsecar line running from the city to Hamilton. Starting with the Thorn Hill Quarry on Hillen Road and the old Ridgely quarries (submerged by the 1912-1914 reservoir expansion), Campbell opened the Texas quarry in 1919. In 1926 Campbell leased the old Butler Quarry on Falls Road and in 1931 commenced operations at White Marsh. Campbell products have been used in innumerable major constructions, such as the Prettyboy Dam, Friends School, the Loch Raven-Montebello water tunnel, the Campbell Building and Calvary Baptist Church in Towson, City College, Loyola High School, and the buildings on the new Goucher College campus, among others.

The Campbell quarry holdings and related enterprises were bought by Flintkote in 1960, which in turn was bought by a wholly-owned subsidiary of Genstar Ltd., a Canadian firm, in 1980. In 1981 the local works were called the Genstar Stone Products. In 1986 Redlands PLC, a foreign company, bought Genstar Stone Products. The Campbell family is now active in Nottingham Properties, Inc., the developers of a 152-acre shopping mall and the town around it, on two thousand acres they own in the eastern part of the county.

497

The quarries around Beaver Dam, now favored swimming places for county youngsters, were operating before 1840. Marble from here was used in the Baltimore City Hall (1867-1875), the Washington Post Office (1865), the U.S. Capitol and the Washington Monument, as well as for many buildings (and door steps!) in Baltimore. The quarries had ceased operation by the end of World War II.

In 1900 Victor G. Bloede, a Catonsville resident and a chemist-industrialist, formed the Patapsco Electric and Manufacturing Company to supply power to the Catonsville and Ellicott City areas, both beyond the service area of the Consolidated Gas, Electric Light and Power Company.

Bloede first located near Gray's Mill on the Patapsco River and then acquired a site near Ilchester, upstream from the Thomas Viaduct at Relay.

Bloede's new 220 feet-long dam, built in 1907, was 40 feet wide at the base and had a height of 26½ feet from normal tail water to the crest. It was described as being an Amburson Hydraulic Construction Company (Boston) type, reinforced-concrete, slab-and-buttress dam. It was the first known instance of a submerged hydroelectric plant, where the power plant was actually housed under the spillway. Light into the engine room was received through glassless windows under the falls—virtually a flowing curtain. The engine room was 108 feet long, 27 feet wide (18 feet at the buttresses) and 10 feet high.

Shown are the original 34-inch Poole Engineering and Machine Company Leffel water wheels with 30-inch Samson turbines. There were Woodward governors attached to the turbines. The turbines ran at 240 rpms, and were direct-connected to an Allis-Chalmer 300-kw, 11,000 volt, three-phase 60-cycle alternator belted at the shaft.

The Gray's Mill plant gave electric power to Ellicott City, Catonsville, Irvington, Carroll, Halethorpe, Arbutus, St. Denis, Elkridge, and parts of West Baltimore, a service area of some six by ten miles. The new plant was intended to extend service to Mt. Washington and West Arlington. H.J. von Schon of Detroit was the consulting hydraulic engineer; Newton and Painter of Baltimore did the electrical engineering. Von Schon was a relative of Charles Wacker, Bloede's Eden Terrace, Catonsville friend and neighbor. Otto Wonder was the first superintendent.

Bloede sold his company to Consolidated in 1912 or 1913.

499

Two pictures of Clayton Seitz's Towson Ice Company show how far the firm advanced in fewer than twenty years. The wagons are lined up outside a site which is now the Subway Shop, at the corner of East Chesapeake Avenue and York Road, about the time of World War I. The firm was in the retail ice and ice cream business in 1909. By the mid-1920s, at a site now occupied by the First American Bank Building, 25 West Chesapeake Avenue, the machinery for providing power and the pipes needed to create a cooling system in ice making were wondrous. The Seitz family ran the business from 1909 to 1942.

500

501

William Henkle Hoffman (1810-1886) was the third generation and most successful of a family of paper manufacturers in Baltimore County. His grandfather, William Hoffman, received a grant of a thousand acres from the colonial governor for producing the first ream of paper in Maryland. He did so by resorting to sharp practices which enabled him to beat a Frederick County man for the prize. William's flagship operation was Clipper Mill in Northwest Baltimore County. Peter Hoffman, William's son, started Gunpowder Mill, near what is now Hoffmanville. William Henkle bought Marble Vale (near Ashland, on Paper Mill Road), built Rockdale Mill (shown in this 1890s photo, and bought back Clipper, which had gone out of the family in the interim. The various mills produced all of the newsprint paper used by the Baltimore Sun, *letter quality paper, and much paper used by the federal government. Legal documents from the last century periodically surface bearing a Hoffman watermark.*

Fires, mismanagement, and failure to modernize caused the family business to fail after William Henkle's death. The fourth generation sold the mills to various developers. Rockdale had a brief history as an explosives manufactory. Nothing now remains of any part of this important Baltimore County business.

Vincent's Dahlia Nurseries had been started in 1856 by Richard Vincent, Jr., in Elizabeth, New Jersey. He moved to Baltimore in 1862. Vincent bought his first farm in Anne Arundel County. In 1869 he bought a fifty-acre farm on Ebenezer Road between Chase and Cowenton. People took the train and in later years motored out to see the annual floral display in his fields and numerous greenhouses. The family was active in the Maryland Horticultural Society. The business closed during the 1930s.

502

HOUSES

Next to fire, termites were the greatest enemy of early wooden structures, which is why old pictures of log barns and cabins often reveal structures with serious sags and leans. Although pitch and tar were tried to counteract this problem, most of the oldest surviving structures were made of brick or stone. These, too, had problems, as the porous quality of some old brick let in dampness, and the coldness of large stone buildings made them poor havens for those with rheumatism and arthritis. The thick walls and high ceilings may have helped keep the lower floors cool in the summer, but keeping warm in the winter was another story, and involved the work of tending fires, carting wood or coal, and removing ashes. The smaller houses were dark, dank, smoky places.

The fashion of landscaping with shrubs and trees near and against a mansion was not usual in the early periods; old photos (such as those of *Clynmalira* and *Perry Hall*) show buildings standing free with nothing around them. When carpet manufacturer Hugh Gelston rebuilt his imposing corbeled mansion *Gelston Heights* in Calverton, there was not a tree or shrub around the place; there was, however, the inevitable privy off to one side behind the mansion. Trees and shrubs attracted damp and bugs; the yard was often that of a working farm and might even have chickens pecking away in the unsodded area.

Nothing was known of the bacterial causes of illness for most of the nineteenth century, so that privies were inappropriately sited near wells, and cleanliness was not then equated as being next to godliness. Typhoid outbreaks were frequent events in every community. When Albert S. Cook, the newly appointed superintendent of schools, moved from Reisterstown into the house at 201 Chesapeake Avenue, Towson (at the corner of Courtland Street, opposite the courthouse), he came down with typhoid a month later (June 1902).

Readers should bear in mind that with all housing, whether log cabin or elegant mansion, the water source and privies were outside. At one Warren house, still standing on the north side of Warren Road about a mile from where the factory once stood, a man who once lived there recalled that as a boy he had to carry every bucket of water used in the house 125 paces from the well, a 250-pace round trip. When it is remembered that every drop of water used for cooking, clothes-washing, and personal cleanliness had

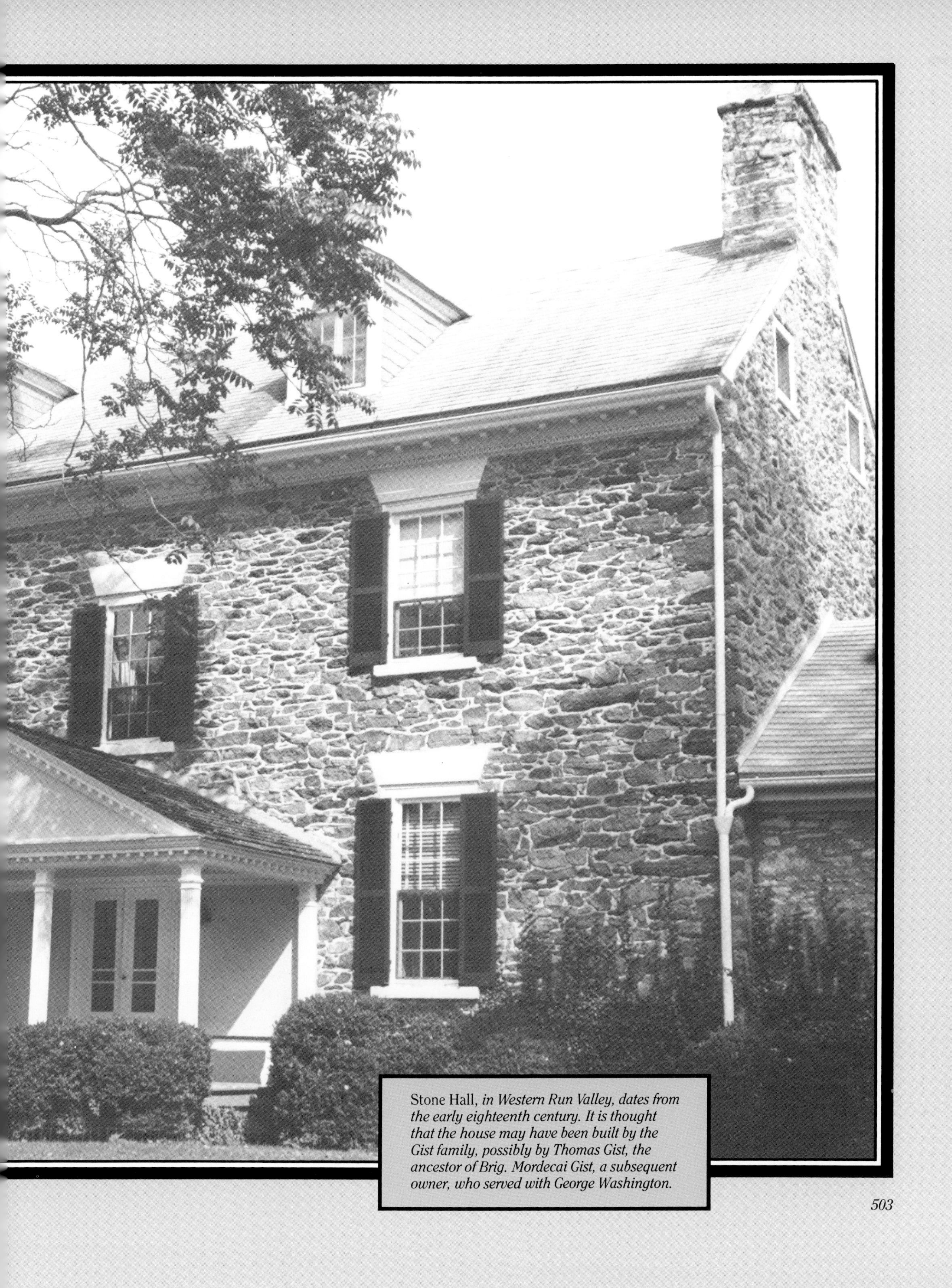

Stone Hall, *in Western Run Valley, dates from the early eighteenth century. It is thought that the house may have been built by the Gist family, possibly by Thomas Gist, the ancestor of Brig. Mordecai Gist, a subsequent owner, who served with George Washington.*

to be carried by bucket, by hand, it is not hard to understand why bathing was not a daily occurrence in rural areas. In most mill villages it was common for five or more families to share water, all carried by buckets, from the same pump. Every backyard had its privy and woodshed, the latter for all the material needed to stoke the various fireplaces, stoves and furnaces the house might have.

Every house, no matter how grand in front, made backyard provision for hanging out sheets, underwear and ever other washed item on lines strung from poles or trees in fair weather. Housework before the age of inside plumbing and electrical and gas appliances was a succession of long hours and back-breaking labor. It is not surprising that husbands often outlived wives, who had been burdened with constant childbearing in addition to their household labors.

504

Hampton Farmhouse *probably dates from the 1730s. It was lived in continuously by Ridgelys or their overseers until the 1980s. Col. Charles Ridgely (1702-1772) and Capt. Charles Ridgely (1730-1790) lived in it before the building of* Hampton *(completed in 1790). William C. Kenney took this 1920s photo.*

505

Construction was almost finished on the main block of Perry Hall *when the owner, Ironmaster Corbin Lee, died in 1773. The house was purchased by Archibald Buchanan, who promptly sold it in 1774 to Baltimore merchant Harry Dorsey Gough. Gough finished the house over the next decade or so as a five-part Georgian house, with one wing housing a chapel. Gough was an early convert to Methodism and was a friend and host to many of the famous circuit riders, including Francis Asbury. He also pioneered in the import of blooded sheep and cattle and was the first president of the first agricultural society in the state. His nephew, Harry Dorsey Gough Carroll, born at* Mount Clare, *inherited the place and moved there in 1822. About two years later, the east wing burned, along with two bays of the main block. Carroll rebuilt the main block as a three-bay house and covered the brick walls with stucco. It served as a farm residence for many years. Here it is shown about 1890, when it was owned by William George Dunty.*

506

Ulm, *100 Painter's Mill Road, was the playful name Samuel Owings, Jr., the miller, gave his large brick house. It was an acronym for his* Upper Mill, Lower Mill, *and* Middle Mill. *The property was subsequently owned by the Painters, who gave their name to the road.*

Old pictures of Ulm *show brick walls, plantings, walks, and outbuildings. While all that has gone, the house itself has been rescued from near ruin and has been sensitively recycled into the* Country Fair Inn, *a successful and acclaimed French restaurant. The picture dates from the 1930s.*

507

Manor Glen, *on the north side of the Jarrettsville Pike at the Harford County line, is on land originally owned by Elijah Bosley. The house (built about 1798) was the home of Ezekiel Bosley. Ann Gittings Emory, wife of Dr. Richard Emory (the owner shown on maps in 1850 and 1877) was the granddaughter of Elijah Bosley. Her grandson, who inherited the property, was S. Davies Warfield (1859-1927), chairman of the International Cotton Mill Corporation (after 1914) and president of the Old Bay Line. He was a financier with wide interests—railroads, gas companies, insurance firms, utilities—and often took on ailing firms and turned them around. In such a fashion he reorganized the Baltimore City Post Office, being appointed postmaster for eleven years under three successive presidents.*

When he died, the Old Bay Line named a new boat the President Warfield *after him. After World War II the ship was sold to foreign interests and used to ferry survivors of the Holocaust to Palestine via Cyprus. It had been renamed the* Exodus.

This portrait shows Richard Caton (1763-1845), for whom Catonsville is named; he was the son of an East Indiaman captain and grew up in Liverpool. By the age of twenty-four young Caton was in Maryland and had fallen in love with Mary Carroll, the eldest daughter of Charles Carroll of Carrollton (known as Charles Carroll the Signer—of the Declaration of Independence, of course—to distinguish him from his cousin Charles Carroll the Barrister). Mary's father was one of the richest men in the country. Although he objected, love won out, and Mary married her handsome, impecunious young Englishman. Carroll built for them a series of large houses, including Brooklandwood *on Falls Road, their long-term residence. The estate was later the home of George Brown, son of Alexander Brown the banker; still later, the home of Capt. Isaac Emerson. Since 1958 St. Paul's School and St. Paul's School for Girls have utilized the estate. Carroll also built* Castle Thunder *at 1100 Frederick Road, a site now occupied by the Catonsville Branch of the Baltimore County Public Library.*

508

509

In 1846, after Richard Caton's death, Brooklandwood *was bought by banker George Brown. Catonsville photographer A. H. Brinkmann caught up with Brown's gardener near the gazebo in the 1880s.*

Hayfields, *north of Shawan Road, on the west side of Western Run Road, can be seen from Interstate 83. The mansion was built by Col. Nicholas Merryman Bosley in 1810.*

The property passed to John Merryman, a prominent farmer, Southern sympathizer and county leader, who was the subject of Chief Justice Roger Brooke Taney's Ex Parte Merryman, *a ringing defense of* habeas corpus *in 1861.*

In the twentieth century, the farm raised polled Hereford cattle under a descendant, Gen. John Merryman Franklin, president of the United States Lines. In 1978 the farm was sold to Hayfields, Inc., and later to Nicholas B. Mangione. There are current proposals, opposed by neighboring landowners, to subdivide some of the acreage for expensive housing and to use the mansion as the clubhouse for an exclusive golf course.

510

Charles R. Mace came from Dorchester County to attend the newly opened Maryland College of Medicine (later, the University of Maryland Medical School). After graduation in 1811 he decided to stay in the area, and set up his practice in Baltimore County.

He married in 1817 and purchased this house, the Echoes, whose exact date of building is unknown, although its core was a log cabin. Several generations of Maces grew up there, all doctors. The family name was given to an important avenue in the Essex area. Appropriately, when Essex Community College and Franklin Square Hospital moved to new, adjoining properties, they came to the Mace estate. In 1968 the college was built on the site of the demolished house. The family burial plot, with its twenty-two graves, is maintained and protected.

511

512

Windcrest, *an early nineteenth-century house in Arbutus, stands high on a ridge. It was built by a member of the Linthicum family. Oregon Randolph Benson (1847-1923), a prominent Democrat and lawyer of the time, was a subsequent owner.*

513

The tax ledgers suggest that William Bishop's land acquired improvements between 1813 and 1823, the date when William's son Elias filed for bankruptcy. In 1844 the building was referred to as a "two-story stone house known as Bishop's Tavern." Numerous owners lived there after that, including William Dunty, formerly of Perry Hall, *and his family, who occupied the building from 1915 to 1929. Later, the house was much altered from its appearance in this picture dating from about 1916. By the 1980s* Bishop's Inn *had been demolished and replaced by a fast food outlet.*

Todd's Inheritance, *on Old North Point Road, was rebuilt in 1816 after the defeated British invaders had burned the 1664 structure on the site. Lookouts in the upper rooms of the house had given Americans early warning of the invasion. The Todd family lived in the house until the 1970s. A family graveyard is part of the property.*

514

Robert Oliver, a merchant whose city estate became Greenmount Cemetery in 1837, built this waterside stone house about 1817. It is known as the Oliver Beach House. *Oliver maintained an adjacent deer park.*

515

516

English Consul Mansion, *a plaster-over-stone house, was built between 1818 and 1830 by William Dawson, the first English consul to Baltimore after the War of 1812. The property originally included three hundred acres. The Dawson family, active in area cotton mills, helped finance the building of the Republic of Texas navy before Texas joined the United States. They lost money on that venture. The house, altered extensively from its appearance in this 1937 photo, is privately owned and surrounded by tight development.*

Clynmalira *on Carroll Road was built in 1822 by Henry Hill Carroll. This unfamiliar view from the 1880s, before substantial later alterations, shows the back of the house overlooking the valley.*

517

518

519

Glen Ellen *was Baltimore County's preeminent Gothic fantasy, a wild design by Alexander Jackson Davis for Robert Gilmor, his twenty-two-year-old wealthy patron. Although Gilmor was mesmerized by Sir* Walter Scott's Abbottsford, *his pockets were not deep enough to finance more than a one-story structure. Bought by the city because of the expansion of the Loch Raven reservoir in 1921, the structure languished, was vandalized, and suffered fires. Finally, it had to be razed for safety reasons at the end of the 1920s. Recycled portions of it were incorporated into the* Cloisters, *now a children's museum on Falls Road, by its builder, Sumner Parker.*

Col. Harry Gilmor, a Confederate cavalryman, grew up at Glen Ellen. *He stayed there overnight on the occasion of his famous raid into the county in July 1864. A small body of 150 men under his command cut two major railroad connections and the telegraph line, but were dissuaded from taking the Federal Arsenal in Pikesville. He paused long enough to down a glass of ale in the old stone Towson Hotel (then called Ady's Hotel) before heading back to his own lines. He had only lost one man, during the scuffle at Ishmael Day's house (on Sunshine Avenue near Fork) which the Confederates burned.*

Stone Row in Ashland, which faced the Northern Central tracks, dated from about 1844, when the Ashland Iron Company was started by Philip and Samuel Small of York, and Joseph and Edward Patterson of Baltimore (brothers of Betsy Patterson). Little changed for 140 years until the houses were bought and renovated, and the vacant land was built upon in 1986 by developer Kim Strutt.

520

521

Robert Taylor, Jr., son of a Dublin-born post-Revolutionary period Baltimore County teacher, built this Bradshaw, Maryland house in 1851. He named it Mt. Peru *and put a pineapple, a symbol of hospitality, on the roof. His son was Benjamin F. Taylor, a Union Army colonel.*

522

Edward F. Jenkins of Baltimore retired early in order to build this house in the Long Green Valley in 1855. Subsequently called Montrose, *Jenkins's house was reputed to be the first private house in the county to have indoor plumbing.*

523

Stoneleigh, *designed by Niernsee and Neilson, was built in 1852 for $15,738.94 by Robert P. Brown, the son of the first president of the University of Maryland's Board of Regents. Parts of the estate were subdivided in 1927. The house was demolished about 1955 and the balance of the estate then subdivided.*

524

Dumbarton *was designed by the Baltimore firm of Niernsee and Neilson for Baltimore merchant Joseph Reiman in 1853. During the Civil War, Rieman was given tightly drawn passes through the Union Army lines ringing Baltimore, which allowed him to go the exact distance from his town house on West Monument Street, next to Enoch Pratt's (and now the site of the Maryland Historical Society), to his county farm. After his death his widow and his daughter and her husband, state senator David Gregg McIntosh, remained there until the estate was sold to James Keelty in 1929 for a subdivision called Rodgers Forge. The Baltimore County Board of Education acquired both the mansion, which it now uses for offices, and sufficient acreage to build a middle school with space enough for several playing fields.*

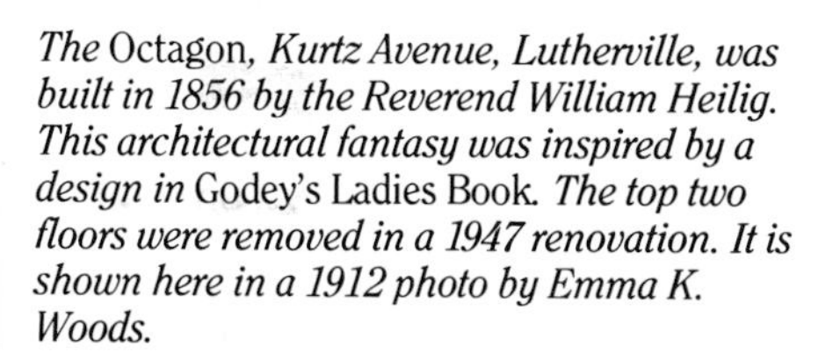

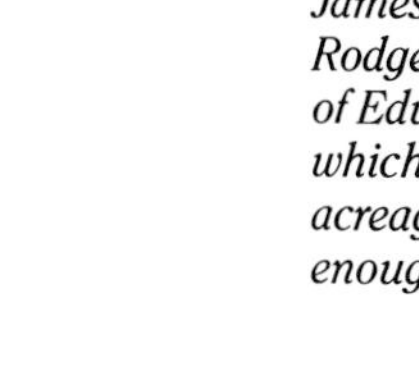

525

The Octagon, *Kurtz Avenue, Lutherville, was built in 1856 by the Reverend William Heilig. This architectural fantasy was inspired by a design in* Godey's Ladies Book. *The top two floors were removed in a 1947 renovation. It is shown here in a 1912 photo by Emma K. Woods.*

527

528

Victorian interiors are fascinating. Drumquhazel's *dining room, and* Dumbarton's *parlor are early twentieth-century photos of even earlier installations. In 1940 Constance Bentley and her sister, Mrs. H. A. Devries, are seated in* Rosland's *chandeliered study.* Rosland's *parlor is a triumph, with marble fireplace, huge gilt-framed overmantel mirror, grand piano and upholstered piano bench, and an Eastlake whatnot at the left. The electrified gas chandelier is impressive.*

529

530

526

A major Gothic extravaganza was Ravenhurst, *built in 1857. Subsequently lived in by ex-Confederate general Isaac Ridgeway Trimble and later by members of the Hoen lithography family, it fell into disrepair after its acreage was sold off. It burned on the night of October 31-November 1, 1985, as a group of owners were making some headway in its restoration.*

Prominent Baltimore brewer Frederick Bauernschmidt built Bauernschmidt's Manor *in 1903, apparently incorporating elements of the earlier* Planters Point Ducking Club. *The club had incorporated in 1877 with sixty acres of land.*

531

532

Bella Vista *stood on a high hill on the east side of Harford Road from 1896 to 1934. It was built by Charles Joseph Bonaparte, a sometime U.S. attorney general and secretary of the navy during the Theodore Roosevelt administration. Bonaparte was a grandson of Betsy Patterson and Jerome Bonaparte, Napoleon's brother.*

When the streetcars arrived on Roland Avenue, Bonaparte fought the service extension as long as he could; then he sold that property and built Bella Vista. *The house was owned by a bootlegger during Prohibition. In 1934, while under new ownership, a faulty electrified fireplace caused it to burn to the ground in a spectacular blaze visible for miles. It was replaced by a poured concrete mansion. There is a cathedral-size 1896 carriage house and stable still on the estate.*

Bonaparte didn't confine his dislike of machinery to streetcars. According to William B. Marye, noted Maryland historian, he never allowed any machinery more complicated than a treadmill on his estate.

533

Arden, *Victor Bloede's bizarre mansion in Eden Terrace, burned in 1898 and was replaced. Graced with carriage paths, formal gardens, greenhouses, and lily ponds, it was a showplace for the German-born industrialist. Bloede (1843-1937) was the son of a doctor who had been forced to emigrate after the revolutionary unrest of 1848. After graduation from school in Brooklyn, Bloede was a chemistry instructor in the Cooper Union for a year. He later established two companies of his own, specializing in products used in the textile and plastics industries. He perfected the gum used by the government on postage and revenue stamps and did important research into colorfast dyes. A founder of the First National Bank of Catonsville, he also organized the Patapsco Electric and Manufacturing Company of Baltimore County.*

Bloede funded Johns Hopkins' first visiting and instructing nurse program, gave his New York house as a manual training facility for blind women, funded a summer home for blind women, and founded a guild for blind actors, which arranged for performances to aid in their support. Bloede was a founder and first president of West Baltimore General Hospital. He left money for chemistry scholarships for needy students.

Eden Terrace was largely obliterated in the 1950s when a swathe was cut for Beltway construction.

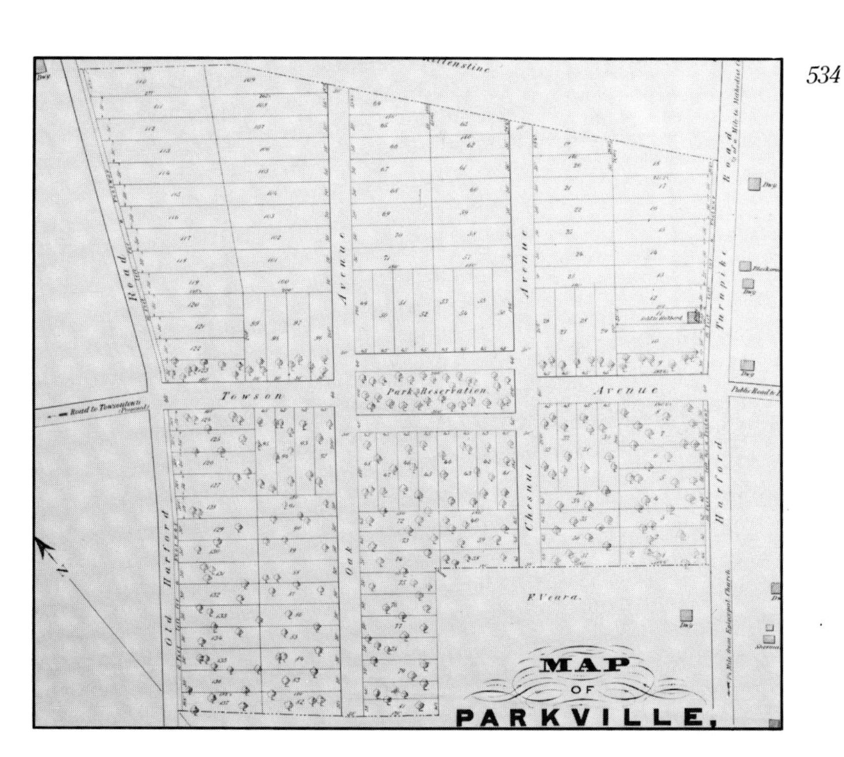

534

Martenet's 1874 plat of Parkville presents a puzzle, since the area had neither business nor industry, the distance to Towson was long and the road bad, and streetcars would not reach the area until 1910. One possible explanation is that the area was an early working-class summer retreat, as there was a hotel on Dubois Avenue off Harford Road. The plat is recognizable today. Towson Avenue is now Taylor Avenue, named for Wilkerson Taylor; the war memorial is located in the park. Joseph Moreland developed an additional 585 acres on Taylor Avenue in the 1930s.

Greenlea, *Long Green, about 1893. The ground was presented to Dr. John S. Green and his bride, Eleanor Lindsey Baldwin, at their wedding. The house built by them stayed in the family until 1968.*

535

Built by Bethlehem Steel for its workers, D. Street, Sparrows Point, was photographed in June 1928, with classic cars and front stoop sitters. It was demolished in 1972.

This 1988 photo by Ruth Schaefer shows 326 Dunkirk Road, Rodgers Forge. James Keelty developed the Dumbarton *tract after he purchased it in 1929.*

537

538

The 3000 block of Dunleer Road, Dundalk, in the winter of 1988, is shown in a photo by Ruth Schaefer. Dundalk, developed by the Dundalk Company to plans drawn up by Edward I. Palmer, was put on the National Register as a historic district in 1983. Plans were developed as early as 1917, although the design and much of the housing as it exists today dates from about 1928 or later.

539

This photo of 502 Riverside drive in Essex was taken by Ruth Schaefer in the winter of 1988. The plat was registered in 1930.

Drive out today and see for yourself

INVERNESS

A DEVELOPMENT OF

200 Homes of refinement and beauty

Handsome up-to-the-minute Homes, 5 and 6 rooms and **Bath, also** Garage, featuring every luxury at extremely low prices—terms same as rent.

Fishing and crabbing and all waterfront sports combined with a PERMANENT year round HOME.

Agent on premises until late in evening — Come out today.

The I. J. Bolton Company

Dundalk 789—Bear Creek and Wise Ave.

Let us build to suit you—Terms very easy.

540

A developer in 1937 was advertising Inverness, located between Lynch Creek and Chink Cove, Dundalk, and directly across the water from the Sparrows Point Country Club. Dollenberg and Company of Towson did the survey; the first plat was recorded on May 5, 1937.

HOSPITALS AND INSTITUTIONS

Although not as susceptible to some health disasters, such as cholera or typhus, as was a congested port like Baltimore City, the county still had no general hospital until 1965. In the nineteenth century health service was delivered by a small corps of dedicated doctors who traveled ceaselessly by horse and buggy. They were backed by local pharmacists.

Tuberculosis was rampant in all classes; typhoid was endemic. Childhood diseases such as scarlet fever and measles were life-threatening at that time. Childbed fever—that is, infection after giving birth—was a significant cause of death. Industrial accidents were frequent and horrendous. Fires were often fatal; hardworking volunteer fire companies were slow to reach a conflagration with horse-drawn equipment on bad roads. In such cases the building was usually gone by the time help arrived.

Agricultural accidents were also frequent. The old newspapers tell of people losing a foot in the reaper, falling off a barn, being trampled by a horse, gored by a cow, badly gouged by an axe. Tetanus was a serious problem; the old accounts report on tragic lockjaw deaths. Diseases mild by modern standards were often fatal. Not mild at all was the 1918-1919 worldwide outbreak of Spanish influenza which claimed 650 deaths out of 7,765 reported cases in the county.

In the nineteenth century there was constant need for almshouses for those made destitute by the bankruptcies, layoffs, and illnesses suffered without health insurance or workmen's compensation. There was also a need for orphanages for children left homeless by the deaths of parents from sickness or accident. Mental illness became an increasing problem, necessitating the opening of such state-run hospitals as Spring Grove in Baltimore County (1872), Springfield in Carroll County (1895), and many private clinics and sanitariums such as Sheppard-Pratt (1891), and Harlem Lodge and the Gundry Sanitarium (both run by the Gundry family).

Diseases were often incorrectly diagnosed in the nine-

The firm of Thomas and James Dixon, with Calvert Vaux as associate architect, designed the main building at the Sheppard and Enoch Pratt Hospital, Towson, which opened for service in 1891, some thirty-one years after construction had started. Construction funds came from a bequest by Moses Sheppard, but since only income and no capital from the

bequest could be used, progress was slow. Sheppard wanted a hospital built for the indigent mentally ill. The architects followed closely a design suggested by Dr. Robert Kirkbride of the Pennsylvania Hospital, known of and approved by Moses Sheppard. The structure was built of locally quarried stone and trimmed with marble from the Hampton *estate, under the supervision of Joseph Camp, who was in charge of construction. In concept and design it was ahead of other mental hospitals of the time. In 1896 the million-dollar gift of Enoch Pratt permitted the hospital to move to the forefront of psychiatric medicine.*

teenth century; paper-maker William H. Hoffman's incompetence and dementia at the end of his life may actually have been what is now called Alzheimer's disease. Iron-founder Horace Abbott suffered from paralysis in his last years; this was doubtless the result of a stroke. When noted Methodist circuit rider Henry J. Slicer got the flu in 1864, he became immobilized with rheumatism and pain and was treated by castor oil, mustard plaster, Seidlitz powders, calomel, and magnesia. Twentieth-century diagnosis might have revealed that he had a virally induced arthritis.

As in the rest of the United States, an increasing number of Baltimore County residents can be classified as elderly. Nursing homes, retirement communities, life care centers, and condominiums and apartments for those who no longer want the cares of property maintenance have proliferated and are monitored by state and local agencies for the care and quality of services offered and delivered.

541

Dr. James Smith (1771-1841) was born in Elkton, Cecil County. He studied medicine at the University of Pennsylvania after graduating from Dickinson College. He became known as the father of vaccination in America because of his lifelong interest in the vaccine for smallpox. Smith named a son for Edward Jenner, after the English medical pioneer who developed the vaccine. It is possible that Smith, who lived on Gay Street in Baltimore 1841, never set foot in Pikesville but merely owned and speculated in land there. He suggested the name Pikesville for the hamlet growing up around the 1816 Federal Arsenal to honor a friend, Brig. Gen. Zebulon Pike, who had been killed during the War of 1812.

Smith had sold the government property for the arsenal, 14 acres and 147 perches (a perch *is an archaic measurement of length, equal to 5½ yards) in 1819 for $895. He left 163 acres and 107 perches to his son. That tract subsequently became part of the McHenry property in Pikesville. The portrait of Smith was painted by Rembrandt Peale and is now in the Baltimore Museum of Art (bequest of Elise Agnus Daingerfield. BMA 1944-97).*

Construction began on "Old Main," Spring Grove State Hospital, Catonsville, in 1853, here pictured in an 1871 Hoen lithograph. The Civil War interrupted the construction and work was not resumed until 1868. The hospital, which opened in 1872, provided vastly improved care for those with mental illness. Heretofore such unfortunates had been minimally warehoused with indigents in almshouses around the state. The building was demolished in 1964.

542

544

Apartment buildings at Court House Square, Burke Avenue, Towson, now occupy the old Stansbury estate known as Eudowood. *The estate had been acquired by a Hospital For Consumptives of Maryland. Named the Eudowood Sanitarium, it accepted its first patient there on June 21, 1899. The hospital closed on July 1, 1964, and the remaining fifty patients were transferred to Johns Hopkins Hospital. As a memorial to his mother, Catonsville industrialist Victor Bloede in 1908 constructed this building named for her in the Eudowood hospital complex. The photo dates from the 1920s.*

A view of a ward at Eudowood Sanitarium in the 1920s.

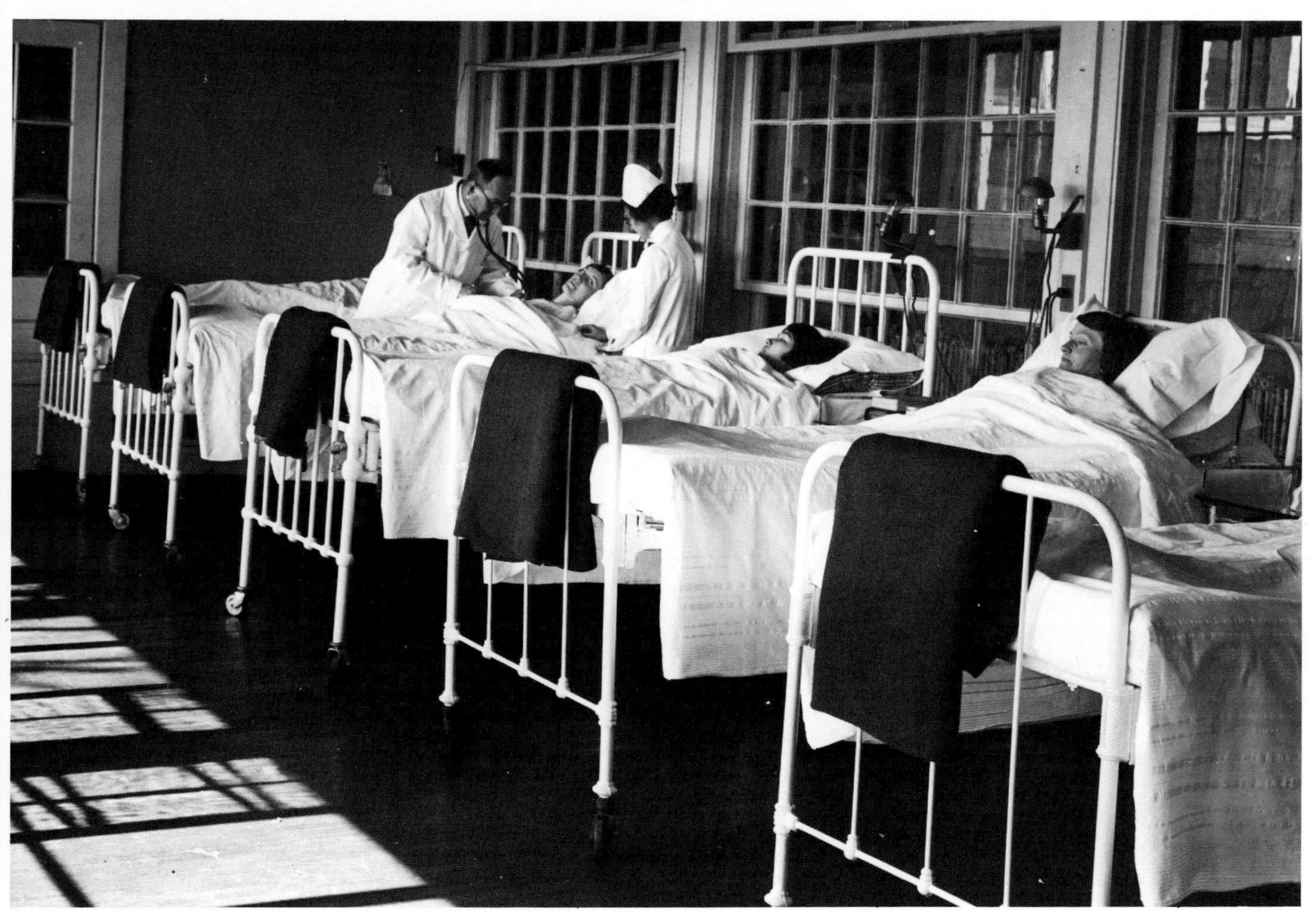

545

546

In the 1940s those living on Liberty Road unlucky enough to need an ambulance were transported by a sedan, which had a side-loading door, through which the stretcher was laid over the passenger-side space of the front and back seats.

The German Protestant Orphan Asylum was established in 1863 by the German Evangelical Lutheran Trinity Church in Baltimore, under Pastor Martin Kratt's leadership. The name was changed in 1866 to the General German Orphan Asylum.

First located at Pratt and North Calvert streets, it moved in 1875 to Aisquith near Orleans Street, where it stayed for fifty years. In 1924 the home (which housed as many as 161 at a time in Baltimore) moved to Bloomsbury Avenue, Catonsville. The school closed in the 1970s. Shown is the dining room as it appeared in the 1940s. The property's original residence was razed in the 1970s after it had served as the administrative building of the children's home.

547

548

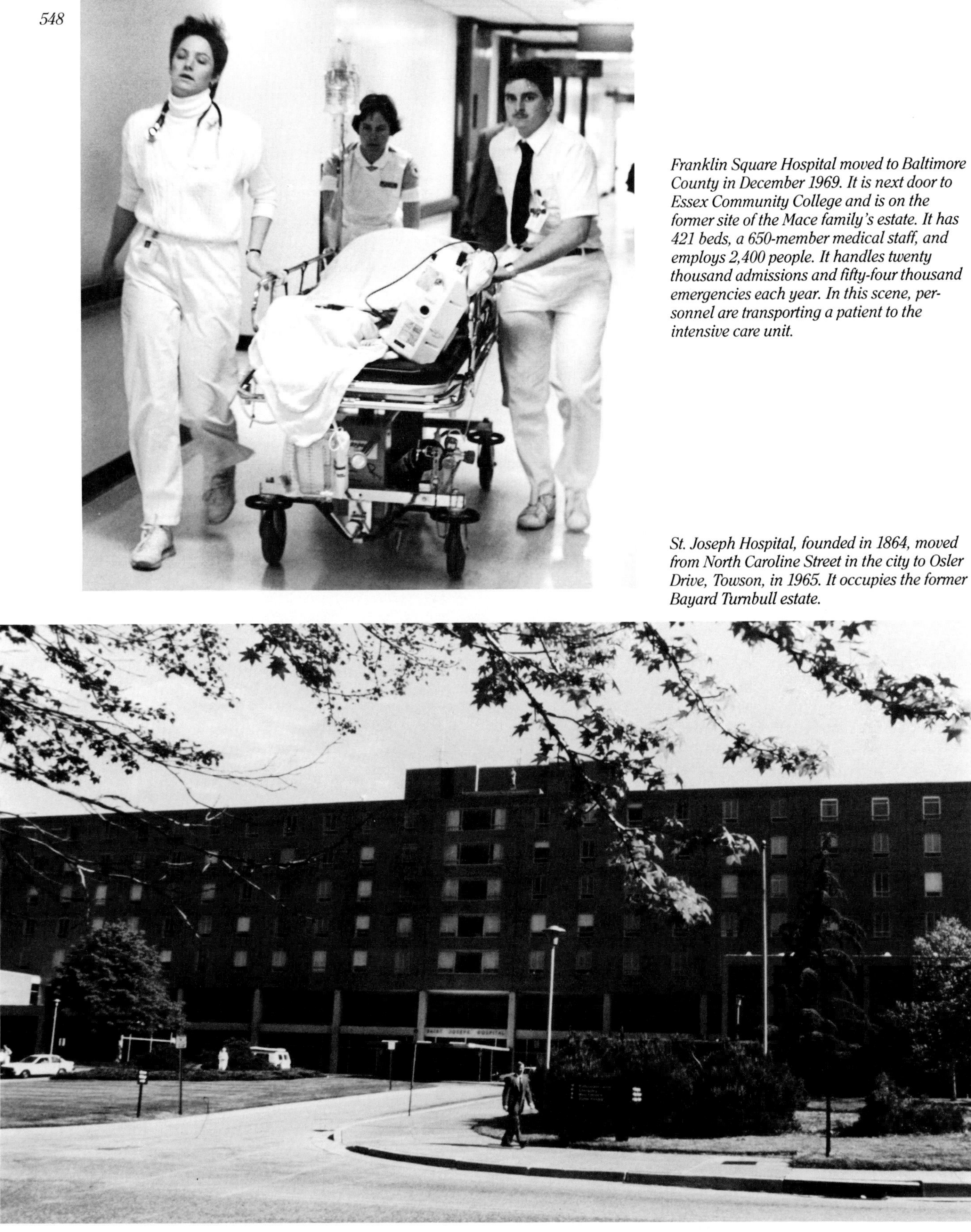

Franklin Square Hospital moved to Baltimore County in December 1969. It is next door to Essex Community College and is on the former site of the Mace family's estate. It has 421 beds, a 650-member medical staff, and employs 2,400 people. It handles twenty thousand admissions and fifty-four thousand emergencies each year. In this scene, personnel are transporting a patient to the intensive care unit.

St. Joseph Hospital, founded in 1864, moved from North Caroline Street in the city to Osler Drive, Towson, in 1965. It occupies the former Bayard Turnbull estate.

549

POSTSCRIPT

Picture No. 1

Baltimore County, by S. J. Martenet, 1866. On this map present-day Parkville is called Lavender Hill and is located on the Harford Turnpike. Essex is in the general area of Rossville, on the Philadelphia, Wilmington, and Baltimore Railroad line. Sparrows Point is the spit between Bear Creek and Old Road Bay. Dundalk is on the other peninsula that ends at Bear Creek and is bounded on the other side by the Patapsco River. Present-day Perry Hall is south of Kingsville on the Belair Turnpike, now called Belair Road or U.S. 1. In the western part of the county, Powhatan is now called Woodlawn. Arbutus is in the southwestern corner of the map and here is called Sulphur Springs. Relay, adjacent to St. Denis, does appear on the map near the Patapsco River. Modern-day Lansdowne, Halethorpe, and English Consul are southeast of Sulphur Springs. Rocky Point Park is located on the most extreme spit of land on Back River as it enters into Chesapeake Bay (opposite Hart-Miller Islands). East of Bear Creek, southeast Baltimore County, is Sparrows Point. The next point east, beyond Old Road Bay, is North Point, site of the British invasion in 1814 and location of present-day Ft. Howard. One and a half miles northeast of Ft. Howard was Bay Shore Park. The new community of White Marsh is due west of Bird River just across the railroad tracks. On this map, Lake Roland near Towson is called by its old name of Swann Lake. It had been named for Thomas Swann, Mayor of Baltimore during the Know-Nothing period when the lake and its dam were approved, who later became Governor of Maryland.

In the northwest part of the county, present-day Liberty Reservoir is now a large man-created lake with inlets on the Carroll County-Baltimore County boundary, between Reisterstown and Harrisonville, but non-existent in 1877. The dam is actually on the county line, at the end of Nicodemus Road which runs on this map more or less due west and south of Reisterstown. Glyndon (and Emory Grove) are one mile northeast of Reisterstown.

Picture No. 9

Towson in 1898, from the Bromley 1898 *Atlas*. The courthouse town was still firmly in the nineteenth century, with blacksmiths and livery stables. Some buildings illustrated elsewhere in this book may be found: the fire house at the top of York Road hill, Bosley's Hotel, and J. Maurice Watkins's tavern on the west side of York Road.

The Baptist church shown near the courthouse burned in 1929 and was replaced by the present Calvary Baptist Church. Nothing remains of any of the buildings which fronted the courthouse or which stood on the two streets beside it except for the former Baptist parsonage, now the offices of a property titling company, and a nineteenth-century house at the corner of Courtland and Chesapeake avenues, used in recent years by a branch of the states' attorney's office. Attorney Robert Boarman's house, at the southwest corner of Washington and Chesapeake avenues, is now the U.S. Post Office. The National Guard is now on the site of the Smedley House, also called the Hampton, a hotel which burned in 1916. The Equitable Bank holds down the corner where the Masonic Temple once stood.

Over ninety years York Road has been changed greatly by additions and deletions. All the old landmarks were taken down in the 1950s, or before; the Towson Hotel, once called Ady's Hotel, was removed in 1929; the Towson National Bank (on the east side of York Road) came down in 1926; and Bosley's Hotel was razed at the beginning of the 1950s. The fire house went at that time, too. The east side of York Road from Chesapeake Avenue south to the railroad (on this map) is now the site of the Towson Branch of the Baltimore County Public Library. The whole of what remains on the west side of York Road, between Chesapeake and Pennsylvania avenues is slated for demolition and intensive development. Of the rest, what remains is a haphazard string of two-story businesses recycled to modern uses, including restaurants, shoe shops, haberdasheries, greeting card outlets, and bars, and other, not always successful enterprises which come and go. Little of what was left after fires in the 1870s and 1880s still remains in the 400 and 500 blocks of York Road other than the stone facade of the I.O.O.F. building. Replacement buildings have followed no particular style and were erected when a lot owner had the funds to put up or replace something already there. None has any distinction although the architects of two are known.

Looking like a small-town main street of the 1940s or 1950s, the 400 and 500 blocks of York Road in Towson exist as an inefficient anachronism in the governmental, legal, and financial centers of the county. They await a realistic, more intensive and profitable use of such valuable land.

The Towson Post Office, now on the site of Robert R. Boarman's house (which was later called the Rider Building), dates from 1938. The Jefferson Building of the 1950s, currently to the west of the post office is on the site used in the 1920s by the Court Garage. The County Office Building of 1958, at 111 West Chesapeake Avenue, occupies the space held from the first decade of the century until the 1950s by the Offutt Building. On the opposite side of the Courthouse grounds, Colonel D. G. McIntosh's house at the corner of Pennsylvania and Washington avenues was replaced in 1951 by the Harry T.

Campbell Building. The house of D. Hopper Emory to the west of it was replaced in the 1960s by the Alex. Brown building. Hopper Emory was a well known late nineteenth- and early twentieth-century attorney. West of the Emory place, now owned by Calvary Baptist Church and rented by Sentinel Title Company, was an Italianate house then owned by another nineteenth-century legal luminary, William S. Keech. Colonel McIntosh's office, at Washington and Pennsylvania avenues, was saved in 1968, and moved when the Mercantile Safe Deposit and Trust Company demolished its marble 1912 building and erected a highrise. Not as fortunate was the Mt. Moriah A.F. & A.M. Masonic Lodge, designed by Frank E. Davis in 1879. The two-story brick landmark, with Asbill's lunch counter and pharmacy in the basement—a meeting place for bureaucrats and politicians for decades—was levelled by 1970 for the Equitable Building, now at the corner of Washington and Chesapeake avenues.

On Allegheny Avenue, next to noted architect Nathan Starkweather's beautiful Trinity Episcopal Church of 1860, land speculator John Burns built a large house in 1873. He sold it to the Union Army veteran and Towson auctioneer, Colonel O. P. Macgill. Real estate man and painting contractor Henry L. Bowen was a subsequent owner, as is shown on the 1898 map. That house, and Sheriff William P. Cole's next to it, were demolished in 1987 to make way for offices for the Legg, Mason brokerage firm. Cole's Italianate house, which he had bought in 1896, had been built between 1857 and 1864 by Enos Smedley, Towson's first town planner, and sold to Edwin Tydings. Dr. James H. Jarrett was a subsequent owner. Cole (1849-1927) had a busy career in Baltimore County, as sheriff and clerk of the court. Still on Allegheny Avenue, but on the other side of Washington Avenue, the present-day, multi-story Penthouse replaces the large frame house and barn of Dr. Jackson Piper. Piper was the son of a War of 1812 colonel who ran the Indian Head Hotel in Baltimore; he was named for one of his father's presidential friends. Before it was demolished, 1973-1974, both the Stieff and Kirk silversmithing firms had had outlets in the Piper house at different times.

Across the street from the Penthouse, still standing though much changed after a 1925 face-lift, is the Craumer-Berry house. It was built in 1895 by J. Maurice Watkins, Sr., for his daughter when she married William C. Craumer, cashier of the Towson National Bank. Across Washington Avenue from the Craumer-Berry house stood Dr. James H. Jarrett's home and office. By 1898 the home had been inherited by his daughter and her husband William A. Lee. The house, then owned by the Nottingham Company, was demolished in the 1980s to make way for an office building.

On York Road at Chesapeake Avenue, Wendy's, in the 300 block, now occupies a site once owned by James J. Linsey. Next door, to the south, the Orient Restaurant stands where Ephraim Almony's house stood until 1948. The Towne and Country Furniture Store took its place, and a succession of bars and restaurants followed that. In the 400 block, at York Road and Pennsylvania Avenue, the southeast corner is now furrier Mano Swartz' parking lot. Dukehart and Stevenson's Towson Horse Company, a livery stable, was on the site by 1908; it's sign may be read at the extreme left of picture No. 298 in this book. Further out York Road, at 617, is the stone Solomon Schmuck house, built, say the tax records, between 1833 and 1841. On this map it is shown as being owned by William Galloway; long before that, Dr. William Bode had lived in it. Subsequently, from about 1912 to 1926, Charles E. Treadwell lived there. In recent times the building was the Valley Gun Shop and is currently a bridal store. On the east side of York Road, next to Prospect Hill Cemetery, the brick Towson Methodist Episcopal Church of 1871 gave way that the Investment Building might rise, in 1967, having served its last years out as a funeral establishment. Also on York Road, at 418, Mykonos Restaurant is the current replacement to Henry Dienstbach's saddlery shop shown on the 1898 map. It was on the site of the house of Towson's postmistress of the 1870s, Sarah Feast, at 408 York Road, that Ellis Finkelstein erected his new store in 1923.

On east Chesapeake Avenue, both the property of Charles E. Fendall, who grew prize strawberries commercially, and that of the two-story brick Towson school house of 1873, were demolished by 1972, and are now part of the parking lot of the public library. The library itself occupies a tract which includes the former property of William H. Ruby, editor of the *Maryland Journal*, a Towson newspaper with strong Southern (and Democratic) leanings published between 1865 and 1905. The newspaper's offices, according to the 1898 map, were on the site of the present-day Maryland National Bank branch. The bank, a stone pillbox, was built in 1926 by Towson contractor William H. Sands. Its design may be blamed on John Ahlers of the Baltimore firm of C. Norbury Mackenzie III; he was also responsible for designing the Towson Theater in 1927.

The 1898 map shows the property of the clerk of the Circuit Court, William Moore Isaac, on the west side of York Road, in the 200 block. His house, called *The Beeches*, was subsequently lived in by his son-in-law, Edward B. Passano. It later became the first Towson YMCA building. It had been built by Dr. William Bode in the late 1860s; he used it and a stone building closer to York Road for his Hydropathic Institute, a water cure establishment.

Picture No. 21

Bendix moved from Baltimore to Towson in March 1941. Since 1983 the company has been part of the Allied Corporation, with the Signal Aerospace Company on Joppa Road and the Environmental Division (formerly known as Bendix-Frieze) on Taylor Avenue.

Picture No. 22

The Ward Machinery Company started in 1962 out of William F. Ward's garage on Kurtz Avenue, Lutherville. By 1964 the company was in larger quarters on Falls Road, and by 1969 had made the journey to its present plant site at 10615 Beaver Dam Road, Cockeysville.

Picture No. 25

The Boordy tract, owned in 1798 by James Gittings, was noted for the quality of its timothy hay. Mr. Wagner, Boordy's founder, actually began winemaking in 1938; commercial production began in 1945.

Picture No. 38

The figures surrounding this tragedy are astonishing: 507 firefighters, 135 pieces of fire equipment, 509 county police, 185 state police, 60 Amtrak police, 200 Red Cross workers and hundreds of volunteers, and 619 Chase residents were involved at one time or another. Terry Turchin, a member of the Baltimore Radio Amateur Television Society (BRATS) and the Baltimore Amateur Radio Club (BARC), and some 60 ham radio operators played a crucial role, augmenting or replacing local police and fire communicating systems when they could not perform (*Sun*, July 30, 1988, 8D). A positive result of the disaster was the significant upgrading of the Baltimore County Police and Fire departments' radio transmitting systems, including the installation of very tall and very noticeable relay towers around the county, so that for the first time police or fire department officials on site could talk directly to *both* departmental headquarters, as well as to other field units of both services.

Picture No. 39

The Dundalk Marine Terminal absorbed the site of Harbor Field, a soggy landfill-made airport which opened in 1941 and closed after the end of World War II.

Picture No. 86

At the age of 95 in 1938, E. Scott Dance was one of three ex-Confederate States Army veterans from Maryland hale enough to make the seventy-fifty anniversary encampment of the survivors of the battle of Gettysburg.

Picture No. 90

Mr. Miller rented the basement of Ellis Finkelstein's store on York Road for a billiards hall. Later, for some fifteen years in the 1950s and 1960s Morton Chideckel ran his Towson Billiards Academy in the same place.

Picture No. 123

The *official* Maryland State Fair at Timonium dates from an act of the Maryland Legislature in 1937. Before that, there were various agricultural fairs dating from early in the nineteenth-century. We are told, for instance, of a plowing match in 1841 on the grounds of Robert Ramsey, opposite the Govans Hotel. The Govans Hotel is still there, having been called at various times Lewis Ritter's, and Eli G. Ulery's; it is now Epiphany House, at the intersection of York Road and Bellona Avenue. Other fairs took place near the Mt. Clare mansion in west Baltimore, and on Charles Street at Twenty-seventh Street.

By 1866 John Merryman of *Hayfields* had started the Maryland State Agricultural Society which met at Pimlico, though only irregularly and not every year. A major fair was held in Ridgely's Woods in Lutherville, September 5, 1878, attracting some five thousand people and was, for all intents, a state fair.

That same year Dickinson Gorsuch, Samuel Brady, William B. Sands, and Col. Benjamin Taylor (of *Mt. Peru* in Bradshaw) started the Agricultural Society of Baltimore County, and had a fairground laid out in Timonium in the summer of 1879. In 1881 there were rival fairs being held at Pimlico and Timonium. In 1890, the State Fair doubled up with the Harford County Fair at Bel Air; that year the management of the State fair leased the permanent grounds at Pimlico for trotting races (see picture No. 8).

In 1897 the Baltimore County Agricultural Society and the Maryland State fair held a joint program at Timonium. In 1906, the county organization changed its name to "Maryland State Fair and Agricultural Society of Baltimore County, Maryland," and mentioned "horse racing and trials of speed" as one of its objectives (John W. McGrain, *Agricultural History of Baltimore County*. Towson, Maryland, Unpublished Manuscript, 1978). From 1893 to 1913 another fair opened a week after Timonium at Prospect Park on Eastern Avenue near Back River.

Picture No. 191

By July 1988, the three new stops of Milford Mill, Old Court, and Owings Mills were adding eight thousand new riders daily to the subway's ridership, contributing 15 percent of the subway's revenues. The trip from Owings Mills to Charles Center took about forty minutes. A survey taken in December 1987 showed that 60 percent of the riders were between thirty-five and forty-five years old, 55 percent were male, and 80 percent used park and ride facilities. Fears that the subway would import more inner city crime to the suburbs were said to be unproven, according to Captain Allan Webster of the Garrison Police precinct. (*Owings Mills Times*, July 21, 1988.)

Picture No. 193

The Loyola Federal Savings and Loan Building on West Pennsylvania Avenue, started in 1961, was open by November 1963.

Picture No. 215

Liberty was the third of Baltimore City's great dam projects. The first was Loch Raven (begun 1874, completed 1881), with enhancements in 1914 and 1922; the second, in 1933, was Prettyboy (near Paper Mills, now called Hoffmanville. See map, picture no. 1, page 19).

Picture No. 317

Oscar Grimes was from Catonsville.

Picture No. 324

Chief Lally was appointed by Governor Spiro T. Agnew to head the state police in 1966.

Picture No. 359

Vauxhall had belonged to Charles Jessop (d. 1828).

Picture No. 364

John McGrain, in his unpublished manuscript on the county's

agricultural history, *op cit*, quotes Charles Gilbert, overseer of the Marye farm near Franklinville.

> *The hay was hauled up into the hay mow for storage by a rope pulled by horses. The hay mow (ed. note:* mow prounced like cow*) was called a hay rick over towards Towson. Farm boys would be tempted to slide down hay stacks or the piles in the hay rick, but they got spanked if they did, because their fun wore a trough in the hay which caused it to get wet and rot. Another farm building, the barrack, was the storage place for wheat before it was "thrashed." (ed. note: barracks also stored hay).*

Picture No. 216

The Rouse Company, creators of Harbor Place and Columbia, have built Owings Mills's Town Center, a mall, residential communities, and office structures. McDonogh School is participating in the development of part of its land as Owings Mills's Corporate Center.

Picture No. 377

McGrain, *op cit*, says:

> *The wheeled thresher machines were usually pulled by eight-horse teams to the site of employment, and some ingenious farmers had hitched the great fly wheel on the engine to power the wheels—making a sort of automotive vehicle. In the late 1870s, thresher engine manufacturers developed a train of iron gears to make their machines self moving, thus eliminating four to six horses. One pair of horses was still needed to steer the engine and to prevent frightening other teams on the road. Finally, in 1881, it was possible to buy thresher machines that were both self-moving and steerable, leaving the farmer free to do without any horses, unless he kept a pair to prevent stampeding other skittish animals with the sight of a vehicle moved by unnatural power.*

McGrain says later:

> (Senator) *O. E. Weller of Reisterstown, chairman of the State Roads Commission, complained in a letter to the county paper that it was illegal to run engines with cleated wheels on public roads: the law was not being enforced, said Weller, and added, "the threshermen have convinced the farmers that engines will not run on smooth wheels."*

Picture No. 397

In the agricultural writings of the 1880s, alfalfa was referred to as "lucerne." Councilman's was one of the very early silos in the county. The 1907 American edition of the *Encyclopedia Britannica* had this to say about the farm structure:

> *A modern silo is a pit or erection in which green crops are preserved in an undried condition for fodder.*

And:

> *A silo should have a depth of at least fifteen feet, and may be either a pit or a building above ground, provided it is water-tight and as far as possible, air-tight. The crops suitable for ensillage are the ordinary grasses, clovers, lucerne, vetches, oats, rye, and maize. . . .*

Picture No. 408

Charles Lyon Rogers (1827-1907) was the nephew of Edward and Charles Lyon who owned *Wester Ogle*. He began to run his uncles' large farm at an early age; by the time he was thirty he had been given part of the *Wester Ogle* tract, and had built *Forest View* (illustrated in Scharf's *History of Baltimore City and County*, p. 838). The house survives as part of the Ner Israel Rabbinical College on Mt. Wilson Lane, Owings Mills. Rogers may have had one of the first silos in Baltimore County (1883). He raised Holsteins, and, with Charles K. Harrison, founded the Pikesville Dairy Company which had an outlet on Argyle Street in Baltimore. The milk was moved from the farm to the outlet by the Western Maryland Railroad. Part of Rogers' estate was leased to the railroad for the Greenwood Amusement Park which flourished for ten years until 1885; the more popular Pen-Mar, built in 1878, took away its trade.

Picture No. 456

Mrs. Wright had bought the hotel in 1912 for $45,000 from the Glenwood Springs Company, the owners since 1901. She sold the land and the ruins to Mrs. Eva Roberts Stotesbury of Philadelphia in 1913. In 1917, a $1 million mansion was erected for Louise Cromwell, her daughter by her first husband, and Louise's husband, Walter B. Brooks, Jr., president of the Canton Company (among several), the son of the owner of *Brightside*. Mrs. Brooks' second husband was Maj. Gen. Douglas MacArthur, then commandant of Ft. Meade, who renamed the house *Rainbow Hill*, after his famed World War I Rainbow Division. Mrs. Brooks' third husband was the actor Lionel Atwill. The Atwills sold the ninety-acre estate to the president of Crown Central Petroleum, Henry Rosenberg and his wife, Ruth Blaustein Rosenberg, in 1940. Sold after Mr. Rosenberg's death, the estate and its thirty-three-room mansion has been used since 1964 by the Baptist Home of Maryland, Incorporated, as a refuge for elderly Baptists.

Picture No. 503

In the mid nineteenth-century *Stone Hall* was owned by Alfred J. Gent. The *Baltimore County Union*, June 6, 1874, reported at length on a visit of the Gunpowder Agricultural Club to the estate. After a tour of the farm and its holdings, followed by supper in the house, papers were read by members, including one entitled "Management of Manure" by Joshua M. Gorsuch. This dealt with the importance of the surface spreading of applications of liquid manure, widely used in Europe but neglected in America.

Picture No. 510

By 1823 the Maryland Agricultural Society was meeting at the estate, admiring Colonel Bosley's Indian corn. Under John Merryman's stewardship, and that of his successors, the farm became famous for breeding Herefords.

ADVERTISEMENTS.
YORK ROAD RAILWAY.
CHANGE OF TIME TABLE.
ON AND AFTER OCT. 9, 1883,
eave Baltimore and Holliday streets as follows:
BALTIMORE TO WAVERLY.
Every 15 minutes from 6.30 A. M. to 8.30 P. M.
t 9.00, 9.30, 10.00, 10.30 and 11.30 P. M.
E. H. LACHENMAYER,
MARBLE WORKS,
FREDERICK ROAD,
OPPOSITE LOUDON PARK CEMETERY.
Address:—Carroll, Md.
To Let,
A SMALL HOUSE, with a vegetable garden of nearly an acre attached, situated on the Hillen road, near Towson-town. Rent $5 per month. Inquire of
JOHN E. OWENS,
Aigburth Vale.
Aug. 23.—3t
Dr. William Bode's
HYDROPATHIC INSTITUTE,
FOR the cure of disease by the exclusive application of water, air, diet, exercise and rest. Boarders taken.
Aug. 23.—tf
Notice.
A NUMBER OF HANDCUFFS belonging to Baltimore county, are in the possession of the former Deputy Sheriffs. I hereby respectfully request them to return them to the Warden of the Prison, or otherwise pay the price of the same.
JOSEPH WALKER,
Sheriff of Baltimore county.
Aug. 23.—3t
Immaculate Conception
Cemetery
Towson, Md.
Inspection Invited
Be Prepared—Purchase
Your Lot Now!
Perpetual Care—Terms If
Desired
Office: No. 1 Reckord Bldg.,
Phone: Towson 954.
Change of Management,
Complete Renovation,
Extensive Additions,
Sanitary Surroundings,
Cuisine Unexcelled,
Bar supplied with Established
Brands of Wines, Liquors, Beers,
Comfort of Guests,
Partially embrace the inducements offered to the traveling public to accept the hospitality of
THE CENTRAL HOTEL,
LEE J. HOBBS, Proprietor.
REISTERSTOWN, MD.
Extensive Stabling.
Teams for Hire.
Livery Service.
ADVERTISEMENTS.
Ammenheuser & Praetoriu
BUILDERS OF
Wagons, Carriage
BUGGIES, ETC.
Coach Painting a Specialty
PERSONAL ATTENTION GIVEN TO
HORSE SHOEING
Blacksmithing of all Kinds.
Frederick Avenue, CATONSVILLE, MD.
THE YOUNG FOLKS OF
St. Stanislaus' Church, Alberton, Md.
PRESENT
Legacy Hunters" a Play in three acts
AT THE COMMUNITY HALL
SUNDAY, DEC. 22, 1929 2.30 P. M.
Proceeds to be given over to the removal of Church det
Adults Ticket 15c
NEW
Harvest Home Park
The Delightful Suburban Family Resort.
Wilkens and Beachfield Avenue
BALTIMORE, MD.
30 ACRES OF GROUNDS,
Beautifully Illuminated by 500 Electric Ligh
MUSIC AND DANCING PAVILION.
LARGE AND COMMODIUS HOTEL AND RESTAURANT.
Cusine Unsurpassed. American and European Plan.
FERDINAND GOEBEL, Proprieto
WILKENS AND BEACHFIELD AVENUES.
C. & P. Phone, Gilmor 283 K.
KEEP COOL! DON'T WORRY!!
If the Weather Man turns on the Heat, checkmate him by going to
GEORGE F. NAYLOR'S
ICE CREAM PARLORS,
(Opposite Central Hotel)
REISTERSTOWN, MD.
and partake of his unrivaled Ice Cream, prepared with all the favorite flavors.
Orders for
FESTIVALS AND PARTIES
promptly filled at short notice.
Ice furnished in large or small quantities

KLEIN'S
[SH]ORE LINE PARK,
Westport Md.

HARRY KLEIN, Proprietor.

[F]REE VAUDEVILLE
AFTERNOON AND NIGHT.

[SA]NDWICHES OF ALL KINDS.

[ME]ALS AT POPULAR PRICES.

[J]OHN TYRIE,
[St]eam Marble Works
Cockeysville, Md.

ALL KINDS OF
[M]ARBLE AND GRANITE
[M]ONUMENTS
A SPECIALTY.

[All] orders in other Classes of Stone Work [prom]ptly filled.

James D. Slade,
UNDERTAKER,
UNIONVILLE, BALTIMORE CO., MD.,
Old Manor Road, 15 miles from Batimore city.

KEEPS constantly on hand a large assortment of material for making COFFINS, such as Mahogany, Walnut, Cherry and Poplar. Silver Plate and Engraving, if required.

Coffins made at the shortest notice, and finished in as good style as can be done elsewhere.

Jan. 24.—6m

Dr. J. F. Ensor

HAVING located at RANDALLSTOWN, BALTIMORE COUNTY, Md,, offers his professional services to the public.

Reference, for qualifications, &c.—Prof. N. R. Smith, Baltimore.

Aug. 9.—tf

Negro Farm Hand for Sale.

AT a very low price—21 years old, 2½ years to serve, as good, strong and healthy a farm hand as any in the county. Will be sold a great bargain to any one living at some distance from this place. Apply at this office.

Aug. 2.—1t 1860

PLASTERING

First class work; all jobs given prompt attention; reasonable rates. HERMAN WILHELM, Beckleysville, Hampstead P. O. 4-2-4t

---

Lutherville Female Seminary.

THIS Institution will re-open Monday, September 1st. Staff of teachers able and experienced, course of instruction thorough, accommodations ample, situation healthy and accessible from all directions by railroad.

Annual expense for Boarding and Tuition in all English branches and Latin, $150; half session of five months, $75. For circulars or further information, address

REV. B. SADTLER, A. M., Principal,
Lutherville, Baltimore county Md.

Aug. 2.—4t

MACHINE SHOP,
DAVISVILLE, BALTIMORE COUNTY, MD.

THE proprietor of this establishment is prepared to manufacture all kinds of AGRICULTURAL IMPLEMENTS, including Threshing Machines and PLOWS of the most approved patterns. He is prepared to manufacture THE PELTON IMPROVED POWER, to run with strap or rod. Also, Plows of the improved Woodcock, Wiley, and Atwood patterns.

CASTINGS kept constantly on hand at wholesale and retail.

All kinds of REPAIRING done at the shortest notice.

Apply to EVAN DAVIS, Butler Post Office, Baltimore county, Md. EVAN DAVIS.

July 21, 1860.—1y

Mules. Mules.

I OFFER for sale, at the farm of John O. Price, near Cockeysville, FIFTY LARGE FINE KENTUCKY MULES.

Aug. 16.—3t J. A. J. LEE.

[C]ATONSVILLE RAILWAY

Cars Leave Baltimore, each hour, from 6 A. M. to [8] P. M., and at 11.30 P. M. On Sundays at 8 A. M. to 10 P. M.

[L]eave Catonsville, each hour, from 6 A. M. to 8 P. M., [an]d 10 P. M. On Sundays, 8 A. M. to 10 P. M.

[To] and from Loudon Park, Mount Olivet, Irvington, Saint Agnes Hospital and Cathedral Cemetery, Every Half Hour from 2 to 6 P. M., Daily.

JOHN C. HOLLAND, President.

THE OLD CORNER STORE,
C. F. FUSTING, Proprietor.

Corner Frederick and Ingleside Avenues,

Will be pleased to have his friends and patrons call and inspect his large and varied assortment of

Toys, Skates, Breech & Muzzle Loading Guns,

Pocket and Table Cutlery, and Christmas Goods Generally.

IN ADDITION TO HIS USUAL LARGE STOCK OF

Groceries, Hardware, Queensware, Boots and Shoes,

HATS, CAPS AND NOTIONS BEFORE BUYING.

If you want good Cakes for the Holidays, use the Best Flour, B. Select or Volunteer, and Pure New Crop New Orleans Molasses, together with Strictly Pure Spices, and you won't fail to have a Merry Christmas for the want of good Cake.

"...or they tried to beat the Volunteer, but they couldn't do it you know."

ROUTSON HOUSE,
[Ma]in Street, near Bond Ave., REISTERSTOWN.

A. J. ROUTSON Proprietor.

[Hou]se recently refitted and refurnished, the table always supplied with the best in the market, and the bar stocked with choicest

LIQUORS, WINES, ALE, BEER, CIGARS, Etc., Etc.

[A]MPLE STABLING ATTACHED.
CHARGES MODERATE.

Try Sherwood Horse and Cattle Powders.

Cockeysville, Md., near Depot.

MANUFACTURERS AND DEALERS IN FAMILY MEDICINES. MERCHANTS CAN BE Supplied from Wagon, free of Freight or Breakage. We invite those wishing Drugs in our line to call, as we feel assured we can make it to their interest to purchase from us. Prescriptions carefully compounded at all hours.

May 14-1y.

BIBLIOGRAPHY

BOOKS, GENERAL AND LOCAL

Baltimore and Ohio Transportation Museum. Baltimore: Baltimore and Ohio Railroad, ca. 1960.

Bicentennial Souvenir Program June 20, 1976, Boring, Maryland. Fowblesburg, Md.: Boring Volunteer Fire Company and Farmers and Merchants Bank, 1976.

Bickell, Fran. *A Historical Account of White Marsh, Baltimore County, Maryland.* [White Marsh, Md.]; Privately printed, 1974.

Bedini, Silvio A. *The Life of Benjamin Banneker.* New York: Scribners, 1972.

Bromley, George W. *Atlas of Baltimore County, Maryland, From Actual Surveys and Official Plats*. Philadelphia: G. W. Bromley, 1915.

Bromley, George W. *Atlas of Baltimore County, Maryland, From Actual Surveys and Official Plats*. Philadelphia: G. W. Bromley, 1898.

Brooks, Neal A. and Rockel, Eric G. *A History of Baltimore County*. Towson: Friends of the Towson Library, 1979.

Burgess, Hugh F. Jr. and Smoot, Robert C. III. *McDonogh School: An Interpretive Chronology*. McDonogh, Md.: McDonogh School, 1973.

Cadwalader, Mary H. *A Short History of Saint John's Episcopal Church of Baltimore and Harford Counties.* Kingsville, Md.: Privately printed, 1967.

Celebration in God's Grace. Long Green, Md.: St. John's Lutheran Church of Blenheim, 1974.

Centennial Celebration Services for St. Stephen African Methodist Episcopal Church. Essex, Md.: St. Stephen AME Church, 1978.

Clemens, S. B. and Clemens, C. E. *From Marble Hill to Maryland Line: An Informal History of Northern Baltimore County*. Monkton, Md.: Privately printed, 1976.

Crewe, Amy C. *No Backward Step Was Taken: Highlights in the History of the Public Elementary Schools of Baltimore County*. Towson, Md.: Teachers Association of Baltimore County, 1949.

Directory, Baltimore, Carroll, and Harford Counties. Baltimore: J. Fred Lewis, 1879.

Dorsey, John, and Dilts, James D. *A Guide to Baltimore Architecture*. Cambridge: Tidewater Publishers, 1973.

Dundalk, Then and Now, 1894-1980. Dundalk, Md.: Dundalk-Patapsco Neck Historical Society, 1980.

Farrell, Michael R. *Who Made All Our Streetcars Go? The Story of Rail Transit in Baltimore*. Baltimore: NRHS Publications, 1973.

Feasibility Study Bloede Dam. Towson, Md.: Century Engineering, 1980.

Forbush, Bliss, and Forbush, Byron. *Gatehouse: The Evolution of the Sheppard and Enoch Pratt Hospital, 1853-1986*. Baltimore: The Sheppard and Enoch Pratt Hospital, 1986.

Foxworth, Thomas G. *The Speed Seekers*. New York: Doubleday & Co., 1974.

Frank, Beryl. *A Pictorial History of Pikesville, Maryland.* Towson, Md.: Baltimore County Public Library, 1982.

Gazetteer of Maryland. Baltimore: Johns Hopkins University Press, 1941.

Goodwin, Louise Bland. *Franklin's Century of Progress 1878-1978*. Reisterstown, Md.: Franklin Senior High School, 1978.

Hahn, George, and Behm, Carl. *Towson: A Pictorial History of a Maryland Town*. Norfolk, Va.: Donning Co., 1978.

Haile, Elmer R., and Wollon, James T. *Historic Long Green Valley*. Long Green, Md.: Historic Long Green Valley, 1981.

Hastings, Lynne Dakin. *A Guidebook to Hampton National Historic Site*. Towson, Md.: Historic Hampton, 1986.

The History of Lansdowne. Lansdowne, Md.: Privately printed, 1987.

History of the Belair Road. Baltimore: Perry Hall, Md.: Belair Road Improvement Association, 1925.

Hollifield, William. *Difficulties Made Easy: History of the Turnpikes of Baltimore City and County*. Cockeysville, Md.: Baltimore County Historical Society, 1978.

Hopkins, G. M. *Atlas of Baltimore County, Maryland*. Philadelphia: Hopkins, 1877.

Jenkins, Mary Eben. *The First Hundred Years: Maryland State Grange 1874-1974*. n. p.: Maryland State Grange, 1974.

Keidel, George C. *Early Catonsville and the Caton Family*. Baltimore: J. H. Furst Company, 1944.

Lansdowne Volunteer Fire Association, #1 Inc., 75th Anniversary: 1902-1977. Lansdowne, Md.: Lansdowne Volunteer Fire Association, 1977.

The Limestone Valley. Timonium, Md.: Heritage

Committee of the Greater Timonium American Bicentennial Committee, 1976.
Martinak, George. *A Short History of Essex and Middle River.* Essex, Md.: Privately printed, 1963.
Maryland Business Almanac. Baltimore: Baltimore Sun Co., 1987.
McCauley, Lois B. *Maryland Historical Prints, 1752 to 1889.* Baltimore: Maryland Historical Society, 1975.
McGrain, John W. *From Pig Iron to Cotton Duck: A History of Manufacturing Villages in Baltimore County,* vol. 1. Towson, Md.: Baltimore County Public Library, 1985.
———. *From Pig Iron to Cotton Duck: A History of Manufacturing Villages in Baltimore County,* vol. 2. Towson, Md.: Baltimore County Public Library, forthcoming.
———. *Grist Mills in Baltimore County, Maryland.* Towson, Md.: Baltimore County Public Library, 1980.
———. *Oella: Its Thread of History.* Oella, Md.: Oella Community Improvement Association, 1976.
McIntosh, J. Rieman. *A History of the Elkridge Fox Hunting Club; The Elkridge Hounds; The Elkridge-Harford Hunt Club, 1878-1978.* Monkton, Md.: Privately printed, 1978.
Marks, Lilian Bayly. *Reister's Desire.* Baltimore: Garamond-Pridemark Press, 1975.
One Hundredth Anniversary 1849-1949. Blenheim, Md.: St. John's Evangelical Lutheran Church of Blenheim, Maryland, 1949.
Pearce, Anne, and Cockey, J. H. *Saint James' Episcopal Church: A History.* Monkton, Md.: St. James' Church, ca. 1980.
Perry Hall: Reflections From the Past. Perry Hall, Md.: Perry Hall Improvement Association, 1979.
Perry Hall So Called Since 1775. Perry Hall, Md.: Perry Hall Improvement Association, 1970.
Phillips, Thomas L. *Orange Grove in 1900: A Maryland Treasure Chest of History.* Washington, D. C.: Privately printed, 1971.
Pollack, Carol. *Reisterstown.* Owings Mills, Md.: Franz Printing Company, 1986.
Pollack, Carol, ed. *Reisterstown 1974.* Reisterstown, Md.: Columbia Office Services, 1974.
Prospectus of the Lutherville Female Seminary near Baltimore City, Maryland. Baltimore: F. A. Hanzsche, 1855.
Reflections: Sparrows Point, Md. 1887-1975. Dundalk, Md.: Dundalk-Patapsco Neck Historical Society, 1983.
Seitz, May A. *The History of the Hoffman Paper Mills in Maryland.* Towson, Md.: Privately printed, 1946.
Scharf, J. Thomas. *History of Baltimore City and County.* Philadelphia: L. H. Everts, 1881.
Siciliano, Sam. *The Preakness: Middle Jewel of the Triple Crown.* Baltimore Maryland Jockey Club, 1980.
Smith, Kingsley. *Towson Under God; a Religious History of the Baltimore County Seat.* Towson, Md., Baltimore County Public Library, 1976.
Step Back into History: Come Visit Ballestone Manor House. Essex, Md.: The Heritage Society Museum, and Essex-Middle River Chamber of Commerce, ca. 1987.
Thomas, Dawn F. *The Greenspring Valley, Its History and Heritage.* Baltimore: Maryland Historical Society, 1978.
Toomey, Daniel Carroll. *A History of Relay Maryland and the Thomas Viaduct.* 2d ed. Baltimore: Toomey Press, 1984.
Von Paris Moving and Storage 90th Anniversary 1892-1987. Timonium, Md.: privately printed, 1987.
Walking Tour of the Dundalk National Historic District. Dundalk, Md.: Greater Dundalk Chamber of Commerce, n.d.
Warren, Mame, and Warren, Marion E. *Maryland Time Exposures 1840-1940.* Baltimore: Johns Hopkins University Press, 1984.
Weaver, Betsy, and Frederick, Gary E. *A Centennial History of the Baltimore County Fire Service.* Towson, Md.: Baltimore County Fire Service Committee, 1982.
Williams, Harold A. *A History of the Eudowood Sanitarium 1894-1964.* Baltimore: Privately printed, ca. 1965.
Woodlawn History Committee. *Woodlawn, Franklintown, and Hebbville.* Woodlawn, Md.: Woodlawn Recreation and Parks Council, 1977.

NEWSPAPERS

Parkville Centennial Reporter 1874-1974, Supplement to *Parkville Reporter,* May 1974.
Power Pictorial and *Baltimore Gas and Electric Company News,* 1923-1930.

Microfilmed sets of the Baltimore *Sun, American, News American, Argus, Baltimore County Advocate, Maryland Journal,* the *Union,* the *Jeffersonian,* and *Baltimore County Democrat.*

YEARBOOKS

High school annuals 1914-1986 from Catonsville, Reisterstown, Patapsco, Chesapeake, and Towson High Schools.

ARTICLES

Clemens, Andrew C. "The Oread Republic" *History Trails* 2, no. 2 (1976-1977), pp. 8-10.
Clemens, Shirley C. "The Water Mills in Monkton," *History Trails* 12, no. 2 (1977-1978), pp. 5-8.
Conklin, Elizabeth. "Is Dundalk Ship Shape? Old Town Plan May Have Caused Myth."*Dundalk Eagle,* 25 February 1898, p. 8.
Davis, Erick F. "Saint Timothy's Hall," *History Trails* 2, no. 3 (1977) pp. 11-15.
Flynn, Ramsey, and Kaye, Stephen. "On the Wrong Track," *Baltimore Magazine* 80, no. 11 (1987), pp. 76-92.
Frank, Beryl. "Dr. James Smith— Land owner in Pikesville," *History Trails,* 15, no. 3 (1981), pp. 8-12.
Haile, Amelia R. Kolk. "Reckord, Maryland," *History Trails* 9, no. 3 (1975), pp. 13-20.
Lehnert, Marie. "The Band Plays On: 100-Year-Old Band Outlasts the Town That Gave its Name," *Sunday Sun* (Howard County Edition) Howard Living section, January 6, 1980, p. 14.
McGrain, John W., Jr. "A Marylander Visits Sir Walter Scott," *History Trails* 6, no. 2 (1971-1972), pp. 5-8.
Parsons, Richard. "A 19th Century Social Service," *History Trails* 19, no. 3, 1985, pp. 8-12.
Parsons, Richard. "Almshouse Revisited, Part 1," *History Trails,* 21, no. 2, (1986-1987), pp. 5-8.
Parsons, Richard. "Almshouse Revisited, Part 2" *History Trails* 21, no. 3 (1987), pp. 9-10.
"Power Plant Inside of a Dam on the Patapsco River," *Electrical World* 1, no. 5 (ca. 1907) pp. 207-210.

MAPS

J. C. Sidney and P. J. Browne, *Map of the City and County of Baltimore, Maryland From Original Surveys* Baltimore, 1850.
Taylor, Robert. *Map of the City and County of Baltimore From Actual Surveys.* Baltimore, 1857.

PUBLIC DOCUMENTS

Baltimore County Courthouse, Towson, Md. Land Records, Tax Ledgers, Orphans Court Records, Incorporation Records, Plats. County Courts Building, Towson, Md.
Landmarks Preservation Commission Nomination Forms.
Baltimore County Police Department Annual Reports 1951-1980.
Board of Education of Baltimore County, Annual Reports, 1852-1950.

UNPUBLISHED SOURCES

Deale, Robert E., Jr., "History of the Baltimore County Police Department, 1874-1985." M.A. thesis, University of Maryland, 1987.
McGrain, John. "Agricultural History of Baltimore County." Cockeysville, Baltimore County Historical Society, 1978.

EPHEMERA

Scrapbooks, albums, files, at the Historical Association of Dundalk and Patapsco Neck, the Historical Society of Essex and Middle River, the Reisterstown Room of the Reisterstown Branch, Baltimore County Public Library (Louise Bland Goodwin Collection), and the Catonsville Room of the Catonsville Branch, Baltimore County Public Library.

Picture Credits

The numbers listed are those assigned to the pictures and are *not* page numbers.

AAI Corporation—19.
American Bank Stationery Co.—490.
Judge William S. Baldwin—227.
Baltimore Bicycling Club—29.
Baltimore County Council—240, 246, 325.
Baltimore County Chamber of Commerce—4, 10, 11, 13, 14, 15, 18, 21, 22, 26, 30, 31, 32, 34, 37, 40, 41, 42.
Baltimore County Department of Recreation and Parks—33, 133, 147, 148, 153.
Baltimore County Fire Department—35, 292, 328.
Baltimore County Historical Society—112, 113, 114, 166, 252, 259, 263, 518.
Baltimore County Police Department—38, 219, 222, 223, 294, 317, 323, 324, 327.
Baltimore County Public Library—43, 51, 71, 109, 141, 174, 177, 199, 210, 242, 243, 244, 245, 289, 331, 338, 244, 351, 360, 365, 375, 378, 389, 400, 409, 412, 430, 452, 454, 486, 503, 507, 510, 512, 514, 515, 516, 519, 521, 522, 526, 535, 537, 538, 539, 540.
Baltimore County Public Library—George Blakeslee collection—46, 126, 135, 187, 215, 232, 291, 342, 445, 446, 475, 476, 481.
Baltimore County Public Library—Jacques Kelly collection—73, 96, 103, 117, 118, 123, 124, 129, 192, 194, 195, 196, 197, 198, 272, 293, 439, 450, 483, 544, 545.
Baltimore County Public Library—William C. Kenney collection—47, 76, 90, 101, 102, 168, 171, 178, 181, 182, 214, 257, 278, 298, 299, 300, 314, 329, 330, 332, 339, 341, 359, 361, 362, 363, 368, 370, 371, 394, 461, 464, 504.
Baltimore County Public Library—Wilmina Sydnor (Richard Childress collection)—119, 125, 152.
Baltimore County Public Library—C. W. E. Treadwell collection—168, 175, 364, 392, 502.
Baltimore County Public Library—Catonsville Branch—5, 6, 56, 59, 65, 146, 173, 200, 208, 217, 249, 261, 306, 307, 308, 318, 355, 381, 384, 385, 421, 429, 451, 508, 533, 542, 547, back cover.
Baltimore County Public Library—North Point Branch—201, 202.
Baltimore County Public Library—Reisterstown Branch—74, 78, 79, 80, 83, 127, 159, 248, 256, 265, 315, 333, 390, 397, 438, 449, 453, 457, 458, 460.
Baltimore County Public Library—Towson Branch—1, 7, 8, 9.
Baltimore County Public Schools—Division of Staff and Community Relations—150, 273, 274, 275.
Baltimore Museum of Art—374, 414, 541.
Baltimore Museum of Industry—473.
Baltimore Sun Papers—424.
Honorable Helen Delich Bentley—247.
Mrs. Lida May Watkins Berry—49, 77, 447.
Lydia A. Berry—60, 100, 373, 399, 525.
Boordy Vineyards—25.
Gerry L. Brewster—120, 322.
Carsten S. Brinkmann—50, 84, 164, 165, 170, 386, 455, 509.
Neal A. Brooks—23, 319.
Vernon Bush—111.
Mrs. Benjamin H. Bussey—211.
Mrs. Katherine Held Buxton—75, 176, 440.
Bruce Campbell—269.
Mrs. Roberta Carter—269.
Mrs. Mildred S. Cassen—462.
Catonsville Times—66, 95, 136, 137, 139, 140, 142, 144, 145, 151, 155, 157, 276, 277, 280.
Shearman Dance—86, 212, 305, 376, 413.
Miss Marie Duncan—436.
Dundalk-Patapsco Neck Historical Society—61, 64, 67, 91, 110, 130, 131, 160, 185, 188, 189, 190, 229, 230, 301, 366, 367, 395, 396, 484, 488.
Mrs. Margaret East—81, 367.
Essex Community College—12, 511.
Franklin Square Hospital—548.
Mrs. Marie Fulker—264.
General Instrument Corporation, Worldwide Wagering Systems Division—493.
Georgetown University—Dept. of Special Collections—172, 281, 282, 283, 284, 285, 286, 287, 346, 347, 348.
Mrs. Edna Gorfine—442.
Grumman Aerospace Corp.—20.
Mrs. Amelia L. Kolk Haile—425.
Robert Bruce Hamilton, Jr.—70.
Louis Hergenrather--441.
Heritage Society of Essex and Middle River—98, 99, 205, 218, 233, 236, 237, 238, 262, 302, 309, 316, 352, 431, 435, 437, 448, 466, 468, 471, 477,478, 479,

480, 482, 494.
Mrs. C. S. Hewitt—489.
William Hollifield—204.
Mrs. Douglas Horstman—87, 340.
A. Michael Isekoff—203.
Mrs. Robert W. Johnson—411.
Mrs. John Kade—88, 408, 444.
Gary Kadolph—28, 546.
Mrs. Dale Kief—89, 505, 513.
Jacques Kelly—68, 69, 72, 97, 104, 105, 106, 107, 115, 121, 122, 138, 163, 180, 184, 193, 209, 213, 223, 271, 295, 296, 297, 313, 320, 321, 326, 334, 335, 350, 391, 423, 456, 463, 470, 472, 532, 543, back cover.
Mrs. Thomasine F. Kibbe—226.
Lansdowne Historical Society, Inc.—62, 93, 216, 220, 353, 354.
League of Women Voters of Baltimore County—239.
Legum Chevrolet—493.
James K. Lightner—39.
Lovely Lane Museum/Library—Balto. Conference, United Methodist Historical Society—3.
Robert Lyon—55, 288, 383, 529, 530.
Jay Lyston—108, 279.
Marriott's Hunt Valley Inn—24.
Maryland Marathon, Inc.—154.
Maryland Public Television—235.
Maryland State Archives—162 (Md. G-1477-6590), 206 (Md. G-1477-4826), 207 (Md.-1477-6680), 304 (Md. G-1477-6057), 443 (G-908-158), 467 (A-908-149), 506 (F-908-192).
Maryland State Police—36, 224.
Mass Transit Administration—Maryland Department of Transportation—191.
McCormick and Co.—491.
McCormick Properties—17.
McDonogh School—253, 254, 255.
Norton C. McDonough—85, 517.
John W. McGrain—2, 186, 345, 366, 377, 398, 520, 531.
J. Rieman McIntosh—57, 58, 524, 528.
Marjorie E. Miller—156, 266, 534.
Jeff Morgenstern—420.
Nottingham Properties, Inc.—16, 496.
Honorable Sandra A. O'Connor—241.
James D. Officer—250, 343, 393.
B. E. Von Paris—358, 379, 487.
Patapsco State Park, Maryland Department of Natural Resources—134, 290, 415, 498.
Peale Museum—169, 183, 401, 402, 419.
Peale Museum—Bodine collection—303, 426, 427.
Peale Museum—Brown collection—94, 337, 369.
Peale Museum—Reis collection—53, 382, 388.
Carroll Radebaugh—27.
Judge John E. Raine, Jr. (ret)—270, 465, 469, 485.
Julia Randall—82.
Dorothy Maisel Reis—44, 48, 250, 251, 343, 344, 393
Roland A. Rockel—161.
Francis Roberts—497.
Walter Rubeling—92.
St. Joseph Hospital—549.
St. Stephen's A.M.E. Church—349.
Raymond Carton Seitz—63, 499, 500, 501.
Regina B. Shepherd—336.
Mrs. Samuel M. Shoemaker III—179, 225, 380, 422.
George L. Small—474.
Crompton Smith, Jr.—128.
Social Security Administration—234.
Angie Spicer—45, 132.
Towson Senior High School—149.
Towson Times—143, 434.
Trustees of the *Bunker Hill* Foundation—52, 54.
University of Maryland—Department of Special Collections—158, 231, 268, 310, 311, 312.
Charles L. Wagandt II—416, 417, 418.
M. Cooper Walker—387, 523, 527.
Mrs. Jean S. Walsh—77.
Mrs. Helen Hale Weed—258, 404, 405, 406, 407.
Madeline Weis—432, 439.
Harold Witmyer—536.
A. Leister Zink—267.

Many of the photos from the Baltimore County Public Library Collection were taken by Geoffrey W. Fielding, 1975-1978.

DENTISTRY.

DR. JAMES A. DUNCAN

'AS established himself at the above profession at the residence ıs brother, JOHN D. C. DUNCAN, BUTLER, TIMORE CO., MD., where he is prepared o all all kinds of work connected with his ession, upon the most reasonable terms.
e has received a diploma from the Balti-e College of Dental Surgery, and can give rences to persons who stand high in that 'ession, if required.
(ay 10.—3m

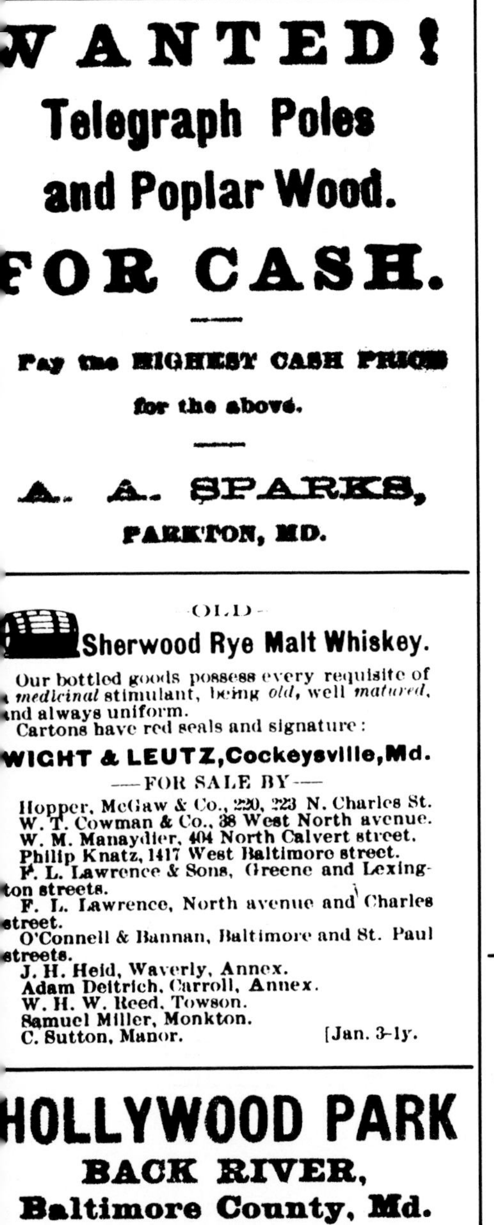

HOLLYWOOD PARK

BACK RIVER,
Baltimore County, Md.

The Most Popular and Delightful Family Resort.

The Cleverest and Most Refined Vaudeville Company to Entertain.

A VERY GOOD

Fish and Fowl Dinner,
(With all the Season's Delicacies)

For 50 Cents.

Dancing from 2.30 to 11.30 P. M., in Electric Pavilion.

JOSEPH GOELLER,
Proprietor.

UNITED RAILWAYS AND ELECTRIC COMPANY.

TOWSON AND CATONSVILLE LINE.

WEEK DAY SCHEDULE.

LEAVE TOWSON FOR CATONSVILLE

Every twelve minutes from 6.00 A. M. to 10.48 P. M., then 11.03, 11.18 P. M.
To Irvington only, 11.26, 11.34, 11.50 P. M.
To Waverly Barn only, 11.52, 12.04, 12.12, 12.27, 12.42 midnight.

PASS CITY HALL FOR CATONSVILLE

Every twelve minutes from 5.30 A. M. to 11.30 P. M., then 11.45, 12.00 midnight.

LEAVE CATONSVILLE FOR TOWSON

Every twelve minutes from 6.01 A. M. to 10.37 P. M., then 10.45, 11.00, 11.15 P. M.
To Waverly (Arlington Avenue) 11.23, 11.31, 11.47 P. M.
To Irvington Barn only, 11.54, 12.06, 12.18, 12.33, 12.48 midnight.

PASS CITY HALL FOR TOWSON

Every twelve minutes from 5.34 A. M. to 11.18 P. M., then 11.30, 11.45, 12.00 midnight.

SUNDAY SCHEDULE.

LEAVE TOWSON FOR CATONSVILLE

Every twelve minutes from 7.00 A. M. to 10.48 P. M., then 11.03, 11.18 P. M.
To Irvington only, 11.24, 11.36, 11.46, 11.56, 12.08
To Waverly Barn only, 12.12, 12.27, 12.42 midnight.

PASS CITY HALL FOR CATONSVILLE

Every twelve minutes from 6.30 A. M. to 11.30 P. M., then 11.45, 12.00 midnight.

LEAVE CATONSVILLE FOR TOWSON

Every twelve minutes from 7.01 A. M. to 10.37 P. M., then 10.45, 11.00, 11.15 P. M.
To Waverly (Arlington Avenue) only, 11.23, 11.30, 11.43, 11.54, 12.06 midnight.
To Irvington Barn only, 12.18, 12.33, 12.48 midnight.

PASS CITY HALL FOR TOWSON

Every twelve minutes from 6.34 A. M. to 11.18 P. M., then 11.30, 11.45, 12.00 midnight.

PRICES OF ADS IN THE BULLETIN

Single Space,	*$1.00 per month*
" "	*5.00 for 6 months*
" "	*10.00 for 12 months*
Half Space	*.50 per month*
" "	*2.50 for 6 months*
" "	*5.00 for 12 months*

ADS GO TO PRESS THIRD THURSDAY OF EACH MONTH

THE THOMAS PRESS
PRINTING

ATTENTION! VOLUNTEERS!

83 Men Wanted.

To form a Company in the 4th Regiment Maryland Volunteers.

THE undersigned have been authorized by Col. Wm. Louis Schley, to raise one Company of volunteers, for service in the 4th Regiment of Maryland Volunteers, called out and authorized by the Governor of Maryland, in his proclamation of the 28th ultimo. A company will be composed as follows: 1 Captain, 2 Lieutenants, 5 Sergeants, 8 Corporals, 2 Musicians, 1 Wagoner, and 64 Privates, and recruits will be clothed and under pay immediately after being sworn into the service. The pay is the same as in the Regular United States Army—Sergeants $17 per month, Privates $13 per month, with rations, clothing, medical attendance, bounty land, extra pay, and a bounty of $100 when discharged. A bill has already passed one branch of Congress allowing recruits one month's pay in advance, and our late Legislature provided for the maintenance of the families of volunteers during their absence.

Now is the time to enlist! The late actions of our Regiments already in the field have caused the patriotism and the bravery of Maryland troops to be properly appreciated and our fuller service is asked. All persons of good health, between the ages of 18 and 45 years, wishing to enlist can apply to the undersigned or to JOHN H. LONGNECKER, at the "American" Office, Towsontown.

CHAS. A. CONNER,
JOHN N. WISNER.

June 14.—tf 1863

R. R. BOARMAN,

ATTORNEY AT LAW,

AND

SOLICITOR IN CHANCERY,
Smedley Row, opposite Court House,
TOWSONTOWN.

WILL promptly attend to all business entrusted to his care.

Jan. 7, 1865.—1y

WOLTERS CARNEY HOTEL

CARNEY, MD.

We desire to call the attention of the general public to our faciliti for **SUPPER BUSINESS**, which are the same as those for noon, th business for latter meal being all we could desire.

If you look for a long, beautiful ride, a call will be appreciated an utmost satisfaction may be had both as to cuisine and prices.

☞ SPECIAL CHICKEN SUPPER, 50 CENTS.

WM. WOLTERS, 8-Mile House.

Take Harford Road Carney Car to its terminal.

INDEX

NAMES AND PLACES

A

AAI Corporation, 30
A & P supermarkets, 186 (Reisterstown), 187 (Essex)
Abbot, Horace, 292
Abbottsford, 279
Acme supermarkets, 187
Ady's Hotel, 279, 296
Agnew, Spiro T. (Vice-President), 16, 102, 190, 191, 298
Agnes (Tropical Storm), 176, 239
Agnus, Felix (General), 54
Agricultural History of Baltimore County (book), 298
Agricultural Society of Baltimore County, 298
Ahlers, John, 297
Aigburth Vale, 23
Aircraft Armaments Industries, 30
Akehurst, Carville, 184
Alberton, 21, 73, 194, 214, 216, 239, 240
Alberton Cornet Band, 53
Albrecht, Elaine, 144
Albrecht, Ron, 95
Alderman, R. Bruce, 191
Allen, William (Colonel), 156
Allen, William H., 132
Allied Corporation, 297
Almony, C. Franklin, 255
Almony, Ephraim, 297
Alpha Theater, 75
Alvida J. (boat), 42
Amann, Michael R., 150
Ambermill, 28
Amburson Hydraulic Construction Company, 269
American Bank Stationery Company, 28, 266
American Bicentennial, 21
American Colonization Society, 156
American Totalisator. *See* General Instrument Corporation, Worldwide Wagering Systems Division
Amoss, William L., 162
Amprey, Walter G., 166
Amrein Brothers, 196
Amtrak, 38, 298
Anderson, Dale (County Executive), 16, 120, 190, 191, 193
Anderson, James C. L., 133
Andrews, G. Clyde, 255
Anne Arundel County, 49, 76, 172, 271
Anneslie, 240
Arbutus, 126, 269, 277, 296
Arbutus PAL Center, 92
Arcadia, 222
Arden, 285
Arlington Presbyterian Church, 209
Armacost, Mr., 125
Armstrong, Ruth, 54
Arnold's Men's and Women's shops, 187
Asbill's Pharmacy, 297
Asbury, Francis (Bishop), 15, 20, 274
Ashland, 152, 271, 280
Ashland Iron Works, 65, 216, 260, 280
Association of Professional Baseball Players, 238
Atwill, Lionel, 299
Avalon Foundation, 20
Avalon Inn, 253
Avalon Iron and Nail Works, 175
Avalon Dam, 19
Azola, Martin P., 235

B

Bachur, Barbara F., 151
Back River, 70, 87, 245, 296, 298
Bacon, Lewis, M., 221
Baker, Greg, 96
Balbirnie, Thomas, 132
Baldwin, Ann Louise, 47
Baldwin, Dorothy, 46
Baldwin, Eleanor Lindsey, 286
Baldwin, Ephraim Francis (architect), 29, 252
Baldwin, H. Streett, 141
Baldwin, Juliet Catherine, 47
Baldwin, Juliet G. S., 47
Baldwin, Summerfield, 46, 241
Baldwin, Mrs. Summerfield. *See* Baldwin, Juliet G. S.
Baldwin (Village), 141
Ball family (Catonsville), 46, 47, 224, 226
Ballestone, 21
Baltimore, Lord, 16
Baltimore Air Terminal of New York, 256
Baltimore Amateur Radio Club (BARC), 298
Baltimore *American,* 54
Baltimore and Delta Railroad, 110
Baltimore and Lehigh Railroad, 110
Baltimore and Ohio Railroad, 15, 103, 108-110, 131-132, 183-184
Baltimore Beltway, 102, 120, 122-123, 216, 285
Baltimore Bicycling Club, 34
Baltimore City Hall, 268
Baltimore City Water Department, 108, 153, 155, 231, 263
Baltimore Company, 214
Baltimore Conference (Methodist), 198
Baltimore County Bank, 114
Baltimore County Bar Association, 133
Baltimore County Board of Library Trustees, 9, 150
Baltimore County Chamber of Commerce, 29
Baltimore County Council, 148, 150-151
Baltimore County Court House, 29, 34, 115, 132, 191, 296
Baltimore County *Democrat,* 234
Baltimore County Dept. of Public Works, 107
Baltimore County Dept. of Recreation & Parks, 21, 39, 97
Baltimore County Fire Department, 37, 94, 138
Baltimore County Health Department, 37
Baltimore County Office Building, 92, 192, 296
Baltimore County Police Department, 139, 190, 298
Baltimore County Public Library, 149-150
Baltimore County Public Works, 107
Baltimore County Recreation and Parks, 21, 36, 97
Baltimore County *Union,* 172, 177, 222, 299
Baltimore Gas and Electric Company, 73, 126. *See also* Consolidated Gas Light and Power Company
Baltimore Harbor Tunnel, 118
Baltimore Hebrew Congregation, 212
Baltimore Highlands Flower Mart, 98
Baltimore Industrial Museum, 260
Baltimore Manufacturing Company, 239
Baltimore Museum of Art, 292
Baltimore Orioles, 55, 94, 190
Baltimore *News Post,* 82
Baltimore Post Office, 275
Baltimore Raceway, 83
Baltimore Radio Amateur Television Society, 298
Baltimore Subway, 119, 298
Baltimore *Sun,* 135, 146, 209, 241, 271
Baltimore Symphony Orchestra, 36, 216
Baltimore Yacht Club, 43
Banks, Daniel, 252
Banneker, Benjamin, 127
Banneker Festival, 90
Banneker High School, 15, 157
Baptist Home of Maryland Inc., 29, 299
Baptist State Mission Board of Maryland, 203
Barnes, Dan, 93
Barrett, Francis, 191
Barrett, Lester L. (Chief Judge), 191
Barry, James M., 148
Barthel, Mrs. Evelyn, 258
Bartlett-Hayward Company, 260
Barton, William, 176
Bartos, (Coach), 96
Baseball Hall of Fame, 238
Battle of North Point, 19, 128, 129
Bauernschmidt, Frederick, 284
Bauernschmidt's Manor, 284
Bauman, Paul I., 159
Baumgart, Norman, 176
Bay Shore Park, 73, 116, 178, 296
Beaman, Dorothy, 9
Bean Creek, 176
Bear Creek, 296
Beatty, James, 108
Beaver Dam, 35, 268
Beaver Dam Road, 29, 200, 297
Beckley, John, 216
Beckleysville, 216
Beeches, 297
Beer, William, 210
Bel Air, 241, 298
Belair Road, 177, 197, 296
Bella Vista, 285
Bellona Powder Works, 108
Beltway. *See* Baltimore Beltway
Ben Franklin store, 187, 245
Bendix Corp., 31, 297
Benjamin Banneker High School. *See* Banneker High School
Benlion, Mrs., 86
Bennett, Benjamin Franklin, 199
Benson, Oregon Randolph, 277
Benson, Thomas B., 156
Benson family, 59
Bentley, Constance, 282
Bentley, Helen Delich (Congresswoman), 146, 151
Bentley, William, 245
Bentley Springs, 245
Benton, Richard, 236
Berliner-Joyce, 256
Bermuda Clipper, 259
Bernard, Simon, 260
Bernie Lee's Penn Hotel, 251
Berrigan, Daniel, 190
Berrigan, Philip F., 190
Beth El, 213
Beth Tfiloh, 213
Bethlehem Steel Corporation, 73, 118, 260-265
Betz, Mrs., 161
Betz, Virginia, 161
Biard, Henri C., 178
Biays, Nellie, 159
Bickford, Roger, 161

Biggs, J., 67
Bird River, 296
Birmingham, Michael J. (County Executive), 120, 191, 255
Bishop, Elias, 277
Bishop, William, 277
Bishop's Inn, 277
Black Rock Baptist Church, 201
Black and Decker, 264
Blackwell, Eliza Caldwell, 221
Blair, Joseph, 66
Blake Margaret D., 159
Blakert, Mike, 93
Blakeslee-Lane Studio, 43, 249, 261, 263
Blazek, Joe, 43, 87
Blenheim (Sweetair), 222
Bloede, Victor G., 269, 285, 293
Bloede Dam, 269
Bloomfield, 162, 229, 230
Bloomhardt, Paul F. (Reverend), 50
Bloomsbury Farm, 55, 229
Blue Mount, 182
Boarman, Robert R., 296
Bode, Dr. William, 297
Bodine, A. Aubrey, 232, 242
Bodner, M., 67
Bohne, David, 250
Bokkelen, Libertus van (Reverend Dr.), 154, 155, 251
Bollman, Wendel, 178
Bonaparte, Charles Joseph, 285
Bonaparte, Jerome, 285
Bonaparte, Napoleon, 260, 285
Bonnie Blink, 29
Boone, A. Gordon, 120, 190
Boone, Dorothy, 120, 173
Boonsboro, 104
Boordy Vineyards, 33, 297
Booth, John Wilkes, 154
Boring, 101, 182
Boring Volunteer Fire Department, 182
Bosley, Aquilla C. T., 64
Bosley, Catherine, 64
Bosley, Charles, 64, 172, 249
Bosley, Clinton, 64
Bosley, Eleanor, 64
Bosley, Elijah, 275
Bosley, Ezekial, 275
Bosley, John E. Hurst, 64
Bosley, Mrs. M. Eliza (Hahn), 64
Bosley, Nicholas Merryman (Colonel), 276, 299
Bosley, William Henry, 64
Bosley (village of), 109
Bosley Building, 234
Bosley's Hotel, 172, 180, 249, 296
Bossle, Francis X., 191
Bowen, Charles, 58
Bowen, George Vinton, 44, 58
Bowen, Henry L., 297
Bowen, Mary G., 58
Bowen, Mrs. George Vinton, 58
Bowen, Rebecca Jemima, 58
Bowie, Oden (Governor), 23
Bowley's Quarters, 45
Bowser, G., 67
Boy Scout Troop 32 A., 50
Bradford, Augustus (Governor), 49
Bradshaw Road, 200
Brady, Samuel, 298
Bragg High School, 15, 157
Bread and Cheese Creek, 128
Brewer, George, 161
Brewer, Linda, 161
Brewer, Mrs., 161
Brewster, Daniel B. (U.S. Senator), 120
Brewster, Gerry L., 80, 190
Brightside, 62, 106
Brinkmann, A. H., 42, 45, 105, 225, 276
Brinkmann, Arnold, 45
Brinkmann, B., 53
Brinkmann, Helmuth, 45
Brinkmann, Walter, 45
Brockmeyer, Danny, 161
Broening, William F. (Mayor), 117, 231
Brooklandville, 49, 56
Brooklandwood, 56, 276
Brooklandwood Dairy, 56
Brooks, Violet, 144
Brooks, Walter B., Jr., 299
Brooks, Walter B., Sr., (Professor), 106, 299
Brotman, Benjamin, 213
Brown, Alex & Sons, building, 296
Brown, Alexander, 276
Brown, Clara, 46
Brown, George, 276
Brown, George S., 49
Brown, Percy, 156
Brown, Robert P., 281
Brown, Terry
Brown vs. Board of Education of Topeka, Kansas, 157
Buchanan, Archibald, 274
Buck, D., 57
Buckel, Rick, 96
Buckmaster, T., 67
Bullet, Eugene de, 159
Bunker Hill Road, 107
Burbank, Randolph, 159
Burgess, Hugh F., Jr., 185
Burke, R., 57
Burns, John, 297
Burnside, 112, 140, 219, 223
Burton, Gail, 92
Bush, Vernon, 76
Buskirk, Jean, 144
Butler, 201
Butler Quarry, 268
Butsch, Louisa Weber, 251
Butsch's Gardens, 251
Butt, William, 245

C

Cadle, Ethel, 161
Caldor store, 226
Calloway, Catherine, 60
Calvary Baptist Church, 268, 296, 297
Calvert family (Lords Baltimore), 194
Calvert Hall College, 122
Camden Station, 177
Camp Chapel, 16
Camp, Joseph, 291
Campbell, Bruce S., 267
Campbell, H. Guy, 255
Campbell, Mrs. H. Guy, 54
Campbell, Harry Tyler, 267, 268
Campbell, Ross, 239
Campbell, Harry T., and Sons Stone Products Company, 54, 121, 255, 268
Campbell Building, 121, 268, 296
Canton Company, 216, 299
Carr, Robert, 176
Carroll, Anna Merryman, 62
Carroll, Charles, of Carrollton, 169, 214, 276
Carroll, Charles, the Barrister, 214, 276
Carroll, Harry Dorsey Gough, 274
Carroll, Henry, 62
Carroll, Henry Hill, 279
Carroll, Mary, 276
Carroll, Miles, Jr., 31
Carroll, Miles, Sr., 31
Carroll, Mrs. William S., 62
Carroll, Perry, 30
Carroll, Thomas, 31
Carroll County, 18, 135, 206, 264, 296
Carroll's store, 31
Carson, Charles L., 209
Carter, Gertrude, 144
Carver High School, 15, 157
Cassen, Samuel P., 255
Casteel, Danny, 96
Castle on the hill, 41
Castle Thunder, 276
Catholic Center of Relay, 209
Catiton, James M., 156
Caton, Richard, 276
Catonsville, 15, 44, 90, 96, 99, 125, 127, 152, 167, 169, 194, 204, 224, 225, 242, 243, 251, 269, 276, 292, 294, 298
Catonsville Branch, Baltimore County Public Library, 276
Catonsville Casino, 55
Catonsville Community college, 26, 168
Catonsville Country Club, 55
Catonsville Garden, 251
Catonsville High School, 55, 159, 165
Catonsville High School orchestra, 53
Catonsville Knights of Columbus Building, 190
Catonsville Middle School, 55
Catonsville Nine, 190
Centennial Grange No. 161, 234
Centerville, 198
Central Hotel, 252
Central Vocational Technical Center, 157
Charles Center, 90, 298
Charlestown (retirement community), 169
Charley Irish's Chevrolet. *See* Legum Chevrolet
Charlton, Richard E., 156
Chase, 38, 271, 298
Chattolanee (hotel and railroad station), 105
Chautauqua, 253
Chesaco Avenue, 175
Chesapeake Aircraft Company, 256
Chesapeake and Potomac Telephone Company, 29, 187
Chesapeake Bay, 38, 296
Chesapeake Bay Bridge, 146
Chesapeake Business Park, 216
Chesapeake Senior High School, 165
Chestnut Grove Presbyterian Church, 15, 201
Chideckel, Morton, 298
Childress, Richard, 80, 83, 97
Chizuk Amuno, 212
Choate, Pearce, 61
Church of the Immaculate Conception, 113, 180
Cinnamon Tree Restaurant, 32
Citizens National Bank, 240
City College, 268
Clayton, Corliss, 236
Cleveland, Mary, 86
Clipper Mill, 271
Cloisters, 279
Cloman, Gwen, 161
Cloman, Mrs., 161
Clynmalira, 18, 272, 279
Cockey's Mill, 214
Cockey's Mill Road, 59
Cockey, Thomas Beale, 55
Cockeysville, 31, 35, 102, 231, 254
Cockeysville Branch, Baltimore County Public Library, 150

Cockeysville Elementary School, 162
Cockeysville National Bank, 255
Codd, R., 66
Coke, Dr. Thomas, 20
Cole, Abraham, Jr., 221
Cole, Lewis R., 221
Cole, Miss Stewart, 247
Cole, William P., Jr. (Judge), 133
Cole, William P., Sr. (Sheriff), 297
Coleman, J. Cameron, 178
Coleman, William C. (Judge), 148
College Manor, 173
Collins, Delores, 144
Colosino, Daniel L., 191
Columbia, 299
Comprehensive Zoning Maps, 192
Conestoga wagon, 183
Confederate Soldiers Home, 36, 129, 132
Conley, Terry, 46
Conrail, 38, 298
Consolidated Gas Light and Power Company, 73, 101 240, 269
Cook, Albert S., 272
Cook's Boston Light Artillery, 131
Cooper Union, 285
Cooper, Clarence G., 255
Corbin, Elmer, 180, 244
Councilman, Charles A., 162, 229, 299
Country Fare Inn, 275
County Courts Building, 29, 33, 193
Court Garage, 296
Court House Square, 293
Cowen, Gertrude, 144
Cowenton, 271
Cowenton Permanent Building Association, 184
Cox, Mr. & Mrs. Frank, 60
Cox's Bowling Alley, 75
Cox's Point, 87
Crabel, Don, 99
Cradock, Thomas (Reverend), 15
Craumer, William C., 297
Crease Restaurant, 250
Cromwell Bridge Road, 106
Crosby, Michael, 90
Crosby School, 152, 159
Crouch, John W., 255
Crowding, Ed, 95
Crown Central Petroleum Corporation, 299
Crown Department Store (Reisterstown), 246
Cub Hill Road, 106
Cuba, 261
Cull, Mrs. Roger W., 77
Curtis, H. R. (Reverend), 207
Curtiss Flying Service, 256
Curtiss-Caproni, 256
Curtiss-Wright Corp., 256

D

D Street (Sparrows Point), 287
Dance, Beulah, 63
Dance, E. Scott, 63, 235, 298
Dance, Ernest, 63
Dance, Gilbert, 63
Dance, Joseph G., 63
Dance, Lawrence, 63
Dance, Milton, 63
Dance, Mrs. Sue, 63
Dance, Willard, 63
Dance Farm, 222
Dance Mill Road, 49, 63, 235
Dance's Mill, 235
Daniels, 176
Daniels, C. R., Company, 239
Daniels Town Band, 53, 194
Darrell, J. Cavendish, 148
Darst, David, 190
David (Hurricane), 235
Davis, Alexander Jackson, 279
Davis, Billy, 159
Davis, Clara, 144
Davis, Erick F., 115
Davis, Evan, 201
Davis, Frank E., 297
Davis, J. Robert M., 255
Davis, John, 235
Davis, John K., 148
Davis, Kerry, 115
Davis, L., 57
Davis Cup, 55
Dawson, William, 278
Day, Edward, 197
Day, Ishmael, 114, 279
Day, Nicholas, 251
Deans, Hugh (Reverend), 251
Deem, Blaine, 210
Deford, Robert, 33
Deily, Grace, 54
Devereux, James P. S. (Brigadier General), 191
Devon Horse Show (Back cover)
Devries, Mrs. H. A., 282
Dewberry, Frederick (County Executive), 193
Deyle, Gilbert (Police Chief), 190
DiBenedetto, Jack, 95
Diamond Ridge, 89
Dickey, William J., 237
Dickey, W. J. Company, 73, 237
Dickeyville, 216
Diedeman, Herbert C., 156
Diekman, Lorraine, 210
Dienstbach, Henry, 248, 297
Dieter, Robert, 89
Dietz, Austin (Fire Chief), 176, 193
Dietz, Lingard, 161
Dillman, Ron, 165
Dimpsey, George W., 156
Dixie (song), 23
Dixon, James, 29, 132, 290
Dixon, Thomas, 209
Dollenberg, P. Douglas, 150
Dollenberg and Company, 289
Donet, C., 165
Dolittle, Jimmy (General), 178
Double Rock Park, 63
Doughoregan Manor, 49, 169
Douglass High School, 157
Downs, Shorty, 265
Doyle Aero Corporation, 256
Doyle, Tom, 192
Druid Ridge Cemetery, 10
Drumcastle Apartments, 226
Drumquhazel, 226, 282
Dryden, Bob, 93
Ducker, Ephraim, 254
Ducker, John, (Major), 254
Duddington, 62
Dugan, Sallie Love Merryman, 62
Dukehart and Stevenson, 297
Dulaney Valley Road, 155
Dulaney Valley School, 155
Dumbarton, 240, 281, 282, 287
Dumler, Hilda M., 159
Duncan, Frank I. (Judge), 133
Duncan, John D. C., 133
Dundalk, 50, 117, 118, 120, 126, 137, 210, 264, 267, 288, 296
Dundalk Branch, Baltimore County Public Library, 264
Dundalk Building, 264
Dundalk Community College, 26
Dundalk Company, 288
Dundalk Marine Terminal, 38, 124, 298
Dunkirk Building, 264
Dunleer Building, 264
Dunty, Beth V., 65
Dunty, Edith R., 65
Dunty, Florence M., 65
Dunty, Hazel W., 65
Dunty, James H., 65
Dunty, Mary E., 65
Dunty, Hannah Elizabeth Ransom, 65
Dunty, Osborne Yellott, 65
Dunty, Robert P., 65
Dunty, William George, Jr., 65, 274, 277
Dunty, William, III, 65
Du Pont Company, 108

E

Earhart, Amelia, 117
East, Henrietta, 60
East, R. Walton, Jr., 60
East, Walton, Sr., 60
Eastern Airlines, 117
Eastern Regional Health Center, 26
Eastern Stainless Steel, 66, 263
Ebaugh, Zachariah C., 157
Ebbert, W., 67
Ebenezer Road, 271
Echoes, 277
Eckenrode, Quentin, 146
Eden Terrace, 90, 269, 285
Edgemere, 126
Edmunds, James R., 249
Edwards Mill. *See* Dance's Mill
Eklo School (Middletown), 152, 157, 158, 232
Elk Neck, 197
Elkridge, 131, 269
Elkridge Fox Hunting Club and Elkridge Hounds, 49
Elk's Lodge (Towson), 179
Ellicott, Andrew, 127
Ellicott, George, 127
Ellicott City, 21, 22, 49, 56, 175, 176, 269
Ellicott's Mills, 21, 22
Elliot, Cecil, 96
Elms, 61
Ely family, 239
Emerson, Isaac (Captain), 56, 276
Emerson Farms, 56
Emerson Hotel, 56
Emory, Ann Gittings, 275
Emory, D. Hopper, 297
Emory, Dr. Richard, 275
Emory, John (Bishop), 198, 199
Emory Grove, 16, 199, 296
Employment Security Administration, 190
Endicott and Swett (engravers), 128
English Consul, 296
English Consul Mansion, 278
English, Jim, 93
Ensor, Lawrence E., 133
Enterprise Laundry, 265
Epiphany House, 298
Equitable Bank, 296, 297
Erhardt, Donna, 161
Essex, 126, 137, 146-147, 181, 184, 208, 243, 245, 277, 289
Essex Community College, 27, 277, 295
Essex Community College's Ethnic Festival, 151
Essex Elementary School, 160
Essex fire, 187
Essex Road, 113
Essex Vietnam War/Korean War Memorial, 190
Eudowood, 293
Eudowood Sanitarium, 247, 293
Eudowood Shopping Center, 122, 247
Eureka Mill. *See* Groff's Mill
Eutaw Place Temple, 212
Evans, William R., 150, 151
Executive Plaza (Hunt Valley), 29
Exeter Hall (Baltimore), 212
Exodus (ship), 275

F

Fair of the Iron Horse, 183-184
Fallon, George (Congressman), 120
Feast, Robert, 248
Feast, Sarah, 297
Feder, Fred, 24, 168
Feder, Jane, 74
Feder, Mrs. Josephine, 74
Feder, Mrs. Pauline, 74
Federal Arsenal (Pikesville) see Pikesville Arsenal
Federal Hill, 124
Fellers, Mr., 137
Fendall, Charles E., 297
Fielding, Geoffrey, 306
Filston Farm, 160
Finkelstein, Ellis, 297, 298
Finkelstein, H. Bruce, 213
Finn, Darileen, 161
First American Bank (Towson), 270
First National Bank of Catonsville, 285
First Unitarian Church, 237
Fisher Tavern (Reisterstown), 253
Fisher, Elizabeth, 54
Fitze, Joshua, 59, 84, 227
Fitzell Farm, 261
Fitzgerald, F. Scott, ,74
Fitzgerald, Zelda, 74
Flaherty, Sean, 245
Flamm, Butch, 96
Flintkote, 268
Flood of 1868, 175
Foley, Timothy, 243
Foley, William, 243
Fontenai, 200
Ford, Mary, 144
Forest View, 299
Fornoff, William, 120, 193
Fort Armistead, 142
Fort Carroll, 260
Fort Garrison, 124, 126
Fort George Meade, 299
Fort Howard, 116, 124, 142, 296
Fort Howard Army Band, 52
Fort McHenry, 124
Fort Smallwood, 142
Fosler, Rich, 95
Fosler, Scott, 95
Fowble, C., 66
Fowblesburg, 182
Frames Methodist Episcopal Church, 241
Francis Scott Key Bridge. *See* Key Bridge
Frank Leslie's Illustrated Weekly, 45
Franklin, John, 59
Franklin, John Merryman (General), 276
Franklin Academy, 157, 252
Franklin Elementary School, 161
Franklin High School, 16, 57, 161, 252

Franklin Middle School, 137
Franklin Square Hospital, 26, 277, 295
Franklinville, 194, 200, 214, 299
Franklinville Cotton Factory, 200
Frantz, Etha M., 161
Frazier Episcopal Church, 241
Frazier, Lou, 95
Freddie (horse), 85
Frederick Douglass High School. *See* Douglass High School
Frederick Turnpike, 104, 190
Freedmen's Bureau, 163
Friends of Benjamin Banneker Historical Park, 127
Friends School, 268
From Pig Iron to Cotton Duck (book), 216
Front Street (Lutherville), 220
Fuller, Mike, 192
Fullerton Hotel, 184
Fullerton Police/Fire Station, 137
Fullerton School, 164
Furnace Farm, 58
Fusting, Joseph P., 77

G

Gagliano, R., 66
Galloway, William, 297
Gambrill, Charles A., 47, 214, 236
Garland, Charles, 161
Garrison Forest School, 152
Gary, James Albert, 240
Gary, James S., 239
Gary, Wilson Eugene, 156
Gates, Ricky, 38
Gaudreau, Inc., 29
Gayhardt, Bill, 99
General Dynamics, 29
General Engineering, Inc., 30
General German Orphan Asylum, 294
General Instrument Corporation, Worldwide Wagering Systems Division, 267
Genstar Ltd., 268
Genstar Stone Products, 268
Gent, Alfred J., 299
George Bragg High School. *See* Bragg High School
George Washington Carver High School. *See* Carver High School
Georgetown University, 205
Gerar, 32, 162
Gerber, Damon P. (Captain), 192
German Evangelical Lutheran Trinity Church, 294
German Protestant Orphan Asylum, 294
Gessford, Elizabeth (Watson), 41
Gettysburg (battle), 298
Giant (Supermarkets), 216
Gibbons, James Cardinal, 169
Gilbert, Charles, 299
Gilmor, Harry (Colonel), 114, 279
Gilmor, Robert, 279
Gist, Branford C., 160
Gist, Mordecai (Brigadier), 273
Gist, Thomas, 273
Gittings, James, 297
Gittings family, 33
Glatfelter, Philip H., 216
Glen Arm, 30
Glen Ellen, 279
Glencoe, 217
Glenn L. Martin plant. *See* Martin, Glenn L. Company
Glenwood Springs Company, 299
Glyndon, 16, 49, 111, 126, 152, 162, 194, 199, 230, 252, 290
Godefroy, Maximilian, 237
Godey's Ladies Book, 18, 281
Gonce, W., 66
Gonce family, 98
Gontrum, John (Chief Judge), 191
Good Corn Lecture Train, 162
Goodwin, Frank P., 253
Goodwin, Mrs. Louise B., 161
Goodwin's Livery Stable, 253
Gore, Mrs. William, 59
Gore's Mill, 214
Gorfine, Benjamin and Edna, 248
Gorsuch, Alice, 58
Gorsuch, Dickinson, 298
Gorsuch, J. Fletcher H. (Judge), 133
Gorsuch, Joshua M., 299
Gorsuch, Nellye M., 161
Gosnell, Orville T., 191
Goucher College, 27, 36, 244, 249, 268
Gough, Harry Dorsey, 20, 274
Govanstown Hotel, 298
Governor's Cup Regatta, 87
Grady, Mrs. J. Harold, 54
Grand Army of the Republic, 208
Grand National (Baltimore County), 85
Grand National (England), 85
Grand United Order of the Nazarites, 163
Granite (village), 103
Granite Cotton Factory, 21, 175, 214
Grason, C. Gus (Judge), 133
Gray, Blanche Shurlock, 61
Gray, David William, 61
Gray, Ellen Ely, 61
Gray, Ellen Hepburn, 61, 161
Gray, Frances Noyes, 61
Gray, Joseph Percy, 61
Gray, Mary Rebecca, 61
Gray's Cotton Factory, 21, 175, 214, 269
Greater Baltimore Medical Center, 37, 44, 58
Green, Dr. John S., 286
Greene, Samuel, 148
Greenlea, 286
Greenmount Cemetery, 278
Greenmount/Carroll County stage coach, 105
Greenspring Valley, 56, 105, 112, 156, 253
Greenspring Valley Hunt Club, 49, 140
Greenwood Amusement Park, 299
Greenwood Springs Company, 253
Grglewski, Steve, 96
Grimes, Margaret A., 161
Grimes, Oscar (Police Chief), 190, 298
Grissenger, Myers, 156
Groff's Mill, 235
Grumman Corporation, 30
Guild, Stanley, 191
Guilford, (Daniels), 239
Guise, Stu, 192
Gundry, Martha, 159
Gundry Sanitarium, 252, 290
Gunpowder Agricultural Club, 299
Gunpowder Meeting House. *See* New Gunpowder Meeting House
Gunpowder Mill, 271
Gunpowder River, 50, 101, 107, 109, 124, 231
Gunpowder State Park, 126
Gunther brewing family, 142
Guttenberger, Henry, 243
Gwinn's Falls, 236, 239
Gwynn Oak Park, 79
Gwynn Oak junction, 115

H

Habberkorn, William, 136
Haberkorn, A., 67
Haberkorn, Otto, Sr., 136
Hafer, M., 165
Haile, Elmer R., 133
Haile, LeRoy Y., 255
Hale, John H., 157, 232
Halethorpe (Maryland), 126, 137, 183, 184, 269, 296
Halethorpe Air Show, 177
Hall, Jim, 95
Hall, Mr., 161
Hamilton, 172, 179
Hammon, George, 96
Hammond, Hall (Chief Judge), 191
Hammond, Mike, 96
Hampden, 214, 217
Hampton, 20, 58, 215, 274, 291
Hampton (hotel), 296
Hampton Farmhouse, 15, 274
Hanna, Emma K., 161
Hannah More Academy, 152, 154
Hanover Pike, 182
Harbor Field Airfield, 298
Harbor Place, 299
Harbor Tunnel, 118
Harford County, 33
Harford County Fair, 298
Harford Road, 114, 286, 296
Harlem Lodge, 290
Harper's Weekly, 175
Harris, B., 67
Harris, J., 57
Harris, Walter B., 162
Harrison, Benjamin (President), 45
Harrison, Charles K., 299
Harrisonville, 196, 296
Hart, C., 66
Hart, Charles, 80, 251
Hart, James, 146
Hart-Miller Islands, 296
Hartley's Mill, 61, 214
Hatch, Ernest C., 133
Haussner's, 33
Hayes, B., 165
Hayfields, 62, 162, 276, 298
Heales, C., 67
Hechingers, 216
Hechts, 216
Heeter, Nellie, 86
Heilig, William (Reverend), 281
Heilman, Merle, 54
Held, John Seng, 247
Held, Louis W., 247
Helfrich, Jack, 159
Henryton State Tuberculosis Hospital, 206
Hereford, 107, 219
Hereford High School, 164
Hergenrather, Dr. Louis, 248
Heritage Society of Essex and Middle River, 137, 190
Herman, Emmanuel Weiser, 65, 260
Hess, Rebecca Sewell, 218
Hess, Thelma, 41
Heubeck, Robert, 161
Hickernell, Ronald B., 151
Higgins, William J., 156
High German Lutheran Church (Reisterstown), 196
Highland Park, 49
Highlandtown, 250
Hildebrandt, Eva F., 159
Hill, Ron, 98
Hillside Farm, 46, 47
Hilltop Theater, 56
Hisleir, Wayne, 86
Hiss, Dr. William, 202
Hiss Methodist Church, 202
Ho, Raymond K. K., 145
Hobb's Hotel, 252
Hock, Philip, 250
Hoen, A., 23, 292
Hoen, Frank, 140
Hoen lithography family, 140, 284
Hoffman, Edward, 136
Hoffman, Henry, 136
Hoffman, Peter, 271
Hoffman, William, 271
Hoffman, William Henkle, 271, 292
Hoffmanville, 194, 216, 271, 298
Hogan, Joseph, 188
Holler, E., 67
Holler, S., 67
Hollifield, William, 130
Holloway chemical fire engine, 180
Holmes, J. Gordon (Inspector), 190
Holocaust, 275
Homer, Winslow, 152
Homewood, 77
Hook, Richard (Sheriff), 235
Hope, N., 66
Hopwood, Mrs. Charles, 176
Horner, Joshua, 65, 260
Hospital for Consumptives of Maryland, 293
Houseknecht, Butch, 96
Houseknecht, David, 96
Housely, Mr., 136
Howard, Linda, 161
Howard County, 131, 169, 216, 139
Howaton, Miss, 62
Hubner, John, 23
Huddles, Gary, 191
Hughes, Charles, 253
Hughes, Joseph, 253
Hughes Company, 101, 156
Hull, Charles Wesley, 136, 208
Humphrey's Creek, 261
Hunt, Rich, 95
Hunt Valley, 29, 36, 216, 266
Hunt Valley Inn. *See* Marriott's Hunt Valley Inn
Hunt Valley Mall, 29
Hunter's Mill, 214
Hupfield, E., 53
Hurricane David. *See* David (hurricane)
Hutchins, Nelson, 244
Hutchinson, Donald P. (County Executive), 146, 147
Huttenhauer, Helen G., 161
Hutzler's 120 (Westview), 124, 216, 249 (Towson)
Hyson, Raymond S., 161

I

Ignatowski, Mike, 96
Inauniemi, Delia, 210
Inauniemi, Lalia, 210
Indian Head Hotel, 297
International Cotton Mill Corporation, 275
Inverness, 289
Investment Building (Towson), 211, 227, 297
Irish, Charley. *See* Legum Chevrolet
Isaac, William Moore, 297
Isennock, J. A., 218
Isennock, J. Wesley, 235
Isennock, Mrs. J. A., 218

J
Jackson, Carle A., 54
Jackson, Ken, 266
Jacksonville, 31
Jacobs, Frank Hays, 133
James, Mim, 54
Jarrett, Dr. James H., 297
Jay Trump (horse), 85
Jednoralski, Thelma, 144
Jefferson, Thomas (President), 127
Jefferson Building, 121, 296
Jefferson Lodge, 100
Jenifer, H. Courtenay, 133
Jenifer, R. Moore, 133
Jenkins, Edward F., 280
Jenkins family, 169
Jenner, Dr. Edward, 292
Jensen, Alvida, 42
Jessop, Charles, 231, 298
Jessop, Joshua, 155
Jessop, Norton Merryman, 62
Jessop, Thomas, 222
Jesuits. *See* Society of Jesus
Jewell, Downing and Associates, 150
Johns, Richard, 201
Johns family, 195
Johns Hopkins Hospital, 106, 293
Johns Hopkins University, 146
Johnson, Bradley T. (General), 49
Johnson, E., 67
Johnson, Helen, 86
Johnson, Walter Perry, 238
Johnson, William Fell, 235
Jones, Billy, 95
Jones, Dorothy, 54
Jones, E., 156
Jones, Mildred E., 161
Jones, Willy, 223
Jones Falls, 214
Jordan, John, 161
Josenhans, Frederick W., 245
Joyce, D. F. A., 178
Joyce, Jerome (Colonel), 177

K
Kade, Marie (Bosley), 64
Kadolph, Gerhard, 33
Kahl, Christian H. (County Executive), 120, 190, 191
Kalb, Ernest de, 159
Kane's Hotel, 109
Kann and Ammon, Inc., 212
Kauffman's Pharmacy, 248
Keech, William S., 297
Keelty, James, 281, 287
Keeney Mill, 214
Keidel, Daisy, 77
Keidel, Dr. George Frederick W., 77
Keizer, Lewis R., 231
Kella, Marion, 54
Kelley, James P., 133, 141, 184
Kelly, W., Boulton. *See* Tatar and Kelly
Kemp, Mrs. Betty Merryman, 62
Kenilworth Park, 248
Kennedy, John F. (President), 190
Kenney, Edmund T., 41, 71, 114
Kenney, Mrs. William C., 41, 65
Kenney, William C., 41, 112, 173, 202, 219, 274
Kent, Margaret, 54
Kernan Hospital for Crippled Children, 140
Key, Francis Scott, 61
Key Bridge, 120
Keyes, Michael, 41
Kilchenstein's store, 98
Kimberly, George, 159
Kincannon, Walter H., 156
King, Alvin, 161
King, Billie Jean, 46
King, Mrs., 161
Kingsville, 197, 296
Kingsville Inn, 251
Kirk-Stieff Incorporated (silversmiths), 297
Kirkbride, Dr. Robert, 291
Klapproth, August, 136
Klemm, Kenora, 210
Klingelhofer, G., 57
Kloiber, George, 161
Kloiber, Mrs., 161
Knauf, E., 67
Knoblock, W., 67
Knoebel's Corner, 49, 112
Know-Nothing party, 155, 296
Koppers, 260
Korvettes, 123
Kraft, Fred G., Jr., 120
Kratt, Martin (Pastor), 294
Kronnewetter, Catherine, 144
Krs, Evelyn, 144
Ky, Nguyen Cao, 189

L
La Paix, 74
Ladies Democratic Club of Essex, 144
Lake Roland, 42, 88, 106, 108, 296
Lally, James, 164
Lally, Robert (Police Chief), 191, 298
Lamour, Dorothy, 235
Lancashire Furnace, 214
Lansdowne, 126, 138, 194, 296
Landsdowne Christian Church, 208, 209
Lansdowne Football Team, 67
Lansdowne Volunteer Fire Department, 136
Lansdowne Volunteer Fire Department Band, 51
Lapicki-Smith and Associates, 150
Lassahn, John E., 148
Lassahn Funeral Homes, E. F., 251
Lauder, Miss, 161
Lauenstein, Norman W., 146, 150, 151
Lavender Hill, 296
Lawrence, William H. (Judge), 133
Lawrence Hill, 28
League of Women Voters, 147, 148
Leakin, Alice Woodward, 47
LeBrun, Tim, 115
Lee, Bernie, 251
Lee, Corbin, 274
Lee, Fitzhugh (General), 154
Lee, Ralph, 95
Lee, Robert E. (Colonel), 260
Lee, Ruth Silver, 86
Lee, William A., 297
Legg Mason Center 297
Legum Chevrolet, 266
Lehner, John, 136
Leisenring family, 70
Lesnick, Glen, 96
Letke, Mary, 161
Levering family, 239
Lewis, Roberta, 54
Lewis, Thomas Pohl, 190
Lewis, William C., 156
Liberty Dam, 61, 135, 296, 298
Liberty Road, 196, 294
Lightner, James K., 38
Linsey, James J., 297
Linthicum family, 277
Lintz, Lucille, 161
Lion's Club of Pikesville, 203
Litsinger, R., 57
Little, John Mays, 133
Liverpool (England), 22, 276
Lloyd Street Synagogue, 212
Loch Raven Dam, 135, 298
Loch Raven Reservoir, 17, 38, 109, 153, 155, 231, 279
Loch Raven-Montebello water tunnel, 268
Loch Raven Village, 245
Locust Grove Furnace, 214
Logan, Patrick (Lieutenant), 118
Logan Elementary School, 26
Logan Field, 117, 118, 178, 256
Logan Village, 118
Loizeaux, J., 57
Loizeaux, R., 57
Long, Clarence D. (Congressman), 146, 151
Long, Robert Carey, Jr., 203, 212
Long Green, 218, 232, 265, 280
Long Green Academy, 152, 201
Long Green Pike, 30
Long Quarter Farm, 49
Loose, August, 64
Lorman, William, 239
Loudenslager, C., 67
Loveton Center, 216
Lower Brick Row (Daniels), 239
Loyola Federal Savings and Loan Association, 121, 255, 298
Loyola High School, 268
Lozzi, Vince, 96
Luddington, C. T., 117
Lurman, Gustav, 55
Lutherville, 50, 56, 70, 126, 173, 197, 220, 230, 281
Lutherville Female Seminary, 152, 173
Lyal Park, 55
Lynch, Marcus, Jr., 90
Lyon, Charles, 299
Lyon, Edward, 299
Lyon's Mill, 214, 234
Lyston, Jay, 74, 168
Lyston, Mrs. Anne, 74

M
Ma & Pa Railroad. *See* Maryland & Pennsylvania Railroad
MacArthur, Douglas (Major General), 299
McCarron, Pat, 85
McCauley, Lois, 128, 129
McCluskey, Bill, 139
McCormick & Company, 266
McCubbin, J., 67
McCubbin, William, 202
McCurdy, Dr. A. C., 227
McDonaugh, Ruth, 210
McDonogh, John, 156
McDonogh School, 152, 156, 185, 299
McDonough, Norton Carroll, 62
Mace, C., 66
Mace, Dr. Charles R., 277
McEnroe, John, 46
McEvoy, Carol, 150
Macgill, Mary, 159
Macgill, O. P. (Colonel), 297
McGinnis, James, 190
McGowan, Ethelwyn, 58
McGowan, Grace, 58
McGowan, Mrs. William, 58
McGowan, William, 58
McGrain, John W., 216, 222, 298, 299
McGraw, John, 55
McGurie, John, 243
McIntosh, David G., Jr. (State Senator), 133, 281
McIntosh, David Gregg (Colonel), 296, 297
Mack, Connie, 66
McKeldin, Theodore, R., 117, 118, 191
Mackenzie, C. Norbury, III, 297
McKinley, James (President), 240
McLemore, Dennis, 161
McNally, Lawrence, 120-122, 123
McPatrick's Pub, 251
McShane Foundry, 197, 198
Madan, (Coach), 57, 66
Magness, G., 66
Mahan, Charles, 111
Mahoney, George P., 190
Main Street (Reisterstown), 246
Maisel, Frederick (Fritz) (Fire Chief), 94
Malozi, Mark, 96
Mangione, Nicholas B., 276
Mann, Brady, 84
Mann, Carol, 34
Manor Glen, 275
Mantua Mill Road, 49
Maple Hill Farm, 236
Marble Vale, 216, 271
Marley, George B., 133, 134
Marriott Corporation, 32
Marriott's Hunt Valley Inn, 32
Marshall, John, 210
Martin, Glenn L., 177, 257
Martin, Isabelle, 54
Martin, Glenn L., Company, 30, 186, 257, 258, 259, 261
Martin Field, 117
Martin Marietta Baltimore Aerospace, 258
Martenet, Simon J., 19, 286, 296
Martini, Ned, 178
Marye, William B., 285, 299
Maryland and Pennsylvania Railroad, 110, 111, 121, 179, (York Road overpass), 162, 265
Maryland Agricultural Experimental Station, 162
Maryland Agricultural College, 162
Maryland Agricultural Society, 299
Maryland Baptist Union Association, 203
Maryland Center for Public Broadcasting, 145
Maryland Central Railroad, 110
Maryland College for Women (Lutherville), 56
Maryland College of Medicine, 277
Maryland Court of Appeals, 216
Maryland Dental School, 227
Maryland Historical Prints, 128, 129
Maryland Historical Society, 127, 128, 129, 221, 281
Maryland Historical Trust, 127
Maryland Horticultural Society, 271
Maryland House of Delegates, 140, 141, 298
Maryland Hunt Cup, 85
Maryland Journal, 297
Maryland Marathon, 98
Maryland National Guard, 124, 144, 296
Maryland Public Television, 145
Maryland State Agricultural Society, 298
Maryland State Fair and Agricultural Society of Baltimore County, Maryland, 298

Maryland State Fair, Timonium. *See* Timonium State Fair
Maryland State Farm Board, 140
Maryland State Grange, 234
Maryland State Police, 36, 126, 129, 140 (Aviation Divison)
Maryland State Superintendents of Education, 158, 167, 272
Maryland Steel Company, 261
Mason, T. Lyde, 133
Masonic Home of Maryland, 29
Masonic Temple (Reisterstown), 253
Matarozza, Mae Tuchton, 146
Matthews Bridge, 109
Mayer, Brantz, 221
Mayer, Charles Frederick, 221
Mayer, Francis B., 129, 221, 234, 236
Meadowdale Farm, 221
Meadows, 223
Meads, T. Wilbur, 133
Melville Woolen Company, 135
Melville, Mr. and Mrs. Thomas Robert, 190
Memorial Stadium, 98
Menicon, Ruth, 54
Mercantile Bank building (Towson), 255, 297
Merchants and Manufacturers Association, 240
Meredith's Ford Bridge, 109
Merrifield, R., 57
Merritt, Alvah, 228
Merritt, Alonzo, 228
Merritt, Enoch, 228
Merritt, Joseph, 267
Merritt, Joseph, Jr., 267
Merritt Point Elementary School, 228
Merryman, E. Gittings, 32, 162
Merryman, John, 62, 276, 298, 299
Merryman, Mrs. Mary (Wright), 62
Merryman, Nicholas Bosley, 62, 162
Merryman, Nicholas Bosley, II, 62
Merryman, Nicholas Bosley, III, 62
Merryman, Mrs. Nicholas Bosley, 62
Merryman, Sallie Love, 62
Merryman's Mill, 214
Merz, Walter (Pastor), 210
Messina, Frank, 192
Metropolitan Opera Company, 54
Mettam Memorial Baptist Church, 203
Mettam, Joseph, 203
Metzger, Albert F., 159
Middle Mill (Samuel Owings's), 275
Middle River, 41, 126, 184, 186, 257, 258, 259
Milford Mill, 236
Milford Pool, 168
Miller, Frank, 65, 298
Miller, J. Jefferson, Sr., 90
Miller, Joseph, 124
Miller, Katherine, 65
Miller, Marjorie, 161
Miller, Samuel, 252
Miller family, 21
Milling, James and Ida, 184
Milling, W. Howard, 124, 184
Mills, Robert, 239
Milton Academy, 152
Milton Inn, 152
Mintz, Melvin B., 151
Mischle, George Joseph, 190
Mitchell, Eleanor, 139
Mock, Emma, 144
Mohr, Jen, 144
Mondawmin, 49
Monkton, 152, 198, 252
Monkton Hotel, 252
Montessori School, 56
Montevideo Park, 49
Montgomery Ward, 214 (Monroe Street), 247 (Towson Marketplace)
Montrose, 280
Monumental League, 67
Moreland, Joseph, 286
Morgan, Annie C., 160
Morningside Apartments, 56
Morrell, Edward (Colonel), back cover
Morris, Dr. John, 70, 173
Morsberger, Edith T., 159
Mt. Clare, 214, 274
Mt. Clare shops, 103
Mt. de Sales Academy of the Visitation, 152, 155, 228
Mt. Gilboa African Methodist Episcopal Church, 207
Mt. Hope, Ohio, 160
Mt. Moriah A. M. and F. M. Lodge, 296, 297
Mt. Olivet Cemetery, 20, 198
Mt. Paran Presbyterian Church, 196
Mt. Peru, 280, 298
Mt. Pleasant, 231
Mt. Washington Casino, 56
Mt. Wilson State Hospital, 126
Mt. Wilson Lane, 299
Mt. Zion Lodge, Number 87, I. O. O. F., 100
Mowell, Peter, 217
Moylan, Mary Assumpta, 190
Mueller, John, 176
Mueller, Mrs. John, 176
Mullineaux Toll House, 251
Mumma, John, 265
Municipal Airport, 118, 256
Murphy and Olmstead, 169
Murray, J. Howard (Judge), 133
Muscular Dystrophy Association, 192
My Lady's Manor Steeplechase Race, 87
Myer, Anna, 47
Myer, Elizabeth, 47
Myer, Robert J., 47
Mykonos Restaurant, 297

N

Nacirema, 54
Napoleon, *See* Bonaparte, Napoleon
Natchez, 130
National Bank of Cockeysville, 55
National Brewing Company, 181
National Education Association, 155
National Grange of the Patrons of Husbandry, 234
National Parks Service, 20
Natural Food Company, 160
Naylor, Fannie S., 248
Neilson, J. Crawford, 281
Nelson, Gwynn, 133
Ner Israel Rabbinical College, 299
Neuhauser, Brenda, 161
Nevins, Mr., 136
New Gunpowder Meeting House, 200
New Orleans, 23, 156
New Theater, 75
New York Giants, 55
New York Yankees, 94
Newton and Painter, 92, 269
Nicholas, Jesse, 63
Nicodemus Road, 296
Niernsee, Rudolf, 132, 281
Nimmo, Thornton, 41, 102
Nixon, Richard M. (President), 146
Norris, Margaret, 210
North American Airlines, 29
North American Van Lines, 265
North Branch of the Patapsco, 135
North Point-Edgemere School Mother's Club, 86
North Point, 69, 296. *See also* Battle of North Point
North Side (Sparrows Point), 261
Northampton Iron Works, 21, 214
Northern Central Railroad, 106, 182, 245, 280
Northwest Expressway, 120
Nottingham Properties Incorporated, 150, 268, 297

O

O'Connor, Sandra A., 148
Oak Grove, 70
Oak Hill Cemetery, 130
Oakland Mills, 135
Oaks, Evelyn, 144
Obrecht, P. F. (and Company), 31
Octagon, 281
Odell, Mary Osborn, 149
Oella (cotton factory), 17, 21, 194, 207, 214, 237
Officer, James D., 155, 203
Offutt, James P., 133
Offutt, Noah E., 133
Offutt, T. Scott (Judge), 133
Offutt building, 296
Ogle, Benjamin (Governor), 251
Ogle, E., 53
Old Bay Line, 275
Old Court Station, 119
Old North Point Road, 110, 278
Old Road Bay, 296
Old Salem Evangelical Lutheran Church, 204
Oldfields School, 152
Oliver, Robert, 278
Oliver Beach House, 278
Olver, R. T., 67
Olver, W. C., 67
Orange Grove Mill, 236
Oread, 160
Oregon Iron Furnace, 216
Oregon Ridge Park, 36, 216
Orient Restaurant, 297
Ornson, Joseph, 160
Osenburg, W., 66
Oswald, Edward Ingram, 162
Our Lady of Mt. Carmel Church, 208
Overlea School, 152
Owens, G., 57
Owens, John E., 23
Owens, Dr. Joseph R., 162
Owings, Samuel, I, 223
Owings, Samuel, Jr. 235, 275
Owings, Thomas, 223
Owings Mills, 119, 145, 216, 299
Owings Mills Corporate Center, 299
Owings Mills Town Center, 299
Owings Mills *Times,* 298

P

PHH Group, 29
Padgett, Virginia, 54
Painter, D. F., 234
Painter family, 275
Painter's Mill, 214
Palmer, Edward L., 264, 288
Paper Mill Road, 50
Paper Mills. *See* Hoffmanville
Paris, B. E. Von, 210, 223
Paris, Bonaventure Von, 223, 265
Paris, Eligius Von, 265
Paris, Margaret Von, 223
Paris, Marie Von, 223
Park Circle Chevrolet. *See* Legum Chevrolet
Parker, Sumner, 279
Parker, Thomas and Rice, 167
Parkton, 217
Parkville, 63, 124, 126, 202, 286, 296
Parkville Volunteer Fire Department, 98
Parsons, Ethel A., 161
Passano, Edward B. 234, 297
Patapsco Electric and Manufacturing Company of Baltimore County, 269, 285
Patapsco Flour Mills, 17, 21, 175
Patapsco River, 21, 22, 68, 88, 127, 170, 175, 176, 236, 239, 269, 296
Patapsco Senior High School, 93, 96
Patapsco State Park, 126
Patrons' Club (McDonogh School), 185
Patterson, Betsy, 280, 285
Patterson, Dr. H. J., 162
Patterson, Edward, 280
Patterson, Joseph, 280
Peale, Rembrandt, 292
Pearce, Arthur, 61
Pearce, Bill, 61
Pearce, Ellie, 61
Pearce, Frank, 61
Pearce, Greenberry, 61
Pearce, Joe, 61
Pearce, John, 61
Pearce, Martha, 61
Pearce, Mary Jane, 61
Pearce, Stella, 61
Pearl Harbor, 118, 187, 258
Peerce's Plantation (restaurant), 155
Pen-Mar, 299
Pennington, Josias, 29
Pennsylvania Hospital, 291
Pennsylvania Railroad, 110
Pennsylvania Steel Company, 216, 260, 261
Penthouse, 297
Perky, Henry D., 160
Perring Parkway, 123
Perry, Dennis, 96
Perry Hall Mansion, 15, 20, 65, 272, 274, 277
Perry Hall, 16, 245, 296
Perry Hall Elementary School, 161
Peters, Bill, 144
Peters, Theresa, 86
Pfeifer, Steve, 95
Pfeiffer, Eileen, 161
Philadelphia Road, 175, 176
Philadelphia, Wilmington and Baltimore Railroad, 296
Phillips, Mabel Elwood, 236
Phillips, Thomas L., 236
Phoenix, 102, 172, 194, 214, 241
Phoenix Cotton Mill, 17, 135, 160, 241
Piel, Vernon L., 159
Pietrowski, Nick, 96
Pike Theater, 75
Pike, Zebulon (Brigadier General), 292
Pikesville, 30, 55, 56, 75, 100, 119, 120, 132, 137, 194, 203, 211, 212, 236, 243, 292
Pikesville Armory, 144
Pikesville Arsenal, 36, 124, 129, 279, 292
Pikesville Church. *See* Mettam Memorial Baptist Church
Pikesville Dairy Company, 299

Pikesville Fire Department, 138
Pimlico Race Track, 23, 49, 298
Pine, James A., 147
Pine Ridge Golf Course, 34
Pinewood Elementary School, 25
Piper, Dr. Jackson, 297
Pitcairn Aviation Company, 256
Pittsburgh Pirates, 66
Planters Point Ducking Club, 284
Poehlmann, Louis, 242
Polesne, Charles, 176
Ponselle, Rosa, 54
Poole, Engineering and Machine Company, 269
Popke family, 42
Posey family, 62, 106
Pot Spring Elementary School, 35
Poteet, Zephaniah, 102, 231
Power, Gordon G., 148
Powhatan Cotton Mill, 216, 239, 296
Powhatan Road, 225
Pratt, Enoch, 281, 291
Preakness (horse), 23
Preakness (race), 23
Preservation Maryland, 20
President Warfield, 275
Preston, Herbert, 159
Preston, Walter W. (Judge), 133
Prettyboy Dam, 268, 298
Price, Vernon, 263
Priester, Phil (Fire Chief), 125
Primitive Baptists, 201
Prospect Hill Cemetery, 297
Prospect Park, 298
Public Works Administration, 185
Pulaski Highway, 123
Punch (horse), 77
Public Service Commission, 115
Putty Hill, 126

Q
Quaker Bottom, 200
Quality Inn (Towson), 113
Queen Anne's County, 198
Queen Elizabeth II (ship), 15, 38

R
Radebaugh, George W., 33
Rainbow Division, 299
Rainbow Hill, 299
Ramsey, Robert, 298
Randallstown, 115
Raphel, Stephanie, 200
Rasmussen, Dennis F. (County Executive), 8, 146, 150
Raukko, Anio, 210
Ravenhurst, 284
Rayville, 194
Read's drug store, 187
Reagan, Ronald (President), 38
Reckord H., 57
Reckord, Henry, 216, 241
Reckord, 216, 241
Red Rocket (streetcar), 116
Red Run, 223
Redlands PLC, 268
Regional Planning Council, 193
Reich farm (Catonsville), 224
Reinhardt, H., 67
Reinhardt, J. H., 67
Reinhardt, Mr., 136
Reister, John, 248
Reister's Desire, 248
Reisterstown, 15, 19, 56, 57, 198, 227, 246, 252, 254
Reisterstown Branch, Baltimore County Public Library, 157
Reisterstown Fire, 186
Reisterstown Plaza, 119
Reisterstown Volunteer Fire Department, 182
Reitmiller, August, Jr., 136
Reitmiller, August, Sr., 136
Religious Society of Particular Baptists, 203
Relay, 62, 131, 194, 209, 252, 269, 296
Republic Airlines, 29
Richardson, T., 57
Rider, Edward, 141
Rider, Harrison, 141
Rider Building, 296
Riderwood, 33, 126, 141
Ridgely, Charles (Captain), 20, 274
Ridgely, Charles (Colonel), 274
Ridgely, Mrs. Howard, 49
Ridgely, John, 58
Ridgely, Otho, Sr., 58
Ridgely's Woods, 298
Riedel, W., 67
Rieman, Adam, 136
Rieman, Joseph, 281
Riggs, Charlotte, 159
Ritchie, Albert C. (Governor), 267
Ritter, C. E. (Bud), 192
Ritter, Lewis, 298
Ritter, William T., 159
Roberts, Estell, 86
Roberts-Beach School, 152
Robinson, Charles W., 149, 150
Robinson, Mazie E., 159
Robinson, Mrs. Ida, 258
Rockdale Mill, 216, 235, 271
Rocky Point Beach, 70, 296
Rocky Point Golf Course, 20
Rodgers, George, 240
Rodgers Forge, 74, 152, 240, 281, 287
Roe, Cornelius, 133
Rogers, Charles Lyon, Jr., 234
Rogers, Charles Lyon, Sr., 234, 299
Roland Avenue, 285
Rolling Road Golf Club, 55
Rollins, H. Beale, 156
Roosevelt, Franklin D. (President), 186
Roosevelt, Theodore (President), 285
Rodenberg, Henry, 299
Rosenberg, Ruth Blaustein, 299
Rosenthal, H., 53
Rosland, 47, 282
Ross, Robert (General), 129
Rossville, 296
Roszel, Mrs. Eleanor (Merryman), 62
Rouse Company, 299
Rowe, Pete, 82, 164
Rowe's Carriage Works, 254
Roy Rogers Restaurant, 64
Ruark, William B., 156
Rubeling, Albert, 66
Ruby, William H., 297
Ruck, Mrs. Charles, 176
Ruckle, Thomas, 128
Rudolph, Richard, 248
Rukeyser, Louis, 145
Ruppersberger, Charles A. (Dutch), 151
Russell, Dorothy, 161
Russell, William, 254
Russell's store, 246, 254
Rutherford Business Center, 216
Ruxton, 62, 126
Ryan, F., 67

S
Sachse, E., 21, 22
Saffell, Mollie F., 161
Sagamore Farms, 162, 229
St. Alphonsus Rodriguez, 205, 206
St. Charles College, 169, 196
St. Denis, 269, 296
St. Denis Glee Club, 51
St. Francis Assisi Church, 180
St. George's Industrial School for Destitute Children, 152
St. George's School for Boys, 152
St. Helena, 126, 264
St. James Academy, 152, 198
St. James Episcopal Church, 194, 198
St. John's African Union Methodist Protestant, 196, 204
St. John's Evangelical Lutheran Church, 49, 196
St. John's Joppa. *See* St. John's Kingsville
St. John's Kingsville, 194, 197, 251
St. John's in the Valley Episcopal Church, 49, 195
St. Joseph Hospital, 295
St. Louis Browns, 94
St. Mary's Seminary College, 169
St. Paul's Lutheran Church, 50
St. Paul's School, 276
St. Paul's School for Girls, 176
St. Peter Claver's (Sunday School), 205
St. Pius X. Church, 163
St. Rita's Church, 118
St. Stanislaus Church, 239
St. Stephen's African Methodist Episcopal Church, 206
St. Stephen's Church (Upper Falls), 200
St. Timothy's Episcopal Church, 154, 155, 203
St. Timothy's Evangelical Lutheran Church, 210
St. Timothy's Hall, 152, 154
St. Timothy's School, 152, 154, 155
St. Thomas, Garrison, 194
St. Vincent's Male Orphan Asylum, 152
Salem United Methodist Church, 202
Salvation Army, 101
Sander's meat market, 186
Sands, William B., 298
Sands, William H., 297
Sargent, Dr. George F., 23
Sater, Henry, 197
Sater's Baptist Church, 197
Satyr Hill Road, 98
Satyr Hill Shopping Center, 123
Saxon, J., 67
Schaefer, Ruth, 287-289
Schaffer, G., 57
Scharf, J. Thomas, 299
Scheufele, Benny, 225
Schield, Joseph L., 148
Schiller, W., 66
Schmidt, Elmer, 232, 242
Schmidt, George, 242
Schmidt, Karl, 161
Schreefer, Ida Clayton, 217
Schmuck, Solomon, 297
Schmulowitz, Hal, 166
Schneider, Jean, 178
Schneider Cup, 178
Schon, H. Von, 269
Schwartz Avenue, 163
Scott, Rev. Aquilla, 204
Scott, Sir Walter, 279
Security Boulevard, 122
Security Mall, 32
Seitz, S. Clayton, 255, 270
Selby's Funeral Establishment, 254
Sentinel Title Company, 297
Sewell, Juliet Gambrill. *See* Baldwin, Juliet G. S.
Sewell, Mrs. 218
Shaffer, Mrs. Rip K., 176
Shaffer, Rip, 176
Shamel, A. D., 162
Shealey, Mrs. Mary, 180, 249
Sheppard and Enoch Pratt Hospital, 23, 74, 290
Sheppard, Moses, 290, 291
Sherwood Rye Distillery, 250
Sherwood Station, 62
Shipley, Esther, 161
Shipley, Jack, 54, 111
Shoemaker, Samuel Moor III, 112
Shoemaker, Samuel Moor II, 140, 223
Short and Leister (contractors), 195
Shriver, Donald, 192
Shriver, Pam, 46, 156
Shriver, Rosalie, 47
Silvester, Dr. R. W., 162
Simmons, O., 67
Simms, Hugh, 200
Simpson, Mary, 54
Singer, E., 67
Sinkenbring, William, Jr., 136
Sinkenbring, William, Sr., 136
Sizemore, Donny, 96
Slade, James Dixon, 242
Slater, Harry C., 156
Slicer, Henry J. (Reverend), 292
Slothower, George, 239
Small, Philip, 280
Small, Samuel, 280
Smedley, Enos, 297
Smedley House, 296
Smith, Crompton (Tommy), Jr., 85
Smith, Edward Jenner, 292
Smith, George, 226
Smith, Gideon, 125
Smith, Harriet (Jones), 44
Smith, Harry L., 133
Smith, Dr. James, 221, 292
Smith, Jerome, 44
Smith, Margaret, 258
Smith, Milton R., 133, 255
Smith, Samuel (Major General), 128
Smith, Vernon, 191
Smith, W. Gill, 133
Smith Avenue Shopping Center, 256
Smoot, Robert C. III, 185
Snyder, Joyce, 161
Social Security Administration, 124, 145
Society of Friends, 200
Society of Jesus, 103, 169-171
Sombre, Martin de, 176
Sombre, Mrs. Milton de, 176
Sons of Temperance, 200
Souris's Saloon, 247
South Vietnam, 191
Southard, Mrs., 161
Southard, Robert, 161
Southeastern Vocational-Technical Center, 25
Spalding, Frank, 75
Spanish-American War, 240
Sparks, Laban, 133
Sparks Agricultural High School, 160
Sparks School (black), 152
Sparrows Point, 15, 119, 126, 194, 216, 229, 260, 261, 287, 296
Sparrows Point Country Club, 289
Sparrows Point High School Soccer Team, 66, 165

Sparrows Point Methodist Church, 211
Speigel Catalog Company, 248
Spencer, Estell Roberts, 86
Spicer, Harold, 81, 90, 211
Spindler, J., 57
Spittel family, 77
Spring Grove State Hospital, 126, 290, 292
Springfield, 290
Springfield State Hospital, 290
Stall, C., 205, 206
Stamford, 49
Stansbury, Isaac, 21
Stansbury family, 130, 293
Stansbury Yacht Basin, 43
Starkweather, Nathan, 297
State Normal School, 167
State Roads Commission, 104, 107, 108, 109, 114, 134, 140
States Attorney, 81, 148
Stebbins Anderson, 216
Steel Car Company of St. Louis, 160
Steiner, Robert, 168
Stem, H., 67
Stemmers Run, 184, 223
Stephens Hall, 167
Stephens, Morse Bates, 167
Sterling, Grace K., 161
Stevens, William, 125
Stevens Garden Club, 203
Stevenson, 154, 155
Stewart, C. Morton, 140
Stewart, Redmond C., 140
Stone Hall, 273, 299
Stone Row, 280
Stoneleigh, 240, 281
Stotesbury, Eva Roberts, 299
Strack, Gertrude (Bosley), 64
Strand Bakery, 33
Strand Theater, 33, 75
Strasbaugh, C., 165
Strawhat, 251
Stretka, Elsie, 144
Stricker, John (General), 128
Strutt, Kim, 280
Stryker, Goss L., 255
Stump Electric Company, 28
Suburban Club, 55
Subway Shop, 270
Sudbrook Park, 126
Sue Island, 43
Sugars, Lawrence, 176
Sulphur Springs, 296
Sullivan, Katherine E., 36
Summit, 240
Sunshine Avenue, 114, 279
Super Fresh Supermarkets, 216
Suttka, Oscar, 210
Swann, Don, Jr., 56
Swann, Thomas (Governor), 296
Swann Lake. *See* Lake Roland
Swartz, Mano, 260, 297
Sweetair Road, 15, 201

T

Talbott, J. Fred C., 65, 140, 141, 260
Taliaferro, W. T. L., 162
Taney, Roger Brooke (Chief Justice), 276
Tatar, Seymour. *See* Tatar and Kelly
Tatar and Kelly, 149
Tawes, J. Millard (Governor), 120
Tawney, Dr. L. S., 67
Taylor, Benjamin (Colonel), 280, 298
Taylor, Edward, 23
Taylor, Robert, Jr., 280
Taylor, Wilkerson, 286
Tender is the Night (book), 74
Terminal Stores, 264
Texas (Maryland quarry), 268
Therapia Farm, 56
Thistle Mill, 21
Thoebus, Mrs. May, 86
Thomas, Bill, 95
Thomas, Charles Edward, Jr., 71
Thomas, Virginia Merryman, 41
Thomas Viaduct, 131, 175, 269
Thompson, Dr. George A., 102
Thorn Hill Quarry, 268
Thornton, Ellen, 54
Thornton Mill Road, 107
Thorpe, Albert, 161
Tillman, D., 57
Tillman, Irvin C., 30
Timanus, E. Clay (Mayor), 136
Timonium, 25, 34, 35, 298
Timonium State Fair, 72, 77, 80, 81, 82, 227, 267, 298
Tipton, C. Louise, 161
Tivoli, 261
Todd's Inheritance, 278
Tomlinson, Richard, 82
Topp, W., 53
Totten, Joseph G., 260
Tovell, G. Walter, 137
Towne and Country Furniture Store, 297
Townsend, Howard E., 156
Townsend, Samuel, 111
Towson, Ezekiel, 130
Towson, Nathan (Maj. Gen.), 130
Towson, 15, 18, 33, 37, 62, 64, 71, 92, 113, 115, 121, 130, 132, 194, 227, 234, 244, 247, 248, 249, 264, 267, 272, 290, 293, 295, 296-297, 299
Towson Billards Academy, 298
Towson Bootery, 248
Towson Branch, Baltimore County Public Library, 149, 179, 296, 297
Towson Business Association, 83
Towson Demonstrations, 189, 192
Towson Elk's Lodge, 179
Towson Fire House, 121, 180
Towson Guards, 180
Towson High School, 23, 57, 66, 158
Towson High School Band, 52
Towson Horse Company, 179, 297
Towson Hotel, 180, 279, 296
Towson Ice Company, 255, 270
Towson Market Place, 122, 247
Towson Methodist Episcopal Church, 11, 211, 244, 297
Towson Methodist Protestant Church, 211
Towson National Bank, 250, 255, 296, 297
Towson Nurseries, 23
Towson Plaza, 190
Towson Police Station, 161
Towson School, 297
Towson State Teacher's College, 168
Towson State University, 126, 167, 191
Towson Theater, 75, 250, 254, 297
Towson United Methodist Church, 211
Towson Volunteer Fire Parade, 172, 179, 180
Towson water tower, 180
Towsontown Center, 190
Towsontown Gran Prix, 34
Towsontown Junior High School, 157
Towsontown Spring Festival, 83
Tracey, Charles, 247
Tracey, Preston, 247
Trautmann, Walter A., 156
Treadwell, C. W. E., 58, 110, 215
Treadwell, Charles E., 58, 297
Treadwell, Mrs. Charles E., 58
Treadwell, William S., 215
Trenton Mill, 214
Trimble, Isaac Ridgeway (General), 284
Trinity Episcopal Church (Towson), 297
Triple Crown (racing), 23
Tropical Storm Agnes. *See* Agnes (Tropical Storm)
Trostel, Michael F., 155
Trump Mill Farm, 223
Turchin, Terry, 298
Turkey Point, Rockaway, 42
Turnbull, Bayard, 74, 295
Turner, Bill, 192
Turner's Station, 256, 260
Tydings, Edwin, 297
Tyrie, John, 255
Tyrie, Walter, 192
Tyrie & Sons Monument Works, John H., 255

U

Ulery, Eli G., 298
Ulm, 275
Unglesbar, Wilbur, 225
Union Manufacturing Company, *See* Oella
United Electric Railways Company, 116
United States Capitol, 268
United States Congress, 141, 142
United States Lines, 276
U.S. Post Office, 118, 296
U.S. Shipping Board Emergency Fleet Corporation, 264
U.S. Steel, 73
U.S. Supreme Court, 147
U.S. Veterans Administration, 142
United Steel Workers of America, 263
University of Maryland, 140, 162, 281
University of Maryland, Baltimore County, 27, 126
University of Maryland Medical School, 277
Upper Brick Row (Daniels), 239
Upper Falls, 200, 202
Upper Mill. *See* Groff's Mill

V

Vagabond Players, 56
Valley Gun Ship, 297
Vanderbilt, Alfred Gwynne, 229
Vaux, Calvert, 290
Vauxhall, 231, 298
Venetoulis, Theodore G. (County Executive), 149, 193
Vernon's Roller Rink, 76
Veterans Administration, 142
Vetra, Frederick G., 156
Viaduct Hotel, 49, 131, 252
Vietnam War, 190, 191
Vigilant Building Association, 137
Vigilant Volunteer Fire Department, 137
Villa Julie College, 54
Villa Pace, 54
Vincent, Richard, J., 271
Vincent's Dahlia Nurseries, 271
Visitation Order, 155
Vogel, Emma, 73
Vogtman, Mr., 161
Volz, Dale T., 9, 151
Vondersmith, S. B., 252
Vulcan (ship), 262

W

WMAR-TV, 152
Wacker, Charles, 90
Wafer, John, 33
Wagner, Elmer, 136
Wagner, Philip, 33, 297
Walker, Charles, 194, 209
Walker, Elisha H., 226
Walker, Joseph, 216
Walker, Randy, 95
Walker-Gordon Laboratory, 223
Wall $treet Week, 145
Wallen, Ric, 92
Ward, Dean, 96
Ward, James J. III, 229
Ward, William F., 297
Ward Machinery Company, 31, 297
Warfield, S. Davies, 275
Warren, Donald T., 193
Warren (Village), 46, 109, 194, 231, 238, 241
Warren (Cotton factory), 17, 47, 135, 214, 231
Warren Road, 102, 238
Warren Road Bridge, 108, 114
Warren School, 152, 153, 238
Washington, George (President), 273
Washington and Lee University, 156
Washington College, 198
Washington Monument, 239 (Baltimore), 268 (Washington)
Washington Post Office, 268
Washington Senators, 238
Waters, Minetta, 54
Waters Camp Ground, 199
Watkins, Annetta Stitt (Bowen), 58
Watkins, J. Maurice, Jr., 58
Watkins, J. Maurice, Sr., 58, 250, 296, 297
Watkins, Lida, 297
Watson, Don, 265
Watson, W., 57
Webb, H., 57
Webb, William, 53
Webber, Dr., 162
Weber, Dorothea, 251
Weber, Frederick, 251
Weber's Cider Mill Farm, 236
Weber's Hotel, 251
Weber's Tavern, 251
Webster, Allan (Captain), 298
Webster, Daryl, 93
Weir, Michael H., 146
Weis, Albert M., 180, 244
Weis, Henry, 244
Weis, Madeline G., 244
Weiskittel family, 29
Weiss, Charles, 96
Welch, Mrs., 86
Weller, Keith, 92
Weller, O. E. (Senator), 299
Welshe's Cradle, 229
Wendy's Old Fashioned Hamburgers, 297
Wesley, John, 20
West Baltimore General Hospital, 285
West, J., 66
West, Louis Bresee, 159
Wester Ogle, 224, 299
Western Maryland Railway, 111, 152, 182, 234, 299
Western Run, 107, 194
Westview Shopping Center, 120, 249
Wetheredville, 216

Wheaton Place Apartments, 224
Whedbee, James, 47
Wheeler, Betty, 54
Wheeler, Frank I., 255
Wheeler, George G., 133
Wheeler, W. Horace, 161
White, Joe, 96
White, Lucius, 121
White Marsh, 28, 150, 215, 268, 296
White Marsh Branch, Baltimore County Public Library, 28, 150
White Marsh Business Center, 28
White Marsh High Tech, 28
White Marsh Mall, 28
White Marsh Plaza, 28
Whitney, Holbrook, 161
Whitney, Mrs., 161
Whitney, Toddie, 242
Whitney-Gardner butcher shop, 242
Whitworth, Cathy, 34
Wiatrowski, Pat, 96
Wight family, 250
Wilkins-Rogers Company, 214
Williams, Ember, 54
Williams, Mamie, 48
Williams, Oden, 48
Williams Mobile Office, 28
Williams and Wilkins (Publishers), 234
Wilson, Mrs. Hilda, 83, 252
Wilson, T., 57
Wilson and Poehlman, 243
Wilson Lumber Company, John S., 243
Wilton Farm Dairy, 225
Windcrest, 277
Windsor Farm, 226
Wine Warehouse, 251
Wineholt, Winfield (Fire Chief), 191
Wolf, Marjorie, 161
Wolfe, Kay, 144
Women's Choir of Dundalk, 54
Women's Club of Towson, 149, 211
Wonder, Otto, 269
Woodberry, 214, 217
Woodfall, 28
Woodholme Country Club, 56
Woodlawn, 32, 89, 126, 225, 296
Woodlawn Cemetery, 10, 93, 239
Woodlawn Senior High School, 93, 166
Woods, E., 67
Woods, Emma K., 70, 220, 230, 281
Woodstock, 103, 170-171
Woodstock College, 169, 170, 196, 205, 206
Works Progress Administration, 142, 185
Worthington family, 195, 229
Wright, Freddie, 62
Wright, Mrs. Sarah F., 253, 299
Wye, 20

Y

YMCA, 101, 297
Yellott, John (Major), 251
Yellow Tavern. *See* Hobbs' Hotel
York, Pennsylvania, 111
York Road, 107, 113, 180

Z

Zahn, Robert, 161
Zaiser, Louis F., 225
Zalowski, Mike, 96
Zeller, Andrew, 156
Zephaniah Poteet, 102, 231
Zimmerman, Margaret (Bosley), 64
Zink, Nancy, 161
Ziolkowski, J., 67
Ziolkowski, L., 67
Zoning Appeals Board, 102

SUBJECT INDEX

A

Aerial views, 21, 26, 28, 29, 38, 82, 120, 121, 122, 123, 135, 145, 241, 249, 257, 260, 268
Agriculture, 14, 16, 17, 56, 298; buildings, 17, 217, 221, 223, 224, 226, 229, 230-232; crops, 219, 220, 229, 299; education for, 162, 232, 233; farms and farm life, 32, 57, 218, 219; livestock, 219, 220, 227-229; machinery and equipment, 222, 224, 225, 228, 230, 231, 299; orchards, 233; organizations, 234, 298, 299; poultry, 217; practice of, 230, 299; produce, 80, 218, 227, 236; tools, 221, 232
Airlines and airplanes, 117, 118, 171, 178, 256-259
Airports, 118, 298
Alcoholism and substance abuse, 38
Almshouse, 290, 292
Ambulances, 37, 140, 294
American Revolution, 15, 16
Amusement parks, 72, 79, 80, 81, 82, 299
Amusements, 18, 40; billiards, 92, 298; bull roast, 99; cheerleading, 165; crab feast, 39; crokinole, 46; dancing, 165; darts, 90; fireworks, 90; Jump-a-thon, 90; skateboard, 92; snowballing, 90; swinging, 34, 70, 72
Anglican Church, 16, 194
Animals, 23, 45, 47, 64, 71, 72, 77, 81, 84, 85, 97, 105, 112, 180, 181, 217, 225, 227, 228, 230, 231, 244, 270
Annexations, 10, 15
Architects. *See* Ahlers, John; Balbirnie, Thomas; Baldwin, Ephraim Francis; Bernard, Simon; Bollman, Wendel; Brotman, Benjamin; Carson, Charles L.; Cookman, Alfred; Davis, Alexander Jackson; Davis, Frank E.; Dixon, James; Dixon, Thomas; Edmunds, James R.; Finkelstein, H. Bruce; Gaudreau Inc.; Jewell, Downing, and Associates; Kann & Ammon; Lapicki-Smith and Associates; Long, Robert Carey, Jr.; Mills, Robert; Murphy and Olmstead; Newton and Painter, Neilson, J. Crawford; Niernsee, Rudolf; Palmer, Edward L.; Parker, Thomas and Rice; Pennington, Josias; Starkweather, Nathan; Tatar and Kelly; Totten, Joseph G.; Tovell, G. Walter; Turnbull, Bayard; Vaux, Calvert; and White, Lucius.
Architecture. *See* Houses
Armories. *See* Military installations
Arsenals. *See* Military installations
Asians, 18, 46
Athletes, groups of, 57, 58, 66, 67, 95, 96
Auctions, 81
Automobiles and trucks, 18, 56, 65, 70, 87, 99, 100, 113, 117, 158, 175, 255, 265, 266-267, 270, 287-288. *See also* Transportation

B

Bakeries, 33, 170
Baltimore County, overview, 14-18. *See* specific departments. *See also* Public service
Baltimore County Bar Association, 133
Baltimore County Commissioners, 15
Baltimore County Council, 9, 120, 148, 150, 151
Baltimore County Executives, 8, 16, 102, 120, 144, 146, 147, 150, 190, 191, 193, 255 history, 14ff.
Baltimore Harbor, 15
Bands, 51, 52. *See also* Orchestras
Banks. *See* names of specific banks
Barns, 17, 217, 221, 223, 224, 226
Battle of North Point, 128, 129
Beaches, 69, 72, 73
Beltway. *See* Baltimore Beltway in Name and Place index. *See also* Roads; Transportation
Black Churches, 204, 206-207
Black Schools, 15, 157, 163
Blacks, 15, 59, 127, 166, 172, 224, 225, 229, 244
Blacksmiths, 242
Boats and ships, 38, 41, 42, 43, 87, 139
Boy Scouts, 50
Bridges, 106, 107, 108, 109
Budgets, 15
Builders, contractors and developers. *See* Amrein Brothers; Andrew, B. M., Company; Azola, Martin P.; Bennett, Benjamin Franklin; Burns, John; Camp, Joseph; Hubner, John; Keelty, James; Newton and Painter; Nottingham Properties Inc.; Obrecht, P. F. Company; Rouse Company; Sands, William B.; Schon, H. J. Von; Scott, Rev. Aquilla; Short and Leister; Strutt, Kim; Tillman, Irvin C.; and Tovell, G. Walter
Business Parks, 28, 29, 216
Businesses, 31, 33, 99. *See also* Industry
Butchering, 17, 227

C

Catholicism. *See* Roman Catholicism
Celebrations, 83, 90, 98, 151, 157, 179-181
Cemeteries, 20, 130, 239, 297
Census, business, 18; population, 14, 18
Chapels. *See* Churches
Charter government, 239
Chesapeake Bay, 14, 39
Children groups of, 35, 45, 50, 57, 67, 80, 92, 101, 153, 154, 156, 157, 167
Churches, 194, 195, 196-211, 239. *See also* Black Churches
Civil War, 124, 131, 132, 208
Classrooms, photos of, 25, 26, 27, 158, 164, 168
Clergy, 15, 169, 207
Club members, 49, 54, 86, 144
Colleges and universities, 26, 27, 167-171
Company towns, 17, 21, 135, 176, 194, 237-239, 241
Congresspersons and U.S. Senators, 120, 140, 141, 148, 151
Contractors. *See* Builders, Contractors and Developers
Corporations, 28-31, 264, 266, 267. *See* specific names of. *See also* Businesses; Industry
Country Clubs, 55, 56
County Council, formation of, 148; members of, 9, 146, 148, 149, 151
County Executives. *See* Anderson, Dale; Birmingham, Michael J.; Dewberry, Frederick; Hutchinson, Donald P.; Kahl, Christian H.; Rasmussen, Dennis F.; and Venetoulis, Theodore G.
Court House, 29, 132, 191
Courts, 15, 133
Crops, farm. *See* Agriculture
Crowds, 36, 68, 69, 78, 80-83, 115, 116, 179, 180, 184

D

Dairies, 56, 223, 225, 299
Dams, 88, 135, 269, 298
Defense industry, 30, 186, 216, 260
Democratic party, 16, 41, 147, 151
Demonstrations, 188, 192
Depressions, 185, 216
Development, 216
Disasters, 38, 175, 176, 177
Disease, 290-292
Distilleries and wineries, 33, 250

E

Eating, 39, 44, 68, 74, 85, 99
Economic growth and decline causes of, 216
Education, 15-16, 25-27, 152-172; number of years offered, 15, 52, 157. *See also* Colleges and Universities; Private schools; Public schools
Elections, 146, 147, 148, 151, 190, 192
Employment, 17, 18
Environment, 216
Episcopalianism, 195, 197, 198, 202
Ethnics, 18, 151
Events and ceremonies, 83, 85, 99, 120, 168, 176, 179-181, 189-191, 193, 247
Executive. *See* County Executive

F

Fair of the Iron Horse, 183, 184
Fairs, 72, 80-81, 227
Family groups, 39, 42, 44, 45, 47, 48, 58, 59-66, 240
Farm buildings. *See* Agriculture-buildings
Federal Government. *See* U.S. Government
Fertilizer plants, 216
Festivals. *See* Events. *See also* Celebrations
Fire Department, 15, 193; regular, 37, 125, 137, 138; volunteers, 51, 98, 136, 137, 170, 176, 179, 180. *See also* Public Service
Fire Equipment, 127, 136-138, 180
Fires, 74, 173, 186, 187
Floods, 175, 176, 177
Florists, 33, 267, 271
Forts, 126, 142, 143
Fraternal Orders, 100
Funeral homes, 216, 251, 254

G

Good Roads Movement, 102, 140
Government, U.S. *See* U.S. Government
Government Service. *See* Public Service
Great Depression. *See* Depression
Group (persons) pictures), 42, 44-47, 49-53, 57-67, 74, 86, 92, 98, 101,

105, 109, 120, 125, 131-133, 135, 136, 138, 140, 153, 169, 176, 185, 188-193, 206, 209, 210, 250, 255
Gunpowder State Park, 68

H
Halethorpe Air Show, 177
Handicapped, 97, 192
Health, colonial, 14; nineteenth century, 14, 272, 290-292
Health Care, 37, 163, 192, 206. *See also* Hospitals
Hispanics, 18
Home Economics. *See also* Education
Horse racing. *See* Sports
Horses, 23, 77, 81, 83, 85, 227, 228
Hospitals, 26, 37, 74, 291-293, 295
Hotels, 32, 184, 249, 252-253. *See also* names of specific hotels
Houses, 14, 15, 20, 21, 77, 272-281; numbers of, 18; types of, 18; exterior views, 20, 21, 273-281, 284-289; interior views, 68, 108, 282-283. *See* names of specific houses
Hunt Valley, 29
Hydropathic institutions, 297
Hygiene, 126, 272

I
Ice cream parlors, 248, 270
Ice houses, 226
Ice plants, 270
Implements. *See* Agriculture-tools
Immigration, 18
Indians, 14
Industrial Revolution, 17, 214
Industry, 30, 31
Inns and Taverns, 18, 250-251, 260
Interiors, ambulances, 37; bakeries, 33, 170, 247; bands (halls of), 53, 54; barber shops, 99; bars and taverns, 250, 251; blacksmith's shops, 242; bowling alleys, 75; butcher's shops, 242; churches, 203, 205, 211; colleges, 27, 168; County Council chambers, 148; courts, 133; dairies, 223; florists, 33; gymnasiums, 93, 95, 97, 165; houses, 68, 108, 282-283; hospitals and orphanages, 37, 293, 295; industry, 30, 31, 86, 234, 237, 258, 260, 261, 264, 266, 267, 270; labs, 36, 170; laundries, 265; lecture halls, 101; libraries, 149, 150, 171; military installations, 144; offices, 134, 138; pharmacies, 248; pool halls, 92; restaurants and dining halls, 32, 144, 147, 171, 184, 294; retirement homes, 132; schools, 25, 158, 162, 163, 164, 169; shopping centers and malls, 32; stores, 31, 243-246, 248; Television Studios, 145; Timonium State Fair, 80, 81, 299; trains, 162
Iron industry, 214, 216. *See also* Steel

J
Jesuits. *See* Society of Jesus
Jews and Judaism, 16, 55, 56, 212-213
Jousting. *See* Sports

K
Kahn and Ammon, 212
Korean War, 188

L
Labor Unions. *See* Unions
Landholdings, colonial, 14; size, 14
Laundries, 265
Libraries, 28, 149, 150
Lifestyles 14, 16, 17
Livery Stables, 253
Livestock. *See* Agriculture-livestock
Locomotives, 103, 110, 111, 131, 183
Lodges. *See* Fraternal orders
Lumber Companies, 243
Lutherans, 204, 210

M
Malls, 18, 28, 29, 31, 32
Maps and atlases, 19, 24, 104, 286
Methodism, 16, 20, 198, 199, 202, 211, 212
Mexican War, 130
Military, 130, 131, 142-144. *See also* Public Service
Military installations, 129, 142, 143, 144
Mill Towns. *See* Company towns
Mills, 17, 214; grist, 47, 214, 234-236; nontextile, 214; textile, 17, 21, 47, 214, 237-240. *See also* names of specific mills
Minstrel shows, 206
Monuments, 130, 190
Moving Industry, 265
Munitions, 260
Music. *See also* Bands, 27

N
National Guard, 144
Negroes. *See* Blacks
New Deal and New Deal projects, 185
New Towns, 28

O
Orchestras, 36, 53, 170 *See also* Bands
Orphanages, 294

P
Paper industry, 216, 271
Parades, 179-181
Parks, 36, 63, 68, 216
Pharmacies, 248
Photographers. *See* Blakeslee-Lane Studios; Bodine, A. Aubrey; Brewster, Gerry L.; Brinkmann, A. H.; Burton, Gail; Childress, Richard; Feder, Fred; Fitze, Joshua; Hart, Charles; Hollifield, William; Hughes Co.; Kenney, William C.; Kraft, Fred G.; Lally, James; Lightner, James K.; McGrain John W.; McNally, Lawrence; Mahan, Charles; Officer, James D.; Price, Vernon; Rowe, Pete; Schaefer, Ruth; Schmulowitz, Hal; Shipley, Jack; Spicer, Harold; Tomlinson, Richard; Treadwell, C. W. E.; Weiss, Charles; Weller, Keith; and Woods, Emma K.
Planning, 16, 216
Police, 15, 139; county, 16, 190, 192; state, 36, 129. *See also* Public service
Political machine, 141, 147
Politics and politicians, 146, 147, 148, 190; bossism, 16, 140, 141; corruption, 16, 124, 148, 191, 193; elections, 147, 193; patronage, 16, 124. *See also* Public service
Population, by decades, 18; colonial (estimated), 14
Port of Baltimore, 15, 151
Portraits, 20, 23, 48, 59, 71, 94, 134, 140, 141, 146, 166, 257, 267, 276, 279
Poverty. *See* Almshouse
Presbyterians, 196, 201, 209
Presidents, U.S., 45, 186, 190
Printing, 206
Private schools, 153-156, 159, 161, 171, 185
Protestantism, 16
Public Schools, 16, 23, 25, 26, 152, 155, 157-163
Public service, 15, 16, 36, 125, 126, 138, 145, 185

Q
Quakers. *See* Society of Friends
Quarries, 19, 35, 267-268

R
Race courses, 23, 81, 82, 83
Race Relations. *See* Blacks
Railroads, 15, 38, 103, 105, 106, 109-111, 132, 182, 214; location map, 104
Railway stations, 105, 106, 111
Reconstruction, era of, 16
Recreation. *See* Amusements. *See also* Sports
Reform, 15, 146
Religion, 16, 194-213; colonial, 16. *See* denominational names
Republican party, 16, 148
Reservoirs. *See* Loch Raven, Liberty, Prettyboy in Name and Place index
Resorts, 62, 105, 106
Restaurants, 32, 251
Retailing, 247, 249. *See also* Stores; Malls
Retirement homes, 29, 132, 299
Roads, 15, 112, 120, 122, 123, 130, 134; conditions of, 15, 18, 102, 113, 114, 201. *See also* Baltimore Beltway in Name and Place index; individual names; Transportation
Roman Catholicism, 16, 103, 169, 170-171, 196, 200, 205-207, 209, 210
Rural Life Education, 157, 162. *See also* Education

S
Sanitation, 274
Schneider Cup Race, 178
School groups, 52, 53, 57, 67, 95, 153, 154, 156, 158, 159, 161, 163, 169
Schools, 15, 16, 52, 53. *See also* Black Schools; Private Schools; Public Schools
Scenic views, 21, 22
Scientists and Inventors, 127, 269
Seminaries, 103, 169-171, 196
Shopping Centers, 18, 28, 29, 120, 122, 123, 247, 249, 264
Shopping Malls, 18, 28, 29, 31, 32, 247, 249; impact of, 18
Singers and singing, 27, 54, 354
Slavery, 14, 156, 174
Small Businesses, 17, 99
Social Structure, 14-15
Society of Friends, 200
Society of Jesus, 103, 170-171, 196
Sports, 15, 18, 40; ballooning, 78; baseball, 57, 66, 94, 238; basketball, 93, 95; bicycling, 34, 39, 44; boating, 39; bowling, 75; coon hunting, 84; duck hunting, 45; fishing, 88, 89; football, 35, 67; fox hunting, 49; golf, 34; hockey, 93; horse racing, 23, 81, 83, 85; jousting, 97; lacrosse, 57; marathon running, 98; roller skating, 76; sledding, 90; sleighing, 112; soccer, 66, 96; softball, 94; speedboat racing, 87; swimming, 34, 67-69, 72, 73, 143; tennis, 35, 46; tubing, 68; volleyball, 96; wrestling, 165
States' Attorney, 148
Steel Industry, 216, 260-262. *See also* Iron
Stone and marble works, 267, 268
Stores, 31, 243-246, 248, 249, 254, 264, 276; *See also* Malls; Retailing
Streetcars, 15, 115, 116, 249
Suburbanization, 18
Summer places. *See* Resorts
Synagogues, 212-213

T
Taverns. *See* Inns and Taverns
Taxes, 18, 130
Technological Change, in agriculture, 17; in industry, 17, 216; in home living, 126; in transportation, 15, 17
Telephone, 138
Television, 145
Tents, 142, 199
Textiles. *See* Mills
Theaters, 57, 75, 162, 206
Toleration (Act of), 16
Tollgates, 104
Towns, 15. *See also* by specific name of town
Train wrecks, 38, 182
Trains. *See* Railroads
Transportation, 15, 18, 38, 65, 105, 110-112, 117-120, 122, 123, 132, 152
Turnpikes, 102, 104; location map, 204. *See also* Roads

U
Unions, 263
U.S. Government, 124, 142, 143, 145, 185
Universities. *See* Colleges and Universities

V
Veterans, 132, 188, 208
Vietnam War, 188, 189

W
War of 1812, 128-130. *See also* Battle of North Point
Wineries. *See* Distilleries and Wineries
Women, as officeholders, 148, 151, 174; position in society, 126, 174
Workers' benefits, 216
World War I, 140, 260
World War II, 178, 187

Y
Yacht Clubs, 43

Z
Zoning, 16, 79, 141

ABOUT THE AUTHORS

Richard Parsons, born in Victoria, British Columbia, has a history degree from the University of British Columbia and another in library science from McGill University in Montreal. He has worked in the public libraries of Edmonton, Alberta; Brooklyn, New York; and, since 1962, Baltimore County, where he is administrative assistant to the director. The Towson resident has been an officer in many state, regional, and national professional organizations, and has headed or served as an officer in many community organizations, including the Towson Fourth of July Parade, the Greater Towson Council of Community Associations, Historic Towson, Inc., the Baltimore Environmental Center, and others. In the late 1960s, he was an officer of the Maryland Council for Educational Television which lobbied for and got public television into Maryland. Mr. Parsons was chairman for several years of a committee of historians and public, research, and academic librarians, which negotiated the reprinting of classics of Maryland history. He chaired the Publications Committee of the Baltimore County Chamber of Commerce for six years, and is currently on the Board of the Baltimore County Historical Society. He has had articles, bibliographies, and introductions published, was editor of a quarterly magazine for the Maryland Library Association, and edited and compiled the *Guide to Specialized Subject Collections in Maryland Libraries* for the Special Libraries Association in 1974.

Neal A. Brooks has been a professor of history at Essex Community College since 1970. He holds an undergraduate degree from Towson State University and a Ph.D. in history from Case Western Reserve University, Cleveland. In addition to having published articles, Dr. Brooks co-authored the highly acclaimed *A History of Baltimore County* (1979), the first comprehensive history of the county in a century. His book reviews have appeared in the Baltimore *Sunday Sun* and in a wide range of historical publications including the *Journal of American History* and the *Maryland Historical Magazine.* A frequent speaker on county historical topics, he is also an avid photographer of local scenery. Dr. Brooks served on the Board of Library Trustees for Baltimore County for ten years, two of them as president. He is a member of several historical associations including the Maryland Historical Society and the Baltimore County Historical Society. He has been active in community associations and eastern Baltimore County political campaigns, and has served on the Baltimore County Landmarks Preservation Commission. Now a resident of Phoenix, he has also lived in three other areas of Baltimore County.

TOWSONTOWN ACADEMY,

SMEDLEY ROW,

Towsontown, Baltimore County, Md.

RICHARD BURKE, A. M., *Principal.*

THE undersigned, a graduate of Loyola College, Baltimore, having leased the offices Nos. 7 and 8, Smedley Row, and prepared them for the purposes of a schoolroom, is now ready to receive pupils for primary and academic instruction. As a teacher, the undersigned is extensively known in Baltimore county and elsewhere, and appeals to the large patronage which he has had for many years, as the best proof of his efficiency. The terms of this school are extremely moderate, the situation is healthy and delightful, and parents and guardians who wish their children prepared for college will probably serve their purpose as well by patronizing this, as older institutions.

April 12.—tf RICHARD BURKE.

Hance's Sarsaparilla, Vegetable or Blood Pills,

FOR PURIFYING THE BLOOD;
For Costiveness;
For the cure of Dyspepsia;
For Jaundice;
For the cure of Indigestion
For Headache;
For the cure of Dysentery;
For a Foul Stomach;
For the cure of Erysipelas;
For the Piles;
For the cure of Scrofula;
For all Scrofulous Complaints;
For the cure of Rheumatism;
For diseases of the Skin;
For the cure of Liver Complaint;
For Dropsy;
For the cure of Tetter, Tumors and Salt Rheum:
For the cure of Gout;
For Worms;
For a Dinner Pill;
For the cure of Neuralgia;
For Purifying the Blood.

HANCE'S SARSAPARILLA OR BLOOD PILLS,
Price 25 cents per box, or five boxes for $1.
For sale by SETH S. HANCE,
108 Baltimore st.

REMOVAL OF

SADDLE AND HARNESS

MANUFACTORY.

THE subscriber has removed his establishment FROM THE SOUTHERN PART OF REISTERSTOWN to the NORTHERN END OF THAT VILLAGE, opposite to the Odd Fellows' Hall, where he will keep constantly on hand every kind of article in his line of business. The removal has been made for the purpose of obtaining greater conveniences, and for meeting the demands of an increasing trade.

Manufactures and keeps constantly on hand every description of SADDLES, HARNESS, CARPET BAGS, COLLARS, and every other article in his line.

Repairing done with neatness and dispatch. Old Saddles and Harness taken in exchange for new.

☞ The subscriber thanks his old customers, and the public generally, who have dealt with him, for the liberal patronage heretofore received, and pledges himself that if this support be continued, he will sell to them as good articles, and at as cheap a rate as can be obtained in the city, or elsewhere. He respectfully solicits a call.

HENRY F. EMICH.

Reisterstown, Jan. 24.—6m

A GRAND

DEMOCRATIC MASS MEETING,

WILL BE HELD AT

TOWSONTOWN,

THURSDAY, the 27th day of SEPTEMBER, 1860,

COMMENCING AT 10 O'CLOCK, A. M.

RALLY! RALLY! RALLY!

FOR

BRECKINRIDGE AND LANE.

"THE CONSTITUTION AND THE EQUALITY OF THE STATES, THESE ARE THE SYMBOLS OF EVERLASTING UNION; LET THESE BE THE RALLYING CRIES OF THE PEOPLE."

The meeting will be addressed by

Hon. ENOCH LOUIS LOWE,
Hon. JAMES ALFRED PEARCE,
Hon. JOSHUA VANSANT,
JOHN RITCHIE,
JAMES S. FRANKLIN,
T. PARKIN SCOTT,
ELIAS GRISWOLD,
J. BROOKE BOYLE,
RICHARD JACKSON, } ESQRS.

And other distinguished speakers.

A BAND OF MUSIC WILL BE IN ATTENDANCE.

A Free Collation will be Served for all.

☞ THE CRISIS IS NOW AT HAND. ☜

THIS WILL BE THE GREAT MEETING OF THE CAMPAIGN.

The Friends of the Cause are Expected to Turn Out in Their Strength.

A cordial invitation is extended to

THE PEOPLE.

WITHOUT REGARD TO PARTY.

☞ The Committee beg leave to say, that they have received positive assurance from the gentlemen who are announced to speak, that they will be present and address the meeting.